Planning, Environment, Citie

Series Editors
Yvonne Rydin
Bartlett School of Planning
University College London
London, UK

Ben Clifford
Bartlett School of Planning
University College London
London, UK

This series is primarily aimed at students and practitioners of planning and such related professions as estate management, housing and architecture as well as those in politics, public and social administration, geography and urban studies. It comprises both general texts and books designed to make a more particular contribution, in both cases characterized by: an international approach; extensive use of case studies; and emphasis on contemporary relevance and the application of theory to advance planning practice.

    * Andrew Thornley was series co-editor with Yvonne Rydin up to his retirement from the role in January 2017.

More information about this series at
http://www.palgrave.com/gp/series/14300

Yvonne Rydin

Theory in Planning Research

palgrave
macmillan

Yvonne Rydin
The Bartlett School of Planning
University College London
London, UK

Planning, Environment, Cities
ISBN 978-981-33-6567-4   ISBN 978-981-33-6568-1   (eBook)
https://doi.org/10.1007/978-981-33-6568-1

This Palgrave Macmillan imprint is published by the registered company Springer Nature Singapore
Pte Ltd.
The registered company address is: 152 Beach Road, #21-01/04 Gateway East, Singapore 189721,
Singapore

Preface

My undergraduate programme did not require me to do a dissertation or research project, and I missed out on doing a master's degree. So, my first experience of research was some amateur investigations about an interesting area of London that had experienced repeated waves of refugee and migrant populations (Brick Lane, Whitechapel) and some limited consultancy undertaken by the surveying firm where I worked. My curiosity was piqued, and I applied to do a PhD. I had close and careful supervision, but there was no training as such. It was very much learning-by-doing within a community of practice. As with teaching in due course, I found the advice of those of my peers who had a bit more experience, invaluable. A little way into a lectureship, and I was called upon to be a supervisor myself to students undertaking MSc dissertation and PhDs.

Since that time (and I am talking of the 1980s/1990s), the requirement to do a piece of original research and write that up in a dissertation has become a standard element of many undergraduate and postgraduate taught degrees. Almost all professional accreditation in planning and cognate occupations demands a programme with a research project, and such research is bread-and-butter to the consultancies that employ many graduates of these programmes. At the same time, more people are looking for a doctorate to complete their education and/or advance their careers. The level of training at all levels for such research activity has expanded considerably, and yet much of this remains focussed on procedural compliance (as with ethics approval and data protection), the soft skills of self-managing a research project and writing up a long document, or the range of quantitative and qualitative methodological techniques that a researcher may use. There is relatively little on how to ground a research project in a firm theoretical foundation.

This book explores the interface between theoretical writings that are relevant to studying and investigating the operation of planning systems and the research process itself. As such it should be of interest to all who undertake planning research, at all levels (undergraduate, taught postgraduate, research degree) and in both higher education and professional consultancy. The claim of the book is that research is more robust, more generalisable and just more interesting with a clear link to such theoretical writings. It contains both summary accounts of various relevant theories and, centrally, accounts of published peer-reviewed research that allow the relationships between theory, research focus and methodology to be explored. This selection of academic papers provides a potential set of guided readings for anyone using this as a course-book (officially or unofficially).

Readers should begin by reading the introduction that discusses the key concepts of planning, research and theory. You may then wish to skip to a chapter or two of the theoretical framings that seem likely to interest you the most; other chapters can be returned to when your research project has developed and you wish to consider whether other theoretical framings may prove fruitful. Or, you may find it instructive to read through the whole book from start to finish with a view to getting a fuller overview of the theoretical landscape for planning studies. The emphasis on published research findings means that this approach will also give you an instructive account of planning systems, institutions, processes and practices as researched around the world. But I would recommend that everyone at some point—sooner or later—reads the final chapter, which is very much in the nature of a guide to doing research, hopefully a helpful guide.

This book is dedicated to the many students, who I have had the pleasure to supervise on their dissertations and theses. They taught me much, and I hope this book will teach something to future cohorts.

London, UK   Yvonne Rydin

Contents

1 Introduction: Theory and Planning Research   1

2 Governmental Models: The Hope of Rational Public Administration   19

3 Rational Choice Perspectives: Self-Interest and Decision-Making . .   41

4 The Influence of the New Institutionalism: How Culture Shapes
   Planning   61

5 Governance Theories: Stakeholders, Networks and Collaboration . .   83

6 Urban Politics: Conflict, Power and Justice 105

7 Political Economy: Crisis and Response 127

8 Discourse, Knowledge and Governmentality: The Influence of
   Foucault 149

9 Relational Approaches: Assemblages, Materiality and Power 171

10 Conclusion: On Doing Planning Research 193

Bibliography 203

Index 213

List of Figures

Fig. 2.1   The general planning process (following Lichfield). (Source:
            Adapted from Lichfield et al. 1975)..   21
Fig. 4.1   Douglas' grid-group theory...   66
Fig. 10.1   The Golden Triangle of theory-informed planning research............   195

List of Tables

Table 1.1   The relationship of subsequent chapters to the governmental
            approach   15
Table 2.1   Kumar et al.'s indicator set   28
Table 3.1   Payoff matrix in Chiu and Lai   51
Table 10.1 Different framings of planning 194
Table 10.2 Distinctive methodologies associated with different theoretical
            approaches 198
Table 10.3 Theories in planning research: a summary 199

Chapter 1
Introduction: Theory and Planning Research

What Is This Book About?

Research involves finding out about the world. It is interesting, exciting and difficult. It can be argued that research is integral to the activity of planning; in the
nineteenth and early twentieth centuries, key historic figures in the development of
urban planning such as Ildefonso Cerdá y Suñer from Spain and Patrick Geddes
from Scotland emphasised the importance of research through the 'survey' before
preparing a plan. But this book is not about how research fits into the work of professional planners but rather about work within the academy. It is addressed particularly to students—at undergraduate and postgraduate levels, on taught courses with
a dissertation component and MPhil/PhD programmes—and the wider planning
research community comprising academics and researchers in universities and
research institutes. It aims to provide an insightful and useful account of how theories and theorising are a central feature of planning research.

The field of planning research is notable for the great variety of work that is
undertaken under this umbrella. There are a multitude of different topics studied,
different questions asked and different theories drawn upon. This can often seem
confusing to newcomers to planning research. In many scientific disciplines there
appears to be more widespread agreement on the theoretical frameworks underpinning research activity. The word 'discipline' is not accidental; disciplines shape and
constrain the work that occurs within any particular area of academic activity. A key
example here is the discipline of economics with its very strong framework of
micro- and macro-economic theories that dominates the research being undertaken;
only in certain research and pedagogic locations are 'alternative' frameworks such
as behavioural, institutional or Marxist economics readily promoted. By contrast,
the research undertaken within any one planning school is likely to be very varied
in terms of the theoretical reference points being used.

© The Author(s), under exclusive license to Springer Nature Singapore Pte
Ltd. 2021
Y. Rydin, *Theory in Planning Research*, Planning, Environment, Cities,
https://doi.org/10.1007/978-981-33-6568-1_1

Planning researchers, therefore, face a choice between many different theories and versions of those theories. How is that choice to be made? What is at stake? In this book, I will be looking at how theory can be used to guide and frame research, and I will highlight the implications of choosing one rather than another theoretical framework in terms of the research questions that will be addressed, the methodology and the kind of research that is undertaken, along with the way it is presented and the nature of findings that will result. This does involve a particular take on what theory is and how theory fits into research (discussed later). In each chapter a particular theoretical perspective—often a cognate group of theories—is outlined, and then a number of examples of published research are considered to ground this discussion and provide examples that readers can follow up.

A few caveats are in order at the outset to set the scope of the book. First, this is not a book of planning theory. Broadly, planning theory is a body of work that looks at the normative question of how planning *should* be done; the focus here is much more on theoretical frameworks that help us *understand* how planning processes work. There is some overlap between the theories covered here and those that will be found in a planning theory textbook, but there is a fundamental distinction here between a normative and an analytic approach. This book is situated within the latter approach, seeking to support research that analyses planning processes and practices to enhance our understanding. This may give rise to recommendations for changes in those processes and practices; it may—if appropriately communicated—enhance the understanding of practitioners. But, this only arises after much, if not all, of the analysis is done; it is not the primary task of the research. As will become apparent at various points in the discussion, it is not possible to separate the normative and the analytic completely; they are closely entangled. I am not arguing that research is not normative, that it is value-free in some way. Rather, all research—including analytic research—is imbued with value judgements.

Second, the range of theories that are covered are, to some extent, a reflection of my personal knowledge and interests although I have also tried to cover many approaches that I am aware are being used by planning researchers but I have no personal experience of. Nevertheless, this will inevitably be a selection of what a very diverse planning research community is engaging with as the theoretical foundations for their work. For example, I have not included discussion of psychoanalytic approaches drawing, say, on the work on Lacan. Similarly, urban design research has its own distinctive character that falls outside the remit of this book. I have also given more space to some approaches than others, arguably leading to some under-representation. For example, a feminist perspective is rolled up within the category of urban politics in Chap. 6 and is not discussed separately; similarly, postcolonial approaches are explored through the interest in political economy in Chap. 7.

Third, the emphasis here is on research which is seeking to understand how planning as a process works; the relevant theory is, as Faludi termed it, theory *of* planning and not theory *for* planning (Faludi 1973). There will be research undertaken within the planning academy—and plenty of it—that falls into the camp of producing knowledge *for* planning practice. This would cover research, for example, into urban change or transport behaviour or sustainable energy solutions; these would have their own theoretical reference points within geography or social psychology or engineering that are not covered here. Some, Næss and Saglie (2000), for example, argue that planning research should concentrate on contributing a body of knowledge on which planning practice can be based. I agree that such knowledge is important, but it is also important to consider how planning works as a process and theory plays a key role in understanding this.

Fourth, this book is about research that broadly might be considered social science. The kind of research that is being discussed here is based on empirical data collection and analysis. There will be forms of inquiry that do not fit this model. Work informed by philosophy or literary studies, for example, may not recognise a place for 'data' at all. Some academic authors may produce commentaries or works of planning history; here, there will be historical 'data' that is drawn on, but the emphasis may be on developing a narrative that convinces and informs rather than discussing the links with theoretical debates through the interpretation of 'results'. The intended audience for this book are those planning researchers engaged in data-based empirical enquiry and asking themselves: "How do I handle theory within my empirical research?"

Finally, although methodological issues will be touched on, this is not a methods textbook. It is a 'how to' book in terms of research design (which is discussed further in Chap. 10), but it is not a 'how to' book in terms of elaborating specific methodologies of data collection and data analysis. Rather the focus here is on looking at examples of how a particular theoretical framework has been operationalised through empirical research and, thus, methodologies are discussed in the specific instances of research studies.

So, if you are interested in how planning works and want to understand this better through empirical research, then the theory-informed approach that is offered in this book should support your research activities. In this first chapter, the two key terms of the title are discussed: 'theory' and 'planning research'. An account of the structure of the book concludes the chapter.

Researching Planning

In this section, two key questions are tackled: why do planning research, and what are the challenges of such research. But first some consideration must be given to the object that planning research tackles, that is what is planning.

Planning as a Focus for Research

There are numerous definitions of 'planning' and indeed debates about whether such definition is possible. It may be that the research one does counts as 'planning' research simply because one is based within a school or institute or programme of planning. It may be that it seems self-evident that it is planning research because it studies the work of professionals known as planners or of organisations labelled as planning departments. But any definition of planning adopted by a researcher implies a framing of that object of research and that has theoretical implications. Thus, asking the very simple question of 'what is planning?' or 'what am I researching?' already highlights the importance of the theoretical dimensions of planning research.

For example, some may define planning as a form of decision-making that seeks to achieve specific goals through implementing particular actions, plans, policies or programmes. This frames planning as an instrumental process, using means to achieve ends. It lends itself to a view of planning as a public administration activity, downplaying any political dimension. In their argument on the preferred form of planning research, Næss and Saglie (2000: 730) choose the definition: "Planning is future-oriented processes through which the actors attempt to achieve control, with the purpose of implementing their intentions". They privilege instrumental rationality, keeping planning research closely connected to current practices, and, in so doing, take the intentions of planners or planning organisations at face value, aligning themselves with the professed values of such planning practice.

Shift the focus very slightly to define planning as an activity whereby the state seeks to order the environment, and this reframes that activity. In this view, planning shapes both the natural and built environment through influencing new development, infrastructure provision and the pattern of land uses while at the same time protecting and enhancing features considered desirable. The aim of such planning is to promote the public or collective interest. This collective interest may be understood as addressing the imbalances or inefficiencies that arise from change in urban, rural, natural and built environments driven by private sector, market-led processes. This is a view of planning as one that seeks to enhance society through intervention in the natural and built environment.

But it is possible to politicise this definition further by seeing such planning action as not necessarily in the collective or public interest but as engaging with different interests and needing to be judged in terms of the interests that benefit most from such planning action. A broader perspective may be taken by focussing on how planning action is involved in maintaining (or not) systemic features of society. These small shifts in defining planning—from decision-making, to a state action in the collective interest, to an intervention by the state affecting diverse interests and aspects of systems—imply different views of planning processes which are captured and made explicit by a theoretical framework.

The choice of framing carries with it value judgements about what is important and about what planning should be doing. It doesn't make the theoretical framing a normative planning theory but it does mean that analytic research can also be aligned with or against professional and political ideologies and worldviews. Thus, I agree with Næss and Saglie (2000: 732) when they say that "planning researchers play an important role in the discussion about doctrines" and, further, that:

> Planning research should contribute to the on-going, international professional debate on, among others, what sort of planning procedures we should choose, what should be the tasks of planning in society, what values and interests are being promoted through today's planning, and how planning can improve its ability to promote important social objectives, like for instance democracy, sustainable development and a fair distribution of social benefits.

An analytic perspective does not preclude this.

However defined, planning is highly diverse in terms of both planning systems and planning practices. It operates across different geographical locations and scales with different cultures, institutions, economies and environments. I have sought to capture some of this by providing a global geographical spread in the examples of planning research that I discuss in Chaps. 2, 3, 4, 5, 6, 7, 8 and 9 and including examples studying planning at different scales. Planning also operates in a wide variety of domains across the environmental, economic and social. There is planning associated with water infrastructure, with biodiversity in cities, with master planning of new neighbourhoods, with community development, with transport and traffic management, with small businesses premises and so on. Planning can operate across domains, seeking to be comprehensive and synthetic; a strategic planning perspective can integrate different domains. In terms of daily practice, planners may be involved in community and stakeholder engagement, in developing a vision for an area (at a variety of scales—neighbourhood, city, region, even nation) or deciding on specific development proposals. Again, I have sought to reflect this in the planning research covered.

So, to conclude on the kind of planning covered in this book, it is very diverse. It has in common some attention to the future and how this relates to current decisions and plans. It is focussed on aspects of the natural and built environment although always with an eye towards the implications for society, the economy and the environment as a whole. It is both political and technical, although the balance may vary between different instances of planning. Beyond that I cannot go with a generic definition; indeed, I would argue that one of the purposes of using theory to guide planning research is to provide and support a more detailed and specific definition. Hopefully this will become apparent in Chaps. 2, 3, 4, 5, 6, 7, 8 and 9.

Why Do Planning Research?

This may seem to be a question with an obvious answer. Surely you do research about planning in order to find out more about it. This can feed a personal curiosity about how planning processes work. It may fit into a personal strategic plan for a career. It may be part of a mission to improve the way that planning operates, the argument being that we need to know how the current planning system works before thinking about how to improve it. But finding out just any information or facts about planning does not count as sufficient to be a research activity. While better description can fulfil a useful function, the academy places the bar rather higher than this. In most countries, a key criterion for the award of a doctorate is making a contribution to knowledge. So, this moves the focus from research as information-gathering to considering the processes by which knowledge is generated.

What counts as knowledge? And how is this different from information or facts? I would suggest that knowledge is about more than description. It is about understanding a situation and that involves a focus on the dynamics that have generated that situation. In the words of the motto of the London School of Economics, it is about a claim to know the cause of things: *rerum cognoscere causus*. However, this adage can imply a rather linear relationship between cause and effect, and for now, I would encourage the reader to keep a broader view of why change may occur and how to understand the dynamics. Later chapters will introduce alternative perspectives on understanding change.

Research is, therefore, about appreciating the way that processes of change (and indeed stasis) produce an outcome in a specific situation. It is about a combination of generalised understanding of the world and application of that understanding to a particular case, the empirical focus of the research. In the context of understanding planning processes, this is about developing a general view of how planning 'works' (or doesn't) and also knowing more about how planning in this city, on this issue, in this mode 'works' (or doesn't). There is an interplay here between researching the specific case to improve our generalised understanding of planning and using generalised understanding to guide the research into a specific case.

Such research is about more than enhancing personal knowledge. There is a community of planning researchers, and engaging in such research involves a dialogue with others. Planning research may involve long periods of time working on your own—digging into a database, transcribing and coding interview transcripts, reading about others' research and thinking about what your own research tells you—nevertheless doing planning research is an intrinsically social activity. It is about contributing to an intellectual debate about planning that engages a community. Indeed, one strong rationale for using a theoretical framework for research is that it provides an entry point into these discussions, moving across the specifics of any one case to consider more general issues about how planning operates. Dialogue between researchers working on different cases or in specific areas but sharing a theoretical perspective can be fruitful; such dialogue on similar cases or areas within a shared perspective can be particularly fruitful.

Dialogue can (and many argue should) also include practitioners. There has been some suggestion that the expansion of this kind of theorisation about planning has led to a growing gap between the planning academy and the planning profession (Næss and Saglie 2000). Some frustration has been expressed at research which concentrates more on being critical of planning practice and suggesting unrealistic ways forward rather than producing knowledge which could be directly used within such practice. Goodman et al. report on a survey where planners expressed a desire for researchers to focus on "real, tangible issues" rather than "creating a utopia" (Goodman et al. 2017: 9). Meanwhile, Campbell et al. (2014: 46) suggest that "Critical appraisal of the inadequacies of policy initiatives is of course important, and perhaps a prerequisite for progressive change. However, there are intellectual and practical dangers if failure, immutable constraints, and a narrowing of aspiration become the assumed norm, as such perspectives prompt conservativism, erode confidence, and justify inaction".

There are two responses to this argument. First, while research for planning is clearly important, there are some limitations also. Research that is led by a practice agenda is likely to be based on value judgements that are associated with professional practice and/or a current political agenda. Sometime the values that are present within such a perspective seem unassailable: sustainability, justice, economic development. The search for win-win outcomes and satisfactory compromises across such goals is deeply embedded in the planning profession, and yet again and again we are faced with choices between such goals or, at least, about the way we balance them against each other. This involves value judgements. Denying this tends to a view of planning as a technical exercise where practices can be incrementally improved through knowledge of 'best practice'. Yet, again, much planning research shows us the politics, power and values that lie behind the application of apparently neutral technical expertise. These arguments are developed further in Chap. 2, where the governmental approach is discussed.

The second response is to argue that research informed by theory does have an important role to play in debates with practitioners and policy makers. Research about planning processes and their dynamics can support reflection by those professionally involved on how the processes were generated, how they are structured and how they currently operate. Planners do need knowledge of how cities are changing, of why people don't want to cycle or recycle and what the best ways of installing traffic calming measures are. But there is also value in critically analysing and enabling informed reflection on what planners and planning systems do, with a view to suggesting pathways for change, albeit tentatively and with full attention to implied value judgements.

This is an ambition that requires the involvement of and communication with practitioners as an integral element of research. But it also involves theory as an essential part of conducting research, necessary to frame the specific within a broader context, to improve our understanding and to contribute to knowledge. This may result in an analysis viewed by practitioners as challenging. However, there are theoretical approaches—as we shall see—that situate themselves much closer to the detail of planning practice and do not seek to explore structural and political dimensions. Or the planning researcher can decide to engage in more overtly political action on the basis of or even as part of their research. These are choices that the planning researcher must make.

The Challenges of Planning Research

Given this rationale for undertaking planning research, it has to be acknowledged that it is not an easy task. Doing research is difficult. The world is complex and problematic to understand; this point applies to the world of planning as it does to any other area of social activity. Anyone undertaking a research project will encounter pitfalls and experience anxieties about key decisions that have to be made.

Some of these may relate to the focus of the research and whether it is addressing the right question. Is this a sufficiently important issue? Some may be methodological concerns about how one uses a particular methodology, whether it is a method for collecting data—such as interviews or a survey or observation—or for analysing that data—such as statistical analysis, mapping, thematic analysis or discourse analysis. But both of these concerns are tied up with the bigger difficulty of how generalisable conclusions—knowledge—can be generated from the data that is collected and analysed. Researchers may find themselves asking the following questions:

- Is there enough data to support a claim to knowledge?
- Is the data good enough?
- Have I actually found out something from the data that I have been able to collect?
- Is my interpretation of the data too subjective?
- How do I go beyond description to provide an understanding of dynamics?

In practice, planning researchers will find themselves having to negotiate the boundary between a search for rigour in their handling of data and the degree of pragmatism necessary to complete a research project at all, let alone within a given timescale. It is very rarely the case (perhaps never) that the empirical data one collects unequivocally proves a particular finding. Data has to be interpreted, and a narrative developed about what it tells us. That narrative will link a number of threads together, and it is possible that certain empirical data could be used to support rather different narratives. For example, data on housebuilding rates may be interpreted differently if one takes a historical perspective, a focus on behaviour by housebuilders or a record of decisions by planners and their rationale.

Each of these narratives implies certain value judgements, and there may be conflicts or at least tensions in combining different narratives. Thus, the researcher is left with making their own choices and building the most persuasive narrative they can with the data that they have available. In meeting all these challenges, incorporating a theoretical perspective explicitly can make an important contribution.

The Role of Theory

In this section I look at the role of theory and theories, asking whether it is necessary and what its distinctive contribution is to planning research.

What Is Theory?

The term 'theory' has been defined in different ways (Næss and Saglie 2000: 735). Some emphasise the idea of theory as a law, connecting variables together in a systematic way. This mirrors the use of theory in the natural sciences testing laws and searching for empirical evidence to confirm or refute theorised relationships. Flyvbjerg et al. (2012) argue that social science research should not seek to emulate the search for causal laws found in the natural sciences. The complexity of the social world and its interactions with the environment (built and natural) and the 'double hermeneutic' whereby social scientist are interpreting the way that people interpret the world (Giddens 1986) suggest that the natural sciences are not a good model for the social sciences.

In an alternative view, theory is a heuristic aid to understanding a situation, a way to try to know what is essentially unknowable in its completeness. Here the world is irreducibly complex, and we understand it only partially. We aim to understand more by layering up analyses of the world and considering how they relate to each other. A theoretical framework suggests general patterns of how different elements come together to create the world we live in. While empirical research is, of necessity, always limited in some way—time, space, scale, focus—theory seeks to provide an explanation that goes beyond these specific instances of planning practice.

Theory, here, is a narrative account of the world and of planning processes. Theory is, therefore, best seen as a set of ideas that fit together coherently and make general statements about the world or a part of it. The ideas provide an account of the processes at work, an account that is largely textual and therefore narrative but may involve diagrammatic or even formulaic illustrations to convey this account convincingly. The persuasiveness of these accounts—both in themselves and in how they illuminate empirical research—is central.

Each theory looks at the world slightly differently, building different elements into the narrative. Thus, it matters to the researcher which theory they take on board. But theories are not just framings in the sense of an arbitrary selection of a window through which to view the world. They involve fundamental assumptions about how the world is as well as value judgements about how it should be (even if these are not explicitly stated). With these ontological and normative positions goes a view about how knowledge can be generated through empirical research, an epistemological position.

The terrain of theory is, therefore, a contested one because to engage with theory is to engage with alternative conceptualisations of the world. One has to make choices. If this theory seems more convincing to you, its story of how the world works is resonating with you. It is drawing attention to things that you consider important, or perhaps it is drawing your attention to things you had not considered before and are now convinced are important. There is always a range of reasons why any one person finds a particular theory attractive; included amongst these are the (implicit) value judgements that connect the researcher and the theoretical framework. Choosing between theories is a way of making these value judgements an integral element of one's research, and that is often profoundly satisfying. But one needs to understand what theory can and cannot offer to one's research in order to make the best use of it.

Is Theory Necessary?

A good starting point for discussing the role that theory can play is to ask if it is necessary at all! There is a point of view, labelled empiricism, which argues that the facts can be allowed to speak for themselves. The emphasis is on rigorously collecting data and analysing this to let patterns emerge. There is no need for the filter of theory to stand between the researcher and the world as revealed through data collection. In this view, the world exists 'out there' and needs only to be looked at to reveal itself. This is a view that has been called the 'modernist settlement' by sociologist of science, Bruno Latour (1987).

Without going into the theoretical and even philosophical reasons for why 'holding up a mirror to nature' through empiricist practices may not be appropriate, there are more pragmatic reasons for arguing against empiricism. The first is that there are numerous value judgements involved in what seems to be (and often self-presents itself as) a neutral research practice. It is not possible to collect all the data on a topic, and thus the researcher's attention is partial. Why collect this data and not that? Why collect this data in this particular way? And why has the research topic been defined in that way in the first place? Second, there may well be alternative interpretations of the data that is collected. What justifies one interpretation over another? Again, there will be judgements and associated values involved in this work of data analysis. A more general problem with the empiricist position is that the reliance on empirical research results in a rather disparate field of knowledge. Each situation is researched, in detail, but it can become difficult to make connections between different research projects and their findings.

I would argue that a theoretical framing is an essential resource for the planning researcher in response to both these problems. It enables the researcher to focus their attention, but it also helps them contribute to knowledge through a better analysis of empirical findings and through building a broader picture of planning within the world. Before discussing these points, it is worth dwelling on an influential account that suggests a more limited role for theory and puts more emphasis on the value of building an understanding 'bottom-up' from the findings of empirical research. This is the idea of phronesis.

Flyvbjerg et al. propose "producing situated knowledge about how to understand and act in contextualised settings, based on deliberation about specific sets of values and interests" (Flyvbjerg et al. 2012: 2). This turns research into phronesis or the search for practical wisdom. Such research activity is heavily based on the idea of utilising local and tacit knowledges that emerge from practice. To this is added the importance of praxis as seeking change in the context of "an appreciation of the ineliminable presence of power" (ibid.). Such phronetic research involves answering four questions (2012: 3):

1. Where are we going with this specific problematic?
2. Who gains and who loses, and by which mechanisms of power?
3. Is this development desirable?
4. What, if anything, should we do about it?

There are a number of issues with this approach. First, it dispenses too readily with the idea of theory within the social sciences based on a 'straw man' of what theory can be. It presents research as a-theoretical task, and pursuing phronesis successfully "is actually closer to a virtue, or a set of virtues, that is part of the character of the person" [the researcher] (2012: 19). I prefer to consider research as a skill that can be learnt rather than an inherent personal virtue.

Second, phronesis involves theoretical judgements that are not made explicit. For example, the argument for phronesis relies on Giddens' double hermeneutic (Giddens 1986) in which social scientists interpret the way that actors interpret the world. It is a theoretical choice to base research on this argument and not a way of avoiding theory. Similarly, the emphasis on praxis within research and the preference for in-depth case studies with embedded researchers imply an unacknowledged adoption of a theoretical perspective. If the researcher gains the agreement of political leaders and chief executives to be involved in governmental planning and then engages in dialogue with those actors to change planning, this assumes change in planning processes can be achieved through feedback or communicative action (see Chaps. 2 and 5). Or if the researcher's take on praxis leads them to engage with community groups to assist them in struggles over planning disputes, this implies a view of planning as a political process riven with conflict (see Chap. 6).

Thus, phronesis—as a way of influencing change in planning processes—can and, I would argue, should go with a more explicitly theoretical framing of the research. Not all the theoretical approaches discussed in Chaps. 2, 3, 4, 5, 6, 7, 8 and 9 lend themselves to a phronetic approach, but as indicated earlier, there are some that do, and the search for practical wisdom through interpreting planning practice can go alongside acknowledging chosen theoretical foundations.

The Advantages of Using Theory

There are a number of practical as well as intellectual advantages to incorporating a theoretical component within planning research.

First, adopting a theoretical framework can be of immense help to a researcher in early decisions about what to focus on and what to place more or less emphasis on. As will become clear in subsequent chapters of this book, different theoretical frameworks have very different views of what is important and what plays the largest role in shaping planning processes. The theory that a researcher draws on helps to make these judgements explicit. More practically, it enables the researcher to focus their efforts on certain issues, data and empirical sources; to downplay others; and, therefore, to operate within the practical constraints of a time- and funding-limited research project.

Second, given that any empirical account is necessarily going to be partial and provisional, the linking of empirical research to a theoretical account enables the narrative that the researcher develops to fit into a broader pre-existing story about planning. This assists in the task of analysing and concluding from empirical research. The potential for generalising from specific sets of empirical findings also comes with the linking of those findings to a broader account of how planning works. The ability of the researcher to create a persuasive narrative using their empirical findings is reinforced by a theoretical framework that is, in itself, also persuasive. In the examples of research that are discussed in later chapters, I will be particularly looking for the way that the theoretical account is entwined with and used to support the emergence of an analytic narrative based on empirical results.

Third, the intertwining of theory and research points to the possibility of using empirical research to build theory, and to revise and amplify theoretical frameworks. This is a further contribution that theory-led research can make, going beyond the knowledge of the specific empirical focus of the research. Theory is a way of linking the understanding of the particular with an understanding of the general and advancing both. Thus, a broader ambition of planning research is not just to understand a particular aspect of planning practice or the planning system or the planning process, but to contribute to a deeper understanding of society in general through an investigation of planning.

There are other intellectual attractions to engaging with theory. Theoretical writings are often abstract, intriguing and exciting to read. They offer the prospect of working on a broader intellectual scale, with 'big ideas'. There is the possibility of developing a more fundamental understanding of the world that will carry the research across the pragmatic details and tribulations of specific research projects. There is the sense of being involved in something more profound than the individual details and datasets one has accumulated during research. While it is often fascinating to find out how particular planning situations work, many planning researchers are also attracted by engaging with this sense of how the world at large works.

This puts theory at the heart of the academic inquiry into planning systems and the intellectual debates about planning. Let's return again to the question of how such theorising relates to normative concerns and the desire to improve the world through 'better' planning. Reference has already been made to the field of normative planning theory. This is a body of work that seeks to theorise, that is to generalise ways of improving planning practice. There is a degree of overlap between normative planning theory and analytic theory of planning. One example is the links between governance theory (covered in Chap. 5) and collaborative planning theory. The former is an analytic theory deriving from political science that seeks to understand urban policy and planning in terms of networks of relationships between stakeholders; the latter is a normative planning theory that sees the potential for improving planning by developing more communicative action between stakeholders and aiming for mutual understanding and (possibly) consensus. There is clearly scope for overlap given the emphasis of both on how stakeholders interact. Thus, the use of some conceptual frameworks can have both a normative and analytic dimension.

As indicated earlier, there has been some concern from the world of planning practice that the use of theory, both normative and analytic, has driven a wedge between the academy and that planning practice. The suggestion is that the very language involved in using such theories make then unintelligible to practitioners and, further, that they result in rather critical accounts of what planners and planning systems do. The scope of such theories seems too large for specific improvements in practice; the tone is too sweeping in terms of the reasons for the status quo to enable practitioners to change what they do.

I remain optimistic that it is possible to combine the intellectual excitement of a theory-led approach with communication with practitioners and policy makers in a way that can support self-reflection and possibly lead to change in practices and processes. Clear communication and positive engagement with civil society, state and professional organisations and the polity can be an important part of this; language can be translated to move between these domains and the academy. However, it is the role of the academy to do the best job it can of the research task first.

The Structure of the Book

The main body of the book is structured into eight chapters, each of which looks at a particular body of theory that has informed planning research. These are followed by a conclusion in Chap. 10, which provides reflections on doing research. Some readers may wish to pair reading this Introduction with the Conclusion before dipping into the substantive, theory-led chapters. These theory-led chapters cover a range of different theoretical approaches.

Chapter 2 looks at the insights coming from a governmental or public administration perspective, one that has underpinned much evaluation work within planning studies. Chapter 3 then considers the contribution of the rational choice or public choice school of political science, drawing on certain aspects of economic analysis to understand policy processes. Chapter 4 considers the nature of the institutions that constitute the planning system and the contribution that cultural theory has made to understanding how such institutions work. In Chap. 5, attention shifts to the 'governance turn' that characterised political science and much planning studies in the late twentieth century and the links with using networks to understanding planning processes. Chapter 6 puts the concept of conflict centre stage and considers how planning is a form of urban politics and also the value of seeing conflict as agonism. A more structuralist form of analysis is introduced in Chap. 7 with an account of Marxian-inspired political economy and associated recent developments. Chapter 8 looks at the legacy of Foucault's work within planning studies, including the importance of discourse and a reconceptualisation of 'power'. The penultimate chapter, Chap. 9, looks at relational perspectives, including consideration of assemblage thinking and the role of material entities.

This arc across planning research, thus, roughly moves from the ideal of planning as a linear rational activity (as in Chap. 1) through more actor-centred approaches that highlight the agency of individuals and organisations (Chaps. 3, 4, 5 and 6) to more structural accounts (Chap. 7). It then ends with two relational perspectives (Chaps. 8 and 9) that unsettle conventional ideas of agency and even the actor. However, beyond this, the theoretical approaches vary quite considerably in their focus, how they frame planning processes and the dynamics that are identified as important. They can also be distinguished in terms of what scope they see for improving planning and how that improvement might come about. It has been emphasised earlier that this book is not a work of planning theory, since such planning theory is primarily about how planning ought to be carried out; the emphasis here is on supporting research into how planning is carried out. But that does not mean that the theories discussed here do not imply a view about how planning might be made better. As has been repeatedly emphasised, all theoretical endeavours in the social sciences are inevitably value-laden, and a rigorous approach should seek to make this clear and explicit. An aspect of such values is the desire to find and achieve 'good' planning practice. It is here that the conceptual frameworks discussed in this book differ considerably.

For the governmental approaches, the hope is that better action by planners and other governmental officials will help achieve the desired outcomes, both driven by the political process in setting goals for the future. Rational choice sees individual actors as influenced in their decision-making by the incentive structures they are facing, and thus if the current patterns are suboptimal, planning processes can be improved by realigning those incentive structures in various ways. Turning to New Institutionalism, the key dynamics here concern the culture of organisations and how this shapes internal behaviour. Thus, detailed ways of influencing that culture through learning may help promote better planning. Similarly, within governance approaches, the emphasis is on how different actors across different sectors work together, and the assumption is that better planning will result from the planner being more skilled in enabling partnership working, managing networks and underpinning collaborative approaches. All these four conceptual approaches could be seen as looking inward, to the workings of planning actors and organisations for improving planning practice.

The next set of conceptual frameworks look beyond the planner and planning organisation and see the scope for improved planning outcomes as residing in actors, organisations and agency beyond the state. Urban politics, for example, sees certain groups in society as repeatedly disadvantaged within planning processes and thus looks to ways they can be better resourced, listened to more thoroughly and given more power. Political economy also comes from a perspective where socio-economic inequality is seen as central, but it looks to more structural change in society as a way of resolving this. Foucauldian approaches can be argued to tend to the structural, and indeed, their emphasis on hidden forms of power can suggest there is little prospect of achieving improvements in how planning works to deliver on goals such as sustainability or social inclusion or equity. However, there is within Foucault's work the idea of resistance to societal structures, which suggests a possible pathway to better societal outcomes. Relational perspectives including Actor-Network Theory have been criticised for offering more of a detailed description than a fully fledge theory of dynamics at work. This means that the prescriptions they offer for better planning are often small-scale experimentation and nuanced changes in assemblages.

These different theoretical perspectives do not, of course, exist in isolation from each other. They have often been developed through a critical analysis of weaknesses in the different theories. Table 1.1 suggests how the approaches discussed in this book react in different ways to the limitations found in the governmental approach outlined in Chap. 2; this governmental approach could be said to be closest to the self-presentation of planning as a rational, expert-led process. It provides not only a rationale for the actions of the planner and the planning department but also a kind of template. If this template does not work effectively, then it needs to be adjusted at the margin; the solutions still lie within the planning process itself. For many researchers there are other reasons why the ideal of Chap. 2 is not matched by actual planning practice, and different theoretical approaches seek to deepen and generalise those reasons. Table 1.1 summarises this.

Table 1.1 The relationship of subsequent chapters to the governmental approach

Chapter	Theoretical approach	
2	Governmental Models	Planning as a rational, comprehensive and evidence-based process undertaken by the public sector
		Critique of the governmental approach
3	Rational Choice	Does not recognise the prevalence of state failure and the influence of state actors' self-interests
4	New Institutionalism	Lacks a cultural dimension which often drives action including path dependency
5	Governance Theory	Underestimates the importance of stakeholder involvement in the policy process, both formulation and implementation
6	Urban Politics	Need to look outside the state processes at wider political forces in society and the role of power and of conflict
7	Political Economy	Neglects the structural forces, particularly economic forces that shape governmental action and/or its outcomes
8	Foucauldian Approach	The 'taken-for-granted' dimension of societal discourses and their influence is ignored
9	Relational Approaches	The complexity of the inter-relation of elements, including material elements, is underplayed

Because there is this implicit dialogue across the chapters in the book about the strengths and weaknesses of different approaches, I decided not to include a section in each chapter about the limitations of adopting that particular approach. This would be too repetitive, taking the chapters as a whole; it is also not in the spirit of the book which seeks to support the research activities of planning researchers, whichever theoretical approach they find most interesting and persuasive to themselves. It is my view that all these approaches have the potential to bring some insight into planning processes and practice and, further, that researchers have a right to reflect their own value judgements in their research work. Clearly, there are some perspectives that I am personally more drawn too, but I have tried not to let this influence the account that I give.

Each chapter outlines the relevant theoretical perspective, highlighting the key concepts used and the way that the dynamics involved in planning activities is understood. It then looks at some examples of published planning research undertaken within the given theoretical framework to show how the theory has been used and what the implications were for the framing of the research and the methodologies deployed. These papers have been selected after a widespread review of published research. Bibliographic searches using keywords resulted in hundreds of abstracts to review; the most interesting were selected for detailed reading, and those that best exemplified the theoretical approach were selected. At the same time, the categorisation of the theoretical approaches was refined and became more consolidated as these examples of research practice were studied.

The papers are discussed here not for their specific insights into the particular topics studied but for how the researchers have benefited from their chosen theoretical framing. I made the selection by choosing papers where the theoretical focus was explicit, the methods were sufficiently detailed to see how the empirical work was undertaken and where a link between the theory and the method was demonstrated. I also sought to provide a geographical spread in the areas studied (looking across Europe, North America, Africa, the Middle East, Oceania and Asia) and a range of planning issues in terms of the topics discussed. I have not engaged in a critique of each paper; in general, I have chosen papers that seemed strong, but the main interest in presenting these papers is to show how they have related theory and method and the implications for the analysis and results that ensue.

To finish—a note on references. At the end of each chapter, the research papers that are discussed in detail under 'Research Themes' are listed; this collection of research papers, therefore, could support discussion in a seminar, say, as a kind of course collection. This is preceded by background references on the theoretical frameworks discussed. I have chosen, hoping this makes access easier, to draw on a limited set of handbooks and similar collections that are likely to be available in libraries. The following books have been used:

The Routledge Handbook of Planning Theory, edited by Michael Gunder, Ali Madanipour and Vanessa Watson (2018)
Connections: Exploring Contemporary Planning Theory and Practice with Patsy Healey, edited by Jean Hillier and Jonathan Metzger (2015)

Complexity and Planning: Systems, Assemblages and Simulations, edited by Gert De Roo, Jean Hillier, and Joris van Wezemael (2012)
Contemporary Movements in Planning Theory, edited by Jean Hillier and Patsy Healey (2008)
Readings in Planning Theory, edited by Scott Campbell and Susan S. Fainstein (2003)
Explorations in Planning Theory, edited by Seymour Mandelbaum, Luigi Mazza, and Richard Burchell (1996)

All in-text references are, of course, included in the final bibliography for the book.

Bibliography

Campbell, Heather, Malcolm Tait, and Craig Watkins. 2014. Is There Space for Better Planning in a Neoliberal World? Implications for Planning Practice and Theory. *Journal of Planning Education and Research* 34 (1): 45–59.

Faludi, Andreas. 1973. *Planning Theory*. Oxford: Pergamon.

Flyvbjerg, Bent, Todd Landman, and Sanford Schram, eds. 2012. *Real Social Science: Applied Phronesis*. Cambridge: Cambridge University Press.

Giddens, Anthony. 1986. *The Constitution of Society: Outline of the Theory of Structuration*. Cambridge: Polity Press.

Goodman, Robin, Robert Freestone, and Paul Burton. 2017. Planning Practice and Academic Research: Views from the Parallel Worlds. *Planning, Practice & Research*: 1–12.

Latour, Bruno. 1987. *Science in Action: How to Follow Scientists and Engineers through Society*. Cambridge, MA: Harvard University Press.

Næss, Petter, and Inger-Lise Saglie. 2000. Surviving Between the Trenches: Planning Research, Methodology and Theory of Science. *European Planning Studies* 8 (6): 729–750.

Chapter 2
Governmental Models: The Hope of Rational Public Administration

Framing the Research

Planning history accounts tend to present planning as a way of responding to a set of problems in the urban, rural, built and/or natural environments. It emerges in response to the appalling living conditions in rapidly growing cities associated with substandard housing, inadequate sewage, clean water and other infrastructure and pollution of different kinds. This prompts action on housing and other land uses and investment in urban infrastructure, creating the activity of planning. One influential account of the problems that planning addresses comes from welfare economics (Oxley 2004). The key concept here is that of market failure, demonstrating how and why market processes fail to deliver in the broader public interest.

There are a number of different sources of market failure. The term 'externalities' captures the impacts (both positive and negative) that do not register in the price mechanism of the market. Pollution is a typical negative externality. These are linked to missing markets, where the lack of a pricing mechanism to ration use leads to over-exploitation. Beautiful views can often be subject to this mechanism. Another missing market is that in information, where the inability to charge leads to an under-supply of certain types of information in a market society. Welfare economics also identifies certain other kinds of good that tend to be under-supplied under market conditions. These are either welfare or merit goods (those things that a society collectively decides it is useful for people to have) or public goods (which once supplied to some, it is not possible to exclude others from having). Good housing may be considered a merit good; street lighting is a classic public good. Finally, welfare economics alerts us to the dangers of monopolies and oligopolies, seeing them as a source of inefficiency. Given that planning is concerned with the use, development and change of land-based activities, one key monopoly that is of concern is that exercised by landowners. This can provide a justification for the public sector stepping in to protect society from landowners' monopolistic power.

Y. Rydin, *Theory in Planning Research*, Planning, Environment, Cities, https://doi.org/10.1007/978-981-33-6568-1_2

These arguments provide a strong rationale for the public sector creating, becoming involved in and operating planning processes that will meet the broader public interest rather than the more problematic outcomes promoted by market dynamics. Or, put another way, planning redresses problems that market processes alone cannot solve. Thus, planning processes are about meeting the public interest through the control, management and direction of change in the physical environment. This perspective puts the planner and other public sector officials centre stage, in the Weberian tradition. The questions become ones of how public policies are made and how they are implemented. The goals themselves stand outside the planning process; they are set by the political realm, by debate between politicians who—through the electoral process—are subject to public concerns and desires. However, the public administration, thereafter, plays the key role. They interpret the policy goals and consider how they may be implemented. They bring expert knowledge to bear on the options available and how policy instruments may be used.

Planning, therefore, solves problems; it is purposeful. In general terms, it describes a course of action that seeks to achieve something. Urban planning aims to improve towns and cities, environmental planning to protect and enhance the natural environment, transport planning to create an efficient and effective system of mobility and so on. The idea of the smart city might be seen as the latest exemplar of this approach with its integration of technological rationality into the heart of urban planning. The focus of the public administration approach, though, is on the processes by which it achieves these aims. The assumption is that good planning produces the desired outcomes, and the search is for how to improve such planning. Any problems are seen to lie within the planning process and with the way that public sector planners operate.

This chapter looks at approaches that focus on the links between planning as an activity and these public interest goals that justify its existence. From this perspective, planning is a general set of procedures and actions that can guide action (often the action of other actors) to deliver on these goals. It is both specific in that it addresses the built and natural environment and general in that it is about 'planning' as conventionally understood. As such, the public administration approach frames planning as a rational way of linking means and ends, and also as an idealised set of steps to be followed. A good example of this is provided by renowned planner and planning commentator, Nathaniel Lichfield. In this ideal model of planning, data collection and identification of alternative pathways precedes systematic consideration of these alternatives, identification of the preferred path and then effective implementation. Monitoring to see what the outcomes of planning processes are is also important as it enables the cycle of planning to be completed, with the outcomes of the planning process feeding in to revisions in how policy instruments are deployed (Fig. 2.1).

In many ways, the governmental model of planning processes is an ideal that planning policy makers aspire to. It is found as a recommendation within public documentation and professional guidance. This ideal type can be summarised as follows:

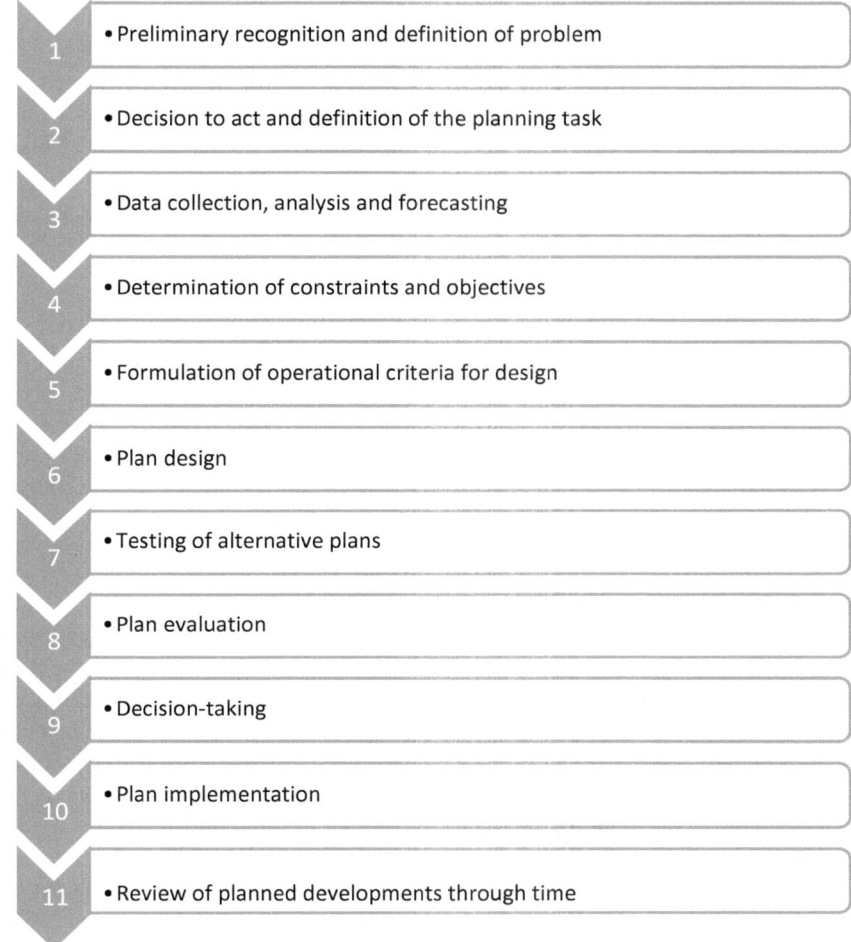

1 • Preliminary recognition and definition of problem

2 • Decision to act and definition of the planning task

3 • Data collection, analysis and forecasting

4 • Determination of constraints and objectives

5 • Formulation of operational criteria for design

6 • Plan design

7 • Testing of alternative plans

8 • Plan evaluation

9 • Decision-taking

10 • Plan implementation

11 • Review of planned developments through time

Fig. 2.1 The general planning process (following Lichfield). (Source: Adapted from Lichfield et al. 1975)

> Planning is future-oriented in its vision and comprehensive in its scope. It emphasises synthesis and integration and is based on information, knowledge and evidence. It responds to the idea of the public interest set in the political sphere and involves stakeholders but only in an instrumental way to increase effectiveness.

The governmental approach keeps its focus firmly on these processes, looking for an understanding of how planning works in terms of its internal dynamics and not straying far into the context within which planning operates.

Dynamics of Analysis and Key Concepts

There are three aspects of these dynamics that are considered important from a governmental perspective: the aim of synthesising a comprehensive body of information; the reliance on evidence; and the importance of implementation of plans, policies and programmes.

Evidence-Based Planning

A key feature of this governmental approach to planning is that it draws on information and knowledge. Planning policy making should be based on the best current state of knowledge. This begins with data about the current situation. But this is not just knowledge about the existing context for planning that is important. Some of this knowledge may be about likely future scenarios, current trends in the economy or society or environmental change. But some may also be about how a particular development (or set of developments) may have an impact. This kind of knowledge is important for the regulation of development projects. Taking the example of major infrastructure projects, such as wind farms, the planning process requires knowledge of how the turbines may impact on local wildlife such as birds through risk of hitting the blades or local residents in terms of noise and flicker; in offshore locations, impacts on fishing fleets and populations of fish and marine mammals due to construction noise and underwater cabling become significant (Rydin et al. 2018a). In Chap. 8 the very concept of 'knowledge' will be questioned, but for the governmental approach, the assumption is that knowledge can be gathered and made available to the planning process in a positive way, supporting decision-making and the development of strategies.

There is some suggestion that the capacities of IT systems will enable better use of very large datasets to the benefit of planning. Kontokosta argues that: "The increasing complexity of urban life also requires that planners bring to bear new data and new computational methods to understand the dynamics of urbanism, forecast and predict future needs, and comprehensively evaluate policy alternatives" (Kontokosta 2018: 11). Rational planning should not just gather as much information and knowledge as possible; rather it needs to actively have a knowledge management approach in the context of rapidly escalating data availability and IT-based decision support systems (Nobre et al. 2016).

Rational planning is also underpinned by knowledge of how planning processes work. This is given clear expression in the phrase 'evidence-based planning', which relies on "the assumption that we can make policies work better if we understand how policy mechanisms bring about change in social systems to achieve desired outcomes" (Sanderson 2002: 2). Sanderson distinguishes between knowledge of such processes to achieve improvement in public sector action and the provision of information about such action, which is designed to improve accountability. While there have been suggestions that policy or planning often leads to the choice of evidence rather than the other way around, the legitimacy of public sector action is clearly based on the idea that planning-based evidence is not the norm (Davoudi 2006). To quote Sanderson again: "it appears to be rational common sense to see policy as a purposive course of action in pursuit of objectives based upon careful assessment of alternative ways of achieving such objectives and effective implementation of the selected course of action" (2002: 5).

The overall logic of rational governmental planning is one that relates means to ends: the planning system will use the means available to it to achieve the ends set by the political system (which may be central, regional or local government or a mix of these). A knowledge-based rationality will enable planners to make the best choice of means available to achieve these goals. Ideally this needs evidence about how the goals set for the planning system can be met by action within that system. Of course, this is not always easy to establish given the multitude of confounding factors that could be involved in generating any particular situation. Market and social dynamics may be relevant as well as specific planning actions and decisions in shaping urban change. Thus, assumptions may be made about planning being able to have the effect it is aiming for; the effectiveness of planning systems may be taken for granted to some degree.

Towards a Comprehensive Synthesis

Another distinctive characteristic of planning as a generic activity is that it seeks to take account of many different dimensions of a problem or activity. Even where the term 'planning' is specified by reference to a descriptor such as 'environmental', 'spatial' and 'transport', there is still a sense that the contribution of planning is to bring a broader perspective to the issue. Thus, transport infrastructure in an area will be planned with reference to easing congestion, promoting public safety, reducing environmental impact, encouraging economic development in certain locations and so on. The planning of an area of urban regeneration will similarly be done in order to promote urban design that fosters a sense of community, is accessible and promotes a mix of viable land uses. Often the 'triple-bottom line' of social, environment and economic goals is used to assess how far a particular planning exercise manages to achieve a truly comprehensive perspective. It is argued that only by being comprehensive in this way can planning fulfil the promise of being in the public interest.

But this is more than just ensuring that all the different dimensions of a development, a plan or a policy are taken into account. It is also about how to integrate these different dimensions, so that their impact on each other is considered. How should the landscape be designed so that it can act as an effective sustainable urban drainage system at the same time as being aesthetically pleasing, safe and accessible for all users, and not taking up too much valuable development land or impeding the road, cycleway and footpath systems. Another way of putting this is to say that planning is a synthesising activity, looking across all relevant issues and impacts to produce a reasoned and balanced overall view.

One way that has been recommended as a means to achieving such integration is to conceive of urban or environmental processes as systems that planning intervenes in or tries to manage. McLoughlin was a key proponent of planning as based in systems thinking (McLoughlin 1969). More recently there has been an emphasis on socio-ecological systems as a way of thinking about sustainability and ensuring that social and environmental dimensions are adequately considered in relation to each other (Domptail et al. 2013; Burayidi et al. 2019). It should be noted that this kind of systems approach is rather different to the complex systems framework that underpins the shift towards more experimental planning discussed in Chap. 10.

To be clear, planning systems and planning actors seek to achieve this comprehensive synthesis rationally; societal preferences as expressed through the political system and public or stakeholder engagement exercises may be an important input into planning, but the legitimacy of plans and planning decisions comes from the rationality of the analysis and propositions that are put forward by planners and planning agencies. As Sanderson says: "The legacy of the Enlightenment is proving robust against post-modern attacks on the notion of rationality" (2002: 1), and within the governmental approach, the gold standard for planning is being seen to be rational.

A range of procedures have been developed which fit within such a rational model of planning and provide means of integrating knowledge into planning processes. Amongst these may be cited environmental assessment and strategic environmental assessment, cost-benefit analysis, multi-criteria analysis and uses of Geographical Information Science. Proponents of these techniques usually emphasise that these are not decision-making tools but rather ways of offering information to the planning system, where the legitimate locus of taking decisions lies.

These are clearly significant ambitions for planners to fulfil, and there have been concerns expressed over the capacity of the state—ministries, agencies or municipalities—to achieve a comprehensive and integrated planning approach in practice. This relates partly to the limits to generating relevant knowledge and partly to the problems of absorbing and appreciating a large body of knowledge. Planning can struggle with both too little knowledge (of the right kind) and too much (to process). This has led to more pragmatic approaches such as disjointed incrementalism, proposed by Lindblom (2010). Here the idea is that rather than seeking to achieve an ambitious vision for the future in one step, there is a focus on incremental steps which together enable progress towards the more comprehensive vision.

Formulation to Implementation

While much of the focus of planning practice is on creating plans and other proposals or strategies, this is not an end in itself. There is a need to consider how the formulation of these documents leads on to implementation. There is a widespread industry inside and outside academe involved in evaluating the performance of planning bodies in terms of the effective implementation of their plans, policies and programmes (e.g. see Chastenet et al. 2016; an example of the French government's evaluation of eco-neighbourhoods). Such evaluation is based on the governmental view of planning as following a linear process of: deliberate—predict—plan—formulate—implement—evaluate. They typically focus on the stated goals or objectives and the stated values and the extent to which these are achieved through the measures proposed. Smith (2018) identifies this kind of activity as plan implementation, as opposed to planning implementation which is closer to integration and deserving of separate process-based evaluation.

Alongside this, there is a body of research that—without disrupting the assumption of a planning process led by politically set goals or rationally linking means and ends—has looked at the detail of how implementation actually occurs. In part this is about the choice of policy instrument and developing an understanding of how the different policy tools work. These policy instruments are a dynamic mechanism within rational planning. A number of such policy instruments are available, and together, they are a measure of the power of the public sector and of the state planner:

- Direct public investment, including landownership and procurement
- Strategic coordination through spatial planning
- Regulation and the granting of authorisations
- Fiscal measures such as taxation and subsidies
- Tradeable market-based permits
- Information and persuasion, including nudge attempts

However, a key insight that has arisen from implementation studies is that planning processes do not just depend on which tools are used but rather on how they are used. There are a range of factors identified here (Smith 2018): appropriateness of the intervention to the context, compatibility between the different elements, the structural context and the scope of agency, resource availability and power, catalysts to implementation, and communication between actors.

Implementation studies also put the emphasis onto the discretion that public bureaucrats such as planners can exercise in the use of policy tools. It highlights the key role that negotiation can play in their deployment. This may be negotiation with actors in civil society or the private sector or with other actors within the public sector. In making a plan, there may be considerable negotiation between public sector departments interested in transport, water, ecology and so on, with the land use or spatial planner seeking to bring the concerns from different quarters together. In deciding on a development proposal, there may be negotiations with the private sector developer and also with the local community over the specific features of the development and how they can be altered to improve outcomes and mitigate negative impacts (Hill 1997; Barrett and Fudge 1981).

This has also led to the questioning of the apparently clear divide between the political and the administrative, with the former setting policy goals and the latter dealing with matters of implementation. Rather research has suggested that policy formulation and implementation are closely entangled with policy goals being reformulated through the implementation process so that planners, as administrators, are inevitably political in their actions. Implementation studies suggest the importance of paying close attention to how planning is undertaken and what planning departments and planners actually do (Clifford and Tewdwr-Jones 2013).

An interesting caveat to this has been proposed by Kaza (2019), who suggests that not all planning activity and, in particular, not all plans should be judged by the extent to which they have been implemented. Some plans have purposes other than achieving their stated objectives, such as framing debates, spreading information or offering a narrative resource. Furthermore, a plan—on its own—is often insufficient to achieve those objectives and should not be judged in isolation. He notes cases of multiple, mutually inconsistent plans being adopted by the same authority, which makes evaluation a challenge! This suggests some modification of evaluation approaches beyond linking stated planning objectives and noted outcomes in a simple manner.

Research Themes in Practice

The framing of planning as a governmental activity thus involves a focus on information or knowledge, synthesis and implementation. In the next section examples of research within this framing are discussed. The specific research themes are support for planning decision-making, implementation including evaluation of planning outcomes, and analysing and promoting integration.

Supporting Decision-Making

Governmental planning often highlights the role of tools designed to assist expert-led planning by adding further or making better use of knowledge, evidence, information and data. These take a variety of forms from those that assess impacts or some aspects of the local baseline to those that support decision-making such as cost-benefit analysis, multi-criteria analysis or other decision support systems (DSS). Here research into two examples is discussed: one looking at vulnerability assessment and one setting out a DSS for neighbourhood energy planning.

Hettinga et al. (2018) sought to develop a multi-stakeholder decision support system for energy planning at the local neighbourhood scale through the design of an addition or amendment to planning procedures and practices and then testing this out in a specific location. The research built upon an established multi-stakeholder engagement platform, Geodesign. This usually involves six steps: mapping current reality, understanding local dynamics processes generating that reality, collecting ideas for improvements and suggesting elements that are to remain unchanged in the future, combining these ideas into scenarios, discussing these scenarios with stakeholders and undertaking impact assessments, and taking the final decision. These steps can be combined iteratively if desired rather than as a single linear run.

This approach was piloted in the Hague, the Netherlands, a city that had set ambitious sustainable climate and energy goals, aiming to be climate neutral by 2040. It particularly focussed on the district of Escamp, chosen because it had potential for clean energy production and savings and because there was a high concentration of housing cooperatives, which reduced the number of potential local stakeholders. In addition, there were mandatory funds available for energy initiatives, making the project more likely to have an impact.

It was found to be necessary to make some amendments to the standard Geodesign process in the context of neighbourhood energy planning in this district. After mapping 'current reality' in Stage 1, Stage 2 was to explore the geodata to understand the processes at work. This took the form of stakeholders remotely (at home or in the office) using a WebViewer to familiarise themselves with the data; the stakeholders here were 12 sustainability officers from different departments of the city administration. This was followed, in Stage 3, by the stakeholders coming together, professionally facilitated, to suggest ideas for improvement, derive a common understanding of the task and identify missing information. The fourth stage set the boundary conditions for a proposal to be acceptable to all stakeholders.

Stage 5 was supported by a touch table or interactive computer interface that could be used to represent and interface with the geospatial data. Ideas from the stakeholders for a clean energy plan for the neighbourhood were gathered together into a proposal by a geospatial expert who also ran impact assessments in real time to allow for modifications to the proposals. In Stage 6 the two separate processes of technical optimisation and collaborative optimisation were combined, leading to the final decision on what was the best option and whether this should be adopted.

The pilot exercise found that the data provided was generally sufficient for the energy planning exercise, but some datasets required additional explanation. Local knowledge revealed previously under-appreciated problems such as the long-standing difficulty of connecting to the existing district heating network. Discussion of this produced potential solutions but also alternative clean energy pathways. Three boundary conditions were agreed identifying the types of property to be prioritised for energy efficiency measures, PV installation and heat and coolth storage. On this basis a neighbourhood energy plan was drawn up.

The conclusion was that the DSS "was shown to be suitable to support the local energy planning for the local municipality" (p. 285). The researchers specifically drew attention to the value of the stakeholders' involvement in setting boundaries and in confronting the technical optimisation with their local knowledge, and to the role of the expert facilitator (an expert in the geodata was deemed necessary). Above all there was considerable benefit in bringing the stakeholders and experts together to share knowledge and devise new boundary conditions together.

The public administration framing of the research was underpinned by assumptions of rationality in this decision-making, on the value of data and the ability to devise a better plan. The research involved considerable technical expertise on the part of the researchers in using geodata and assembling it into a Spatial Data

Infrastructure, developing proposals and modelling scenarios, assessing impacts and also visualisation techniques; however, it centrally involved engagement of local stakeholders also. The project was thus a kind of live experiment in local planning, supporting planners in their administrative and professional tasks.

Kumar et al. (2016) were concerned with incorporating information about climate change vulnerability at the city scale into planning. In particular they looked at vulnerability assessment, a tool to support spatial planning by collating and representing information about the likely effect of climate change on a locality. Their case study was Bangalore in India, but they were concerned to develop a general tool, one that can be standardised and used across different cities. The starting point for the design of the tool was to consider three different aspects of vulnerability, drawing on a socio-ecological systems approach; these were exposure to climate change risks, sensitivity to such risks and adaptive capacity. They reviewed a range of literature on these different dimensions in order to draw together a set of indicators for each one.

The second stage in the methodology was based in Bangalore and involved a review of planning policy documentation, open-ended semi-structured interviews with key stakeholders (n = 16) and a focus group, also with stakeholders. These stakeholders were described as active in the planning and management of Bangalore and comprised a mix of local officials and residents, including residents' groups: "This process aimed at identifying and verifying key indicators that were acceptable by the key stakeholders and represents the socio-ecological and climate change concerns of Bangalore city" (p. 518). These indicators had to be acceptable to key stakeholders and also verified through reported research on other cities. Finally, there was an exploratory survey (n = 58; the nature of the respondents was not clear) to consider the prioritisation of the indicators. The resulting indicator set is summarised in Table 2.1.

The researchers then went on to test the application of the indicator set by combining its use with a spatial analysis of the vulnerability of Bangalore; the combination was achieved through a technique known as Spatial Multi-Criteria Evaluation.

Table 2.1 Kumar et al.'s indicator set

Exposure indicators	Sensitivity indicators	Adaptive capacity indicators
Hot days per annum	Area covered by road	% hshlds who own their home
Mean temperature increase	Fluctuation in ground water	% hshlds with access to banking
Rain range	Number of slums	% hshlds owning any kind of asset
Days per annum with heavy rain	Land use change	% people who are literate
	% people below 6 years	% hshlds with drinking water
	% liveable houses	% hshlds with waste water drainage
	High-density areas	% hshlds with efficient cooking fuel
	Loss of lakes and wetland areas	% areas having road access
		% area under lakes
		Green space per person

Source: Compiled from Kumar et al. (2016)

This process had five steps. First, a criteria tree for vulnerability based on the three dimensions was built with different indicators categorised as benefits, costs or constraints. Second, the indicator measurements were standardised on a 0–1 scale to make them comparable. Third, based on the stakeholder engagement, weightings were applied, and fourth, this was incorporated into the criteria tree. The exposure indicators were weighted 30%, the sensitivity indicators 45% and the adaptive capacity indicators 25%, with further breakdowns within each category. Fifth, the weighted vulnerability indicator metrics were aggregated into an index, and finally, a test was conducted with different weightings. The outcomes were a series of spatial maps illustrating vulnerability (and the component elements of exposure, sensitivity and adaptive capacity) for the city at the ward level.

Cluster analysis was also used to classify different areas in terms of vulnerability: very high, high and medium. The Fraiman measure was calculated to identify which aspect of vulnerability had the greatest impact on the overall result; this suggested that the sensitivity dimension and, further, the social aspects of sensitivity (demographic structure and standard of housing) were most significant. The result was described as "a rational and simple vulnerability assessment approach that is operational at any local spatial scale and can help prioritise response actions" (p. 522). Here a tool was developed that was definitely expert led. It demanded considerable expertise of different kinds, involving multiple techniques. The aim was to provide information for the professional planning. Although there was reference to testing involving stakeholders, the planner remained centre stage.

These two examples show how this kind of research involves a testing-out of new procedures with quite considerable technical demands. Often there is also a need to add a conceptual framework to understand the urban and environmental systems that are being planned; the use of socio-ecological systems thinking is an example here. Because the public administration concentrates on how to plan, it may require additional support for the understanding of what is being planned. These research examples also focus on the value systems of stakeholders as well as their knowledge of planning; this enhances the researcher's understanding of the practicalities of such planning as well as its acceptability. But the frame for research is the planner or planning organisation, the procedures they follow and the role that knowledge, data and information can play.

Implementation and Evaluation

Another major theme within this area of research is the nature of implementation in practice and the extent to which such implementation meets the goals originally set. Some of this research takes the form of evaluating plans, policies, programmes and projects; other looks more closely at the ways in which implementation falls short.

Ma et al. (2018) considered the plan to turn Chongming, near Shanghai, into an Eco Island. Chongming is an interesting case as it was the focus of much international interest when an early eco-city proposal for Dongtan was developed by the global consultancy Arup. However, this proposal was never implemented, and the Eco Island proposal was more based on nature conservation than sustainable urban development, drawing on its ecological characteristics as a wetland. Ma et al. developed a fourfold typology of eco-city projects based on the role of the national government and the involvement of foreign expertise. The Chongming project was characterised as having indirect and limited national support and weak and unstructured foreign support (the other categories were the flagship project, cases of greenwash and the purely nominal project). This meant that the project was heavily reliant on local government action. They then developed an evaluation framework and used this to monitor the success of implementing the policy.

Their research was thus both an evaluation exercise and also an attempt to understand the reasons behind the limited extent to which the policy was implemented. In particular, it was reacting to the extensive use of formal indicator sets within Chinese planning and suggesting a more nuanced way of understanding progress or its lack. In the Chongming case they detailed existing monitoring efforts through indicator sets at the national, provincial and district levels. They noted that the self-assessment of the project by the Ministry of Science and Technology and Shanghai Municipal Government found that 19 of the 22 indicator targets for 2014 had been met. However, they contrasted this with an early and more qualified report from the United Nations Environmental Programme and a later and similarly qualified assessment from the Development and Reform Committee of the municipality; these disparities prompted the researchers' own assessment. In seeking to understand this, they were qualifying the simpler form of the rational planning approach: "Implementation, although potentially served by the presence of clear concepts, indicator systems and guidelines for monitoring project progress, in fact depends at least as much as on taking into consideration the interests and needs other actors in the policy network have" (pp. 873–874).

The methodology involved collecting geographic data on the area, examining the administrative context and mapping existing monitoring evidence, providing considerable descriptive detail: "a vivid narrative and picture of the physical status of the island" (p. 882). Next, they designed an assessment matrix and applied this to the Chongming case through desk-based work and field visits. The framework had two axes. On the first, seven major themes derived from the Shanghai and Chongming master plans were outlined: urban layout, eco and protected areas, agriculture and organic products, transport, solid waste, tourism and connecting the water courses. Using these, the changing nature of the plans for the area could be tracked. The other axis had details of the theme and its contents, observed use of space, observed unanticipated developments and explanation of these unintended consequences. They argued that "since much of the assessment activity is based on comparatively technocratic indicators systems observers, planners and analysts cannot get a 'feel' for what is really happening on the ground and how policy implementation is done in practice" (p. 881).

The framework supported an assessment that led the authors to the conclusion that there were several features contributing to the sustainability of the Eco Island. Foremost among these was the restriction of development to certain locations on the island, thus protecting the rural areas. Industry was constrained to the pre-existing industrial park and had not expanded. A variety of ecological parks had been created, but they were noted to be rather small and not always attuned to protecting indigenous species. However, the work to restore water courses was considered state of the art. Two major problems were the failure to invest in sustainable (or indeed any) transport infrastructure (a significant issue given the island's layout and location) and, despite the construction of high-tech facilities for waste management, the lack of adequate sorting of waste to achieve the goal of sustainable waste management.

Beyond this, though, the quality of life of residents did not seem to be significantly improving, and indeed the project involved limited consideration of the needs of local residents. The plans for low-carbon tourism were not being fulfilled by growth of this sector, and the agricultural activities were not feeding into the eco-plans. While farming was supported by cooperative unions which protected farmers' living standards to some extent and there had been some decline in the use of chemical fertilisers, this sector remained dependent on providing food and urban planting materials for Shanghai and was not becoming a dynamic base for local economic development. Thus, the researchers argued that depopulation was likely to continue rather than the win-win scenario for ecological protection and economic development that was envisaged in the plan. They concluded that developing a low-value, rural eco-island was proving feasible but were much more cautious about a more high-value urban eco-island. These conclusions, they argued, would not be possible without the revised evaluation matrix.

The key focus provided by the public administration framing here is the link between the development of an evaluation matrix and the assessment of a plan or project. This evaluation tool is considered sufficient to gauge the extent of and to understand the process of implementation. No further conceptualisation of the processes leading to outcomes is needed or, indeed, is helpful in supporting improvement in planning practices. Rather the framing emphasises the assumed agency of the plan in producing outcomes and the importance of judging those outcomes in relation to the plan.

Much of the research reviewed so far has provided strong descriptive accounts of the administrative procedures involved in planning and considered how these may be improved to support decision-making and evaluate performance. The research by Pinho (1997) is rather different in nature. Rather than assessing implementation through an extended form of evaluation using matrices and flow-charted processes, Pinho looked at how negotiation is implicated in the implementation of a specific project. Such research focusses on areas where policy and professional actors can exercise discretion and where negotiation that shapes decisions, actions and outcomes is found.

Pinho looked at the regulation of a major development between the Atlantic Ocean and Ria de Aveiro in Portugal and set this in the context of the Portuguese planning system in which the municipal master plan, the Plano Director Municipal (PDM), provides the framework for controlling development and drawing up more localised plans; a full approved PDM removes the need for central government approval of local and detailed development plans. PDMs have proved time-consuming and technically demanding to prepare. In this context, the author argued that this has led to "planning practices characterised by fairly large discretion and relatively large rooms (sic) for bargaining processes" (p. 2039). The weak budgetary situation of local authorities also encouraged them to bargain for social benefits that they could not otherwise finance. At the same time, Environmental Impact Assessment (EIA) processes were independent of the local authority and centralised under the responsibility for the Ministry for the Environment, which appointed a Commission (usually of Ministerial officials) to consider each EIA case. Negotiation within EIA was more focussed on mitigation measures to reduce negative impacts and provide compensation for them and less concerned with local interests and preferences.

The specific case study was a tourism condominium development over 185 hectares on a sandbar of a lagoon alongside the Atlantic coast. The initial proposal was for a holiday housing development of 309 homes, mainly in single-family detached houses in large plots, together with a golf course and an apartment block of 60 flats. The form and content met the general requirements of the local detailed development plan, by virtue of being located in a designated tourist location, and the local municipality of Murtosa was in favour, largely on economic development grounds. The nearby village of Torreira had been slowly developing a tourism industry, but at the time of the research, the area was still largely dependent on small-scale and part-time agriculture, population was declining and the local economy was rather weak. Due to pollution from a nearby chemical complex affecting the lagoon beaches, tourist development was not possible nearer the town of Murtosa, pushing such development towards the sandbar facing the Atlantic, where the proposed project was sited.

However, this was within an ecologically important area, particularly for migrant bird species. The whole Ria de Aveiro area was considered significant under European Union biodiversity designations, and while at the time of the research, only a small area had been classified a statutory nature reserve, there were plans to designate the whole area for nature conservation. That said, the development site was not particularly ecologically important, mainly covered with invasive species of acacia and recently affected by a forest fire.

This was the context in which negotiations on permitting the development proceeded. The EIA report pointed out the potential negative environment impacts and made a number of detailed recommendations for mitigating these. A revised application was produced, proposing horse-riding stables instead of the golf course, a hotel and health club instead of the apartment block, a reduction in the number of houses to 292 with higher-density building types. The overall design was more compact with an extended coastal protection zone and two new lakes. The new EIA report was generally favourable, but the EIA Commission was "uncomfortable" (p. 2047) with the political visibility of allowing this development to be approved. They did not enter into negotiations, and the statutory deadline for the decision passed.

The next event was the election of a new national government; this allowed the Ministry of Environment to commence negotiations with the developer on the basis of the second report. However, these did not prove fruitful. The possibility of a part-nership to implement environmental conservation measures did not go forward. Rather, the Commission no longer felt bound by the first report and its recommen-dations and introduced a new issue—coastal erosion. Two new consultants were hired to investigate this, and following this, the second application was refused development consent.

This detailed planning history was achieved through a methodology that focussed on following the paper trail of the application; interviews with key actors may also be implied (although this was not stated). This supported Pinho's conclusion that implementation of a proposal supported by the local plan and local political inter-ests was stymied by a national political decision (p. 2048).

But he also made a number of more procedural points that reflect on planning as public administration. First, the planning system and the operation of the EIA oper-ated with complete institutional and procedural separation; both allowed for some element of negotiation. Second, the parties to such negotiations could only do so on the basis of their own interests, and this prevented an integrated or balanced approach emerging. Third, he noted the more general separation and conflict between local economic development and nature conservation values and between development planning and environmental planning, calling for more integration. Fourth, this led to Pinho calling for an adaptable management approach, which would allow for feedback of information into the decision-making process and the development of shared understanding and cooperation.

Planning here is a series of steps or stages to be followed chronologically. Points of discretion and negotiation can be identified by following these steps and stages carefully within the research. This can be used to explain how the project unfolded and suggestions for alternative steps or stages can then follow, to achieve the desired outcomes.

Assessing Integration

As emphasised earlier, a key rationale for planning is that it should be comprehen-sive (as far as possible) and be able to integrate different information, assessments and dimensions of an issue or locality. Thus, practices of achieving integration have been a particular focus of attention for researchers within this theoretical approach.

An example of planning research that seeks to combine the idea of planning as fundamentally striving to be rational and objective with an appreciation of the limi-tations of that view is provided by Furlong et al. (2016) with their research on inte-gration of water and urban planning in the Australian context. In particular they sought to incorporate stakeholder involvement as a way of making planning more effective. Furlong et al. framed their research in terms of Integrated Water Resource Management, which is "a strategic long-term planning approach to urban water that considers and includes all potential water sources, services, stakeholders, and impacts in order to create the best possible community outcomes" (p. 2). The link to a comprehensive approach to deliver on the public interest is clear, as is the leading role of the planner: "Planners within water utilities conduct analysis to develop infrastructure recommendations" (p. 2).

Thus, the authors aimed at developing "process instructions, a model, a framework or a heuristic" (p. 3). They wished to acknowledge the reality of planning as not simply linear, rational and expert driven and to create a planning framework more relevant to that reality. This takes on board some of the criticisms coming from what they term sociocratic planning. Their aim was to go beyond the technocratic approach that has particularly dominated infrastructure planning but not to depart completely from it. This was connected to the strong practice link within this research. The methodology that they used was to review and revise existing frameworks for planning, beginning with Lichfield's General Planning Process (see earlier), and combine these with water infrastructure planning frameworks. Four of the six water infrastructure frameworks considered "were based on industry-standard documents from reputable sources" (p. 3) and the remaining two from academia. The revised framework was also subject to extensive consultation with 34 experts from the water infrastructure industry, and it was important that the final version be "consistent with their recommendations" (p. 3).

They developed their proposals by analysis and comparison of the six frameworks, adding further elements identified from a literature review, particularly aspects concerning financing and regulation. The authors highlighted four differences with more technocratic approaches. First, decision-making, leading to recommendation of a preferred option, was separated from decision-taking or implementation, which is seen as involving more actors. Second, financing fed into the selection of the preferred option. Third, evaluation of outcomes and public reactions (including in the media) led to reiterations in a circular rather than linear process. And fourth, there was much greater engagement with community and governmental stakeholders throughout the process and explicit recognition of the influence of government and community preferences. Nevertheless, the key elements of the framework remained decision analysis and decision-taking, with the emphasis on how planners involved in water infrastructure planning can reshape their own planning practice.

The final element of the research was an assessment of the framework in action, using it to collate and organise information on water infrastructure case studies across Australia. The extent to which the categories within the framework aligned with those cases was taken as an indicator of the value of the framework in promoting understanding to support both future research and also more realistic industry practices. This was, therefore, research that is strongly framed by a focus on the procedures of planning, which emphasises the importance of the views of practitioners and stakeholders for judging those procedures and seeks to improve the procedures and practices at the margin. It also saw the use of knowledge and its integration as central to planning activities.

Tajima and Fischer (2013) explored the potential for integration looking at spatial planning in the English context, focussing on the extent to which different impact assessments were integrated within the Strategic Environmental Assessment

(SEA) of plans, which in England is wrapped up within Sustainability Appraisal (SA). The kinds of impact assessment that they were considering concerned natural habitats, health, gender, equalities and transport along with rural areas and age proofing. They were particularly concerned with deriving lessons on whether and how different impact assessments could be integrated across spatial planning as a whole and whether the integration of different assessments was achieving the aim of supporting sustainable development. To do this they produced an evaluation framework to assess whether the values in the SEA were reflected in the plans and whether there was a more balanced consideration of economic, social and environmental aspects as a result.

The methodology for studying this primarily involved document analysis, supplemented with a survey and eight follow-up interviews. To find a sample for this more detailed work, a web-based analysis was undertaken for 325 local planning authorities in England, identifying the number and type of impact assessments used to support the main spatial plan policy document (at that time, called the 'core document' within a Local Development Framework). From this a sample was made of local planning authorities that used three or more such impact assessments (n = 17). For this sample, a survey was sent out; 12 authorities responded. Follow-up interviews were used to clarify any outstanding issues.

The main element of the research was the creation of the evaluation framework, which was applied to each impact assessment and the core strategies. There were two different dimensions to the evaluation. First, the impact assessments were scored according to criteria concerning the timing of impact assessment, the use of the impact assessment in the sustainability appraisal and the organisational location of the key actors. These scores were then summed to produce an Approach to Integration Score.

Second, the effectiveness of the assessments was judged by looking at the extent to which the different sustainability objectives within the Sustainability Appraisal (SA) could be allocated to the different categories: environmental, economic, social, biodiversity, equality, health and transport. This provided an average value score for each sustainability objective category, showing how well a specific value is represented in the plan and its SA.

The evaluation enabled descriptive statistics for integration and for the values in SAs. For example, they showed that Health Impact Assessments showed the highest level of integration in terms of processes undertaken and who the assessors were, while Habitats Regulation Assessments scored highest for integrating outputs; the lowest scoring assessments in terms of process and assessors were Transport Impacts Assessments and, in terms of outputs, Equalities Impact Assessments. Local authorities were allocated to one of three different groups indicating high, medium or low integration. Turning to values, they found that environmental values were considered less than the others. The analysis also enabled correlation of values against integration. This showed, for example, that neither the environmental value score, nor the balance between environment, economic and social value scores, showed any relation to the score for integration. The research suggested that the effort to achieve full integration actually resulted in certain sustainability values being downgraded.

So, the conclusions drawn were threefold. First, the extent to which social, environmental and economic aspects are considered within the SEA does not depend on the integration of other impact assessments into the SEA. Second, there is a parabolic relationship between the willingness to integrate these various impact assessments into the SEA and the individual impact assessments reaching their target values. Third, there seems to be a point beyond which more procedural integration of certain impact assessments may reduce the effectiveness of integration. This may be due to the inherent difficulties of achieving integration across different issues, leading to excessive complexity. It may also be due to the balancing nature of SEA/SA, which could be at odds with efforts towards effective integration across issues. It was also suggested that the affinity of different impact assessments may make a difference, so that integrating quantitative and qualitative methods or values assumed to be in conflict may undermine the effectiveness of integration. The main point that they emphasise is that "while integration may contribute to efficiency, it could also lead to the subordination of certain assessment issues, particularly those that are supposed to have their status raised in decision-making through specific assessment instruments" (p. 29).

This is an example of looking at the detail of the procedural aspects of planning and highlighting the difficulties encountered. It assumes the value of integration and looks for it in examples of practice but then queries how integration works out in such practice. It is framed by the public administration approach but is able to critique it using the research results.

The theme of integration is also highlighted in the research reported by Zhou et al. (2017) on spatial planning at the city scale in Yulin City, China. The aim here was to examine how a new form of spatial planning could operate in this context; this form of planning was described as transformative and integrative, one that "focusses on framing decisions, actions, projects, results, and implementations as well as incorporates monitoring" (p. 32). The issue that the researchers addressed was how this could fit within a Chinese planning system that is highly fragmented. Thus, the researchers looked at a pilot governmental project covering 28 cities and counties and aimed at "integration of multi-planning"; Yulin City is one of these. The purpose of this project was to consider how an overall plan and good coordination of spatial planning could be achieved, thereby hopefully preventing the disorderly urban development that had been occurring.

As is common with research within this framing, there was a close link with governmental actors. Here the authors were part of the pilot project, and they combined this with access to a range of documentation—policy and data based—and other planning actors in the city for interviews. The key planning documents at different governmental scales were subjected to an analysis for similarities and differences, clarification of conflicts and identification of differences in technical standards for information and land classifications. Available data was also subjected to a spatial overlay analysis using GIS. This analysis of Yulin City material was set in the context of the complexity of the current Chinese planning system; they identified five levels from the national, through provincial/municipal, prefectural and county levels down to township. Across these some 26 planning frameworks operated, fitting within four main streams coming from the central government level and led by different government departments; these concerned the National Economic and Social Plan *plus* National Main Functional Planning (concerning patterns of land development), the General Land-Use Planning Outline at National Level (focussed on land and resource management), National Urban System Planning (focussed at the coordination of urban and rural areas) and other national planning for issues including ecology, transportation, minerals, forestry and industry.

Studying this, the researchers found that there was considerable departmental fragmentation and a heavy reliance on national-level policies for guidance. The role of planning in coordinating different aspects of urban development remained weak: "the present planning system does not have a unified, orderly pattern. The separation of departments as well as the lack of platforms and mechanisms for scientific and systematic planning coordination and integration will restrict the effects of the implementation of spatial planning" (p. 39). The ideal of the governmental model was here being used as a benchmark for assessing planning in practice.

The authors were clear that "Every department cannot be united into one planning system if the ingrained administrative system of China is not broken" (p. 41). They designed a new structure for communication and inter-relationships between departments which they termed the 'multi-planning link model'. Specifically, within Yulin City they recommended a level of Comprehensive Planning—incorporating the overarching planning goal, indicators for monitoring and a spatial layout—which would operate at the 'top' level in the city and be the key reference point for all other policy, effectively unifying all elements. They also recommended setting various 'control lines' which would act as protection against development in areas that should be protected for various reasons; five such control lines would be drawn on the 'One Map' to achieve such protection and integration with other aspects of the plan.

Thus, the research identified the ways that the ideal governmental model was failing in this Chinese case and then provided an alternative governmental model which, it was asserted, would work better. However, as they concluded "whether a carefully designed integrated spatial planning system can take effect with these supporting systems already in place remains to be seen" (p. 47), and they point to conflicts at the national level that may prevent this. Here the researchers have taken the design of the planning system as important, reflecting the focus of the public administration approach on examining existing structures and supporting reflection on how they might be improved.

Conclusions

The essence of the governmental or public administration approach to planning is that it frames it as a linear (with feedback loops) and a rational process. This framing is central. It suggests how planning operates and also how it should operate.

This means that research based on this approach also stays within the confines of this model; it typically becomes a form of policy evaluation. Here the goals are taken as given—as they are by the rational planner. The focus is on the steps by which the planning process proceeded and how different policy instruments were deployed. Things that worked well and those that did not are identified. This analysis is set within an understanding of the impact of planning, implying data collection before and after the planning action. In this way, research within this frame tends to mirror the model of planning itself. It becomes a critical friend shadowing the steps set out in the rational planning model. And the outcomes of the evaluation process itself become part of the evidence that helps planning to improve.

This is an extremely attractive vision of planning, particularly to planners. Not only does it make them the main actors within the planning process, it also suggests that planning is something under their control, which demonstrates their knowledge and that is rational and hence difficult to argue with. Of course, planning processes do not always deliver the desired outcomes, and there is a need for constant improvement in how they operate. But this does not detract from the essential power of the planning process and of the planner. If there are problems with planning, they can be solved by change within the planning process, for example, by adopting new tools. This often involves bringing technical expertise into the planning process as with GIS or other mapping techniques or by means of stakeholder engagement supported by new ICT. But even where stakeholders are included in the research, this is usually to garner support, identify values or pinpoint barriers and challenges. The perspective remains that of the planner as leading planning and solutions to solve problems remain within the planning process itself. The benchmark guiding research is a better way of achieving implementation in line with the policies and plans.

Key Theoretical Readings

Mandelbaum (1996), Chs. 3 and 4.

Key Research Readings

Furlong, C., S. de Silva, L. Guthrie, and R. Considine. 2016. Developing a Water Infrastructure Planning Framework for the Complex Modern Planning Environment. *Utilities Policy* 38: 1–10.

Hettinga, S., P. Nijkamp, and H. Scholten. 2018. A Multi-stakeholder Decision Support System for Local Neighbourhood Energy Planning. *Energy Policy* 116: 277–288.

Kumar, P., D. Geneletti, and H. Nagendra. 2016. Spatial Assessment of Climate Change Vulnerability at City Scale: A Study in Bangalore, India. *Land Use Policy* 58: 514–532.

Ma, X., M. de Jong, and H. den Hartog. 2018. Assessing the Implementation of the Chongming Eco Island policy: What a Broad Planning Evaluation Framework Tells More Than Technocratic Indicator Systems. *Journal of Cleaner Production* 172: 872–886.

Pinho, P. 1997. Local Planning and National Environmental Assessment Procedures: The Developer's Mitigated Role in Disjointed Negotiation Processes. *Urban Studies* 34(12): 2037–2052.

Tajima, R., and T. Fischer. 2013. Should Different Impact Assessment Instruments be Integrated? Evidence from English Spatial Planning. *Environmental Impact Assessment Review* 41: 29–37.

Zhou, X., X. Lu, H. Lian, Y. Chen, and Y. Wu. 2017. Construction of a Spatial Planning System at City-level: Case Study of "integration of multi-planning" in Yulin City, China. *Habitat International* 65: 32–48.

Bibliography

Barrett, Susan, and Colin Fudge, eds. 1981. *Policy and Action: Essays on the Implementation of Public Policy.* London: Methuen.

Burayidi, Michael, Adriana Allen, John Twigg, and Christine Wamsler. 2019. *The Routledge Handbook of Urban Resilience.* London: Routledge.

de Chastenet, Cédissia About, et al. 2016. The French Eco-Neighbourhood Evaluation Model: Contributions to Sustainable City Making and to the Evolution of Urban Practices. *Journal of Environmental Management* 176: 69–78.

Clifford, Ben, and Mark Tewdwr-Jones. 2013. *The Collaborating Planner?; Practitioners in the Neoliberal Age.* Bristol: Policy Press.

Davoudi, Simin. 2006. Evidence-Based Planning: Rhetoric and Reality. *disP - The Planning Review* 42 (165): 14–24.

Domptail, Stephanie, Marcos H. Easdale, and Yuerlita. 2013. Managing Socio-Ecological Systems to Achieve Sustainability: A Study of Resilience and Robustness *Environmental Policy and Governance* 23 (1): 30–45.

Furlong, Casey, Saman De Silva, Lachlan Guthrie, and Robert Considine. 2016. Developing a Water Infrastructure Planning Framework for the Complex Modern Planning Environment. *Utilities Policy* 38: 1–10.

Hettinga, Sanne, Peter Nijkamp, and Henk Scholten. 2018. A Multi-Stakeholder Decision Support System for Local Neighbourhood Energy Planning. *Energy Policy* 116 (May): 277–288.

Hill, Michael. 1997. Implementation Theory: Yesterday's Issue? *Policy & Politics* 25 (4): 375–385.

Kaza, Nikhil. 2019. Vain Foresight: Against the Idea of Implementation in Planning. *Planning Theory* 18 (4): 410–428.

Kontokosta, Constantine E. 2018. Urban Informatics in the Science and Practice of Planning. *Journal of Planning Education and Research.* https://doi.org/10.1177/0739456X18793716.

Kumar, Parveen, Davide Geneletti, and Harini Nagendra. 2016. Spatial Assessment of Climate Change Vulnerability at City Scale: A Study in Bangalore, India. *Land Use Policy* 58: 514–532.

Lichfield, Nathaniel, Peter Kettle, and Michael Whitbread. 1975. *Evaluation in the Planning Process.* Oxford: Pergamon.

Lindblom, Charles E. 2010. The Science of 'Muddling' Through. *Emergence: Complexity and Organization* 12 (1): 70.

Ma, Xin, Martin de Jong, and Harry den Hartog. 2018. Assessing the Implementation of the Chongming Eco Island Policy: What a Broad Planning Evaluation Framework Tells More than Technocratic Indicator Systems. *Journal of Cleaner Production* 172: 872–886.

Mandelbaum, Seymour, Luigi Mazza, and Richard Burchell, eds. 1996. *Explorations in Planning Theory*. Rutgers, NJ: The State University of New Jersey.

McLoughlin, J. Brian. 1969. *Urban and Regional Planning: A Systems Approach*. London: Faber.

Nobre, Silvana, Ljusk-Ola Eriksson, and Renats Trubins. 2016. The Use of Decision Support Systems in Forest Management: Analysis of FORSYS Country Reports. *Forests* 7 (12): 72.

Oxley, Michael. 2004. *Economics, Planning and Housing*. Basingstoke: Palgrave Macmillan.

Pinho, Paulo. 1997. Local Planning and National Environmental Assessment Procedures: The Developer's Mitigated Role in Disjointed Negotiation Processes. *Urban Studies* 34 (12): 2037–2052.

Rydin, Yvonne, Lucy Natarajan, Maria Lee, and Simon Lock. 2018a. Black-Boxing the Evidence: Planning Regulation and Major Renewable Energy Infrastructure Projects in England and Wales. *Planning Theory & Practice* 19 (2): 218–234.

Sanderson, Ian. 2002. Evaluation, Policy Learning and Evidence-Based Policy Making. *Public Administration* 80 (1): 1–22.

Smith, Mark C. 2018. Revisiting Implementation Theory: An Interdisciplinary Comparison between Urban Planning and Healthcare Implementation Research. *Environment and Planning C: Politics and Space* 36 (5): 877–896.

Tajima, Ryo, and Thomas B. Fischer. 2013. Should Different Impact Assessment Instruments Be Integrated? Evidence from English Spatial Planning. *Environmental Impact Assessment Review* 41: 29–37.

Zhou, Xiaoping, Xiao Lu, Hongpin Lian, Yuchen Chen, and Wu Yuanqing. 2017. Construction of a Spatial Planning System at City-Level: Case Study of 'Integration of Multi-Planning' in Yulin City, China. *Habitat International* 65: 32–48.

Chapter 3
Rational Choice Perspectives: Self-Interest and Decision-Making

Framing the Research

We have seen how there is a foundational idea of planning as a government activity which brings rationality to bear on the challenges of managing the built and natural environments in the public interest. This is based on the analysis provided by welfare economics or social choice theory to suggest that planning is able to overcome market failure and increase total social welfare. This chapter looks as a set of approaches that challenge this view. They challenge the idea that only the market can fail, looking also for examples and explanations of state failure. This does not mean that all such approaches are hostile to state action such as planning; rather they look for different ways of achieving social welfare, arguing that without careful attention to how state processes work in practice, there is the danger of the nirvana fallacy (Pennington 2000a), which assumes that the state can rectify market failures.

What such approaches have in common with rational planning as a government activity is the emphasis on the rational. But rather than being used as a normative standard for planning decisions, it becomes the analytic tool for understanding how planning works. The emphasis is on how rational decision-making by actors—planners but also landowners, developers, residents and others—underpins the behaviour of these actors and how they interact. When asked how to rectify the problems of state-led planning that it uncovers, many of these approaches argue that the rationality of the market-place should be emulated within state processes. This brings an emphasis on market-style competition inside the state and greater use of tradeable rights to achieve planning goals. This approach has underpinned many of the contributions of think tanks such as the Adam Smith Institute, the Policy Exchange and others in the neo-liberal vein.

In discussing this approach—here labelled rational choice perspectives—it is important to acknowledge that this is a family of theoretical discussions with a common focus on the individual actor (a person or an organisation), rational

Y. Rydin, *Theory in Planning Research*, Planning, Environment, Cities, https://doi.org/10.1007/978-981-33-6568-1_3

decision-making and the value of market-based competition in allocating resources. Welfare economics has already been met in Chap. 2; it provides the analysis of market failure that underpins many of the arguments for planning. Rational choice uses a parallel concept of state failure. The idea of state failure arises from the public choice school which has sought to use the insights of neo-classical economics to advance the understanding of policy processes and politics, together with other cognate theoretical frameworks contributing specific insights. Institutional economics has offered analysis of the problems arising from the absence of perfect, cost-free information and information economics suggests the potential of modelling planning encounters as formal games; meanwhile the work of Coase on property rights has opened up the issue of how the specification and distribution of property rights affects planning decision-making.

If public administration theory presents planning as a rational activity, constrained by a linear process of policy making and implementation, rational choice theory generalises that assumption about rationality and sees it underpinning all sorts of different activities concerning the planning system. Rationality is seen here in fairly simple terms as a basis for decision-making in which advantages and disadvantages, benefits and costs are weighted against each other. Actors are seen as driven by their interests and engaging in a calculus that measures the costs and benefits of particular decisions or courses of action, with maximum net benefit (or minimum net cost) being the aim. This applies to all actors: planners, developers, community members. Rationality, therefore, pervades all sectors: the public sector, markets and civil society. Since planning operates across these sectors—as a public sector activity seeking to control and influence private actions concerning urban development and engage communities in the broadest sense in those activities—it has to contend with rational choice in all these sectors.

In the public sector, rational choice has developed an account of the behaviour of public officials, such as planners, which emphasises the way that individual interest calculations lead to phenomena such as the growth of bureaucracy and also failures of government to deliver optimal outcomes (Dunleavy 1991). The classic question that rational choice approaches address is whether it was in the interest of a planning bureaucrat to grow their bureaucracy; to add staff, functions and responsibilities; and thus expand the remit of planning organisations and the planning system. If straight-forward growth is not in the interests of planning bureaucrats, what kind of planning system does best meet those interests? It also pinpoints the principal-agent problem underlying many failures to deliver on governmental objectives.

What rational choice can also bring to the study of planning is the argument that this economic calculus can be harnessed to deliver public goals. The emphasis here is on using property rights so as to influence behaviour between private sector actors without the need for direct governmental intervention. More critically it explains excessive lobbying by private sector interests in terms of rent-seeking and points to the dangers of regulatory capture affecting planning decision-making. Finally, within civil society, rational choice provides an analysis of why participation in public decision-making often falls short of planners' hopes and even expectations. This so-called collective action problem can also yield insights on how to promote more engagement with planning. More generally, rational choice can extend into game theory with the modelling of specific interactions between actors from all three spheres as examples of mathematical games, which can then be analysed as likely to lead to certain outcomes.

Lord (2012) draws on information economics to consider 'the planning game' and emphasise the negotiation and bargaining that this involves. Again, the context for such gaming is the imperfect nature of information which inhibits cooperation and results in participants in planning (understood as players in the game) having to choose different strategies to try and achieve their objectives and fulfil their interests. Lord favours viewing game theory as a syntax for articulating the vocabulary of interdependent rationality. Game theory is a branch of mathematics that has influenced the social sciences through the suggestion that social and political situations can be modelled as a game, in which different actors have decisions to make or strategies to implement; the decisions and strategies of actors interact as each 'player' in the game takes their turn, and this produces outcomes with 'payouts' for the different actors.

The key research task when using game theory is to appropriately model complex real life so that it fits an already-specified game that can be analysed in terms of the outcomes from the different combinations of strategies that players use, in one and then multiple rounds of the game. Lord distinguishes four types of games: conflict, dissimulation, cooperation (involving teams) and direction. There are a range of names given to such games from the well-known Prisoners' Dilemma through Tit-for-Tat, Chicken, and so on. Game theory has identified how such games tend to develop over repeated rounds of the game, and what are the optimal and likely outcomes for each actor and for the group of actors. The question that is always relevant is not whether the game can be found in mathematical textbooks but whether it is a good approximation of planning practice, identifying the key elements that drive actors' behaviour.

Thus, the rational choice perspective is quite wide ranging. It provides an analysis of key aspects of planning practice such as public participation and bureaucrats' action, and also offers solutions to overcome identified problems such as the principal-agent problem and the collective action problem. It is underpinned in a coherent manner by the focus on the rational individual, in whatever sphere one finds them, and on the implications of decision-making based on such rationality, understood in terms of a clear cost-benefit calculus.

Dynamics of Analysis and Key Concepts

Rational and public choice analyses provide a rich set of concepts for analysing public policy processes such as planning. Here three are discussed in a bit more depth: the view of the planner as a self-interested actor, the collective action problem as a way of understanding participation in planning and the importance of how property rights are defined.

The Interests of the Planner

One of the distinctive features of the rational choice approaches discussed here is that they do not take the role of the planner or planning organisation for granted. The assumption that market failure can be rectified by state action often does just that. But the public choice perspective questions this and asks about the incentives that the planner and planning organisation face and how this shapes their behaviour. Pennington (2000b) expresses this clearly. He argues that planners need information and to be incentivised to act on that information if market failures are to be corrected. However, they are constrained by the lack of an equivalent to market processes for their decisions which would provide feedback on the impact of these decisions and, importantly, on community preferences for those decisions and outcomes. As a result, planners may not accurately deduce what the public interest is. To this one could add the point that Sager (2002) deduces from social choice theory and Arrow's famous paradox that, in many cases, it may not be possible to develop a coherent ranked set of social preferences due to the pattern by which individuals rank their own preferences.

Of more relevance here is the point that Pennington emphasises, that planners may not be incentivised to act on such preferences because they are incentivised to act in quite different ways. This posits that planners' interests are perceived in relation to their work position within the planning bureaucracy, itself positioned within the state. This has a number of implications. These can be summarised in terms of the desire to expand or manipulate their organisational budget and the associated principal-agent problem.

One of the earliest insights that rational choice literature lays claims to is the so-called iron law of bureaucracy, which argues it is in the interests of public sector bureaucrats to expand their areas of activity resulting in the inevitable growth of the public sector bureaucracy. Pennington has seen this as lying behind the extension of regulatory control over land-use decisions. However, Dunleavy (1991) has modified this argument with his 'bureau-shaping' hypothesis. This argues that not all bureaucratic work is regarded equally by public sector workers. Recognising that there are varieties of bureaucrats (such as climbers, zealots, or statesmen) he suggests that a significant group of bureaucrats prefer higher-status work and thus press for greater resources to go into such areas of work as opposed, say, to more routine aspects of bureaucracy. In the case of planning, this could be seen as a preference for higher-status activities developing a plan or strategy for an area over dealing with numerous, often routine applications for development consent. While not exactly contradicting Pennington's argument about the expansion of planning regulations, it could explain why plan-making expands compared relative to the everyday work of planning regulation (see also Poulton 1997).

Pennington goes further to argue that planners and other public sector bureaucrats (in addition to various sectional interests), may manipulate the rational ignorance of the electorate. The electorate always operate with a degree of ignorance; collecting all the information about different candidates' detailed positions would be very time-consuming and even difficult. Votes can only be cast for a candidate on the basis of the policy package that they are putting forward, and yet it is generally not worth the time and effort to collect all the information about their programmes but rather use a short-cut to deciding how to vote based on identity, class, ideology or a dominant policy issue. Even at the local scale, planning issues may not feature very prominently in either the public face of local politicians' campaigning or the local electorates' concerns. Pennington argues that planning bureaucrats may take advantage of that to pursue planning approaches that meet their interests not those of the electorate (should their preferences on this specific planning issue be identified). This is exacerbated by the collective action problem discussed later that shapes the nature of participation in planning consultation exercises.

Given that public choice sees the incentives of planners in terms of these concerns about the nature of their work, it follows that there is not always a close alignment of the interests of different actors within a chain of organisations dealing with a specific topic or problem. A key insight from the rational choice perspective is that problems within policy processes can arise because of the different interests of the actors defining the policy—the principal—and those charged with implementing it—the agents. This difference in interests leads to a difference in decision-making, and hence the divergence of rationalities helps explain some of the problems with the ideal policy model noted in Chap. 2. In particular it identifies the weakness of governing through long chains of principal-agent relations, particularly if these are low-trust relations. In this context, there can be multiple 'breaks' in the movement from policy objective to action and impacts as different actors get involved and take a lead in the process.

The rational choice perspective here has a potential solution, involving the creation of a chain of contracts between actors in principal-agent relationships and setting the terms of these contracts so as to bring the interests of the different actors into alignment with each other. This idea of governing being based on contractual relations has been espoused by the new public management approach (although this is highly contested). Laffin (2016) suggests that there are four dimensions. First, there are benefits from disaggregating large governmental bureaucracies into functionally specialised organisational units. Second, commissioning of services needs to be separated from the delivery of those services, allowing for competition between governmental and extra-governmental organisations to drive down costs and drive up efficiency in service delivery. Third, performance should be measured by explicit performance standards and output or outcome indicators rather than judged in terms of process indicators. Fourth, politicians should focus on steering government through strategic level goals, rather than getting involved in the detail of the means by which those goals are delivered. This suggests a very different kind of planning system to that outlined in Chap. 2.

The Collective Action Problem

One key body of work within the rational choice tradition is that concerned with the collective action problem. This considers the question: is it worthwhile for an actor to participate in a collective decision-making exercise, such as a consultation forum for a new local plan or a protest on a proposed development or even a vote in a local referendum. The answer to this question is seen to arise from a calculus balancing the costs and benefits to that individual actor.

Let us consider the case of attending a meeting on a planning proposal for development near my home. The costs that I will incur will be the time I have given up which could have been spent more profitably or pleasurably elsewhere, doing a piece of paid work or watching a film. In addition, there may be travel and childcare costs. There is the inconvenience of reassigning activities that would be done in that time: laundry, cooking and so on; such inconvenience can be quantified. All these costs are current; they occur now. They are also certain; the exact cost can be calculated or estimated; and they fall on the actor, the individual or perhaps their family and household.

By contrast the benefits of participating have different characteristics. I cannot be sure that my attendance at the meeting will lead to changes in the plans that I desire. Someone else may make my important and insightful point; I could 'free-ride' on their participation without incurring any costs. Or I may make my point, and it could be ignored; it might have no impact at all on the planning proposal. The outcomes of my attendance are, at best, uncertain. In addition, the benefits of an altered planning proposal will emerge in the future, when the development is built (or not) and the local area is changed (or not). And, finally, such benefits will not just be mine but will fall on the wider local community (assuming they want what I want).

So the costs are current, certain and fall on me (or those near to me) while the benefits are future, uncertain and may fall on the wider community. Understood like this, it becomes questionable why anyone participates in planning consultations! Strong values are often cited as the key factor that induces someone to participate: I will go along to the local meeting because I am passionate about urban nature and wish to ensure that key trees and green spaces will be protected. But a close look at the elements generating the collective action problem suggests other factors. It may be that the potential negative impacts are so large that I feel I cannot afford not to attend; this would be the case if my property were to be demolished or very adversely affected by new development. Here the potential benefits of being involved weigh more heavily. If I was unemployed or retired, the cost of my time would be very low. Or it may be that I actually enjoy going along to such events, that I meet neighbours there and feel more like a central member of the local community. This would also discount the costs of going along.

The emphasis on perceptions is important here. The collective action problem is seen from the viewpoint of the actor. So, the perceived benefits will be the change that they hope to achieve; the costs will include how they value time, inconvenience and paying for travel costs. This points to some of the rationale behind a greater turnout among middle-class residents in planning participatory events. Such residents may feel more confident about having an impact on outcomes; they may be more used to affecting others' decisions and actions. They may also be more able to pay for the incidental costs. Thus, the collective action problem can help explain the skewed nature of much participation. Pennington (2000a) argues that the different ways that sectional interests experience the collective action problem can explain the tendency towards urban containment of residential development on greenfield sites noted in British planning. Agricultural interests, construction interests and NIMBY residents can manipulate the planning system by overcoming their collective action problem to achieve representation in the political market of planning decision-making, at the expense of the less organised, more diffuse general urban population and potential housing consumers.

Unpacking the perceived reasons for and calculus about community participation can also lead to suggestions for how to increase levels of participation. Any efforts to keep costs down by making the event accessible and covering incidental costs (say, by providing a crèche) could have an effect. Emphasising the pathways and likelihood of participation actually altering plans and proposals would also help. Identifying benefits that will occur sooner rather than later and highlighting who will benefit can also contribute. Reliance on generalised benefits to the community sometime in the future is, on the other hand, more likely to deter engagement with planning proposals.

A focus on rent-seeking (achieving unearned increments—see more later) provides another analysis of urban containment, so long associated with British planning (Pennington 2000b). Here Pennington examines two alternative explanations, both within the public choice school, for urban containment pressures. The first is a rising preference within the electorate in general for environmental regulation and associated urban containment policies; the second focusses on lobbying by special interest groups, working in conjunction with planning bureaucrats who also favour the expansion of regulation as enlarging their remit of influence. Pennington examines the theoretical arguments for these options and favours the latter on the basis that responses to voter preferences are typically weak due to a low level of collective action among diffuse pro-environmental voters (a classic collective action problem), limited payoffs to politicians of listening to pro-environmental voters and rational ignorance among voters in general. On the other hand, key pro-containment interests have a strong rationale for overcoming their collective action problem and engaging in lobbying activity.

Property Rights as Shaping Interests

The above analysis of the planner as a bureaucrat or the planning organisation as a bureaucracy has assumed that they do not have property interests in the land, buildings and natural assets being planned. For rational choice perspectives, the institutions of property rights are of central importance. They shape the nature of interests that actors hold, and they also underpin market processes. A market is an institutional arrangement for the exchange of elements that are 'owned', that is, that the owner has property rights over. These can be exchanged, typically bought and sold for money. It is the competition for such property rights (to enable direct enjoyment through consumption or as an input into production) that is argued, by rational choice adherents, to promote efficiency, so that maximum benefit is enjoyed at minimum cost.

But since property rights are a social creation, the particular way that they are shaped by property institutions such as legal systems is very important. As Hartmann and Needham (2012: 219) point out: "When land-use planning, or spatial planning, is practised, planning law and property rights interact". They further emphasise though that changing property rights is hard. If there is appropriation of a private property right that is backed by the law, then compensation may be payable. Land readjustment—by which many small plots are brought together into unified ownership to enable a certain pattern of development—can be expensive. Private property owners may resist and use legal channels to challenge a planning decision, whether that is a decision compulsorily acquiring land for development or indeed a decision preventing development on the site that the property owner hoped to realise development value on. But more than the financial implications of seeking to engage with property rights, there are the institutional complexities involved in exchanging and altering property rights; property rights are backed by the power of law in most countries (as opposed to just customary recognition), and any engagement with legal systems is often time-consuming and complex (Reeve 1986).

However, there is another way to look at the role of property rights in planning. Rather than emphasising the difficulties and costs of 'interfering' with private property rights, analysts could look for the ways in which the distribution of private property incentivises and disincentivises the actors involved in planning. This might produce a more nuanced understanding of how property rights interface with planning goals and, by implication, how they might effectively be adjusted to achieve those goals. The aim here is to continue to rely on the market in allocating resources efficiently but to understand how it can be helped at the margin in this activity. For this reason, Hartmann and Needham see planning by law and property rights as not only inevitable but desirable. The challenge is how to anticipated inflexibilities or 'lock-in' that might result and, in the context of this book, that means researching where they arise.

Webster and Lai (2003) set out a comprehensive framework for analysing planning in terms of property rights, drawing on the rational choice approach of institutional economics to, as they put it, "help bring discussions about markets and urban planning into greater balance" (p. 2). They see markets and the state as co-evolving, complementing each other and, by trial and error, distributing responsibilities between public and private sectors, between private and collective action. They particularly focus on the role of transaction costs in shaping the efficiency of allocations, say of development rights. Such transaction costs encompass the costs of searching for partners to an exchange or activity, of making and policing the contracts between parties, of handling the interests of third parties and related compliance of contracts, as well as the costs of gathering information, making rules and policing them and the costs of excluding certain actors from exploiting a resource, including making and policing agreements about this. They argue that all institutions (market and governmental) reduce transaction costs by assigning property rights over scarce resources, but that resources with unclear property rights in the public domain are subject to wasteful competitive consumption. Furthermore, the use of information to promote coordination is constrained by the cognitive ability of individuals and groups and the costs of acquiring information. This particularly affects the public sector as markets are able to respond to price signals, a key form of feedback driving efficiency. The resulting adaptation is more rapid and responsive; the more the competition, the lower the transaction costs and the better the information. Thus, the efficiency with which an institution allocates property rights to individuals and groups depends on the distribution of knowledge, resources and transaction costs.

The property rights perspective argues that it sheds light on two issues of key concern to planning systems. The first concerns the role of externalities, which were seen in Chap. 2 to be a key impetus for planning in order to remedy this market failure. For property rights theorists, the very existence of externalities is a result of the failure to specify property rights appropriately. Ideally property rights would require compensation for any impact of one party on another. Externalities are defined as an impact of one party on another that does not pass through a market transaction. A resident suffers uncompensated air pollution from a nearby industrial premises because they do not hold a property right that the industrialist has to purchase before production activities commence; spatial planning segregating industrial and residential land uses and pollution regulation seek to fill this gap. However, appropriately structured property rights could give the residents a right that industrialist would need to buy in market-based exchanges; in this way the purchase of the right would compensate for the externality. It would not remove that externality, unless the property owner refused to sell her rights at any price; otherwise, it would compensate at a price that the property owner considered commensurate with the negative dimensions of the externality, here the air pollution. Proponents of this approach argue that greater attention should be given to the allocation and specification of property rights as an alternative to state-led planning

The second issue concerns public goods which are analysed as a form of market failure by way of being non-excludable, thus tending to under-supply by the market and over-consumption in general. Here the traditional public administration approach would be to regulate to prevent over-consumption and/or directly provide the good through public sector organisations. Thus, the public good aspects of views over undeveloped areas may lead to such areas being sought after by developers wishing to capitalise on these views for the new housing they will build. Regulation may try to prevent development, or public ownership may take these sites off the market as a means of protecting the views. For the rational choice theorist, this is inefficient. A better solution would be to allocate property rights to these public goods in some way.

This can be quite problematic because of the nature of public goods as compared to private goods, which usually carry with them the right to exclude others from enjoyment of the good—otherwise why bother to own it? Public rights theorists suggest that contractual collective action or entrepreneurial clubs could provide an alternative. This involves enclosing the public good for the collective group and charging a membership fee, so that the larger public good becomes fragmented into a number of small but still public goods. However, these are now managed by a collective institution that has some knowledge of the preference of its members. While this is clearly not suitable for all public goods (such as clear air, say), it does have potential with regard to various land-based public goods and thus, according to the rational choice perspective, contributes to societal efficiency and fulfilment of societal preferences.

Much of the analysis in a property rights paradigm is concerned to make these normative comments about the benefits of a system organised around comprehensive and well-specified property rights being exchanged through markets. However, as the discussion here will show, it can also support research into how the planning system currently operates with regard to the prevailing allocation and distribution of property rights.

Research Themes in Practice

There is, perhaps, less empirical research within planning studies conducted within the rational choice frame than is the case with other frameworks. The papers reviewed here are based on modelling planning as a game, investigating rent-seeking within planning interactions and the role of property interests within planning.

Modelling Planning as a Game

It was suggested above that a rational choice perspective lends itself to seeing planning as a game. A classic example of this is provided by Chiu and Lai's study (2009) of negotiation strategies for siting facilities that are facing NIMBY opposition. Here an experimental approach was adopted, using paid volunteers who played a game based on a given scenario. This scenario involved a proposed landfill site for solid waste in Taipei, Taiwan. This was a multi-billion-dollar project covering not only land acquisition and construction costs but also compensation for local residents, who might be expected to oppose the project. The game was played out by 20 university students, allocated between 'the government group' and 'the residents'. All were briefed on the scenario.

The payoff matrix was established and made known in advance, giving the payout to each group of respectively cooperating or not (defecting). This is illustrated in Table 3.1; the payoff to the government group is given first in each pairing with

Table 3.1 Payoff matrix in Chiu and Lai

		Residents	
		Cooperate	Defect
Government group	Cooperate	(8, 8)	(2, 15)
	Defect	(15, 2)	(3, 3)

Source: Chiu and Lai (2009)

that for the residents second. This payout matrix is based on an assessment of the possible net economic benefits derived from the facilities plan. For the government these net benefits related to the costs of implementing the plan together with the benefits arising from the resolution of a solid waste problem. The delays and uncertainties arising from protests against the facility are also factored into this payout matrix. For residents, the net benefits covered the net losses in public space and also compensation received from the government.

Four strategies were identified: tit-for-tat (doing what the other player does), faithful (always cooperating), trigger punishment (cooperating until the other side decides to defect and then defecting also) and random. Cooperation here involves remaining in the negotiations, while defection involves withdrawal and alternative actions such as protest. These strategies were allocated to the government group; residents were unaware of which strategy was being adopted. Four of eight groups played a limited number of iterations (20) of the game; for the other four, the game was halted once either a maximum time (14 minutes) or a higher number of iterations (30) had been reached.

The results confirmed the deduction from game theory that tit-for-tat was the optimal strategy. This resulted in the highest payoff with a total group average of $601 million for the limited iterations and $679 million for the higher number of iterations. This was followed in both cases by the random group, then the faithful group and finally the trigger punishment group. The games also suggested that residents exhibited low trust at the outset, showing an unwillingness to cooperate. However, this unwillingness declined as the game progressed. This provides some information about how actors in a planning game behave, but the authors also argue that it might enable the planning authority to act more wisely in anticipation of this kind of behaviour when coping with NIMBY issues.

The assumption of this kind of research and theoretical framing is that real-world behaviour can be accurately modelled by the game. The key issue, as this framing posits it, is which is the best strategy to use and which strategy is most likely to be used. Here the research points to the importance of the 'first move' as tit-for-tat is likely to be the approach followed. However, the way that the payoff matrix is specified is central here and will impact on research results; if modelling is attempted, the accuracy of that modelling becomes an important issue.

Lord and O'Brien (2017) use game theory to identify the role of planners as 'market makers'. In line with the rational choice family of approaches discussed here, the focus is "placed on the micro-agential role played by individual actors in shaping and determining the character of the institutions, both formal and informal, that people them" (2017, p. 220) and on identifying the function performed by planning as an intermediary within market processes. Three cases were investigated, which were rather different in kind, deliberately so as to capture the variety of European planning. They were also chosen to explore contexts where planning was explicitly given an economically active role in leading urban change.

The first case was the involvement of coalitions of actors in Lille and neighbouring locations in Nord Pas de Calais, Picardie, France, cooperating on multiple urban projects and seeking to catalyse development. The second focussed on the use of public land development to prioritise strategic bargaining with private actors in Hamburg's HafenCity project in Germany. Finally, the third case considered the introduction of urban land readjustment policies in the Netherlands. The methods involved were semi-structured interviews with key individuals and supplementary document analysis (more details were not provided). The research used game theory to identify three key issues within planning in these case studies: the first mover problem, coalition games and attitudes to risk.

The first mover problem describes a situation where no one actor is incentivised to act first and carry the risk of others not joining in, even when all parties would benefit from their joint action. It often characterises urban development projects, particularly those that require remedial works prior to further construction. The issue here is neatly captured by Lord and O'Brien: "At base, the problem is one of mutual trust versus the fear of free-riding" (2017, p. 221). This can be overcome in various ways, as the case studies illustrated. In Lille, the city-regional governance body, the Métropole Européenne de Lille represented the creation of a state/quasi-state organisation to act as coordinator of the development, building confidence in the overall project. In Lille this involved not only coordination of some 85 communes but also spearheading the Euralille office and retail development as a means of linking the railway station (now served by the London-Paris high-speed rail link) and the city centre. The latter used a *societé d'économie mixte*, a form of public-private development company to take the first move in urban development; private development only then followed, having been reluctant to develop in Lille and favouring other more readily profitable locations elsewhere in France.

In the Netherlands, public land ownership was used to overcome the first mover problem, buying land at existing-use value and servicing it with infrastructure. Here, the profits made by the municipality allowed for cross-subsidisation of improvements at one site by development at another. Another advantage was that this put the municipality in a strong position to influence the nature of the urban development using landownership powers. The downsides appear to have been potentially driving down land prices by oversupply of development sites (particularly post the financial crisis of 2008) and a form of market restructuring in which it became accepted and even anticipated that the state would accept key elements of risk in urban development. The response to this was to shift towards a land readjustment approach, which provides for a temporary pooling of land held by different landowners to enable servicing and reconfiguring the site making it more suitable for development.

Looking at coalition formation, the case studies showed how planning can support this and encourage stability within coalitions through behavioural prompts. This built on the insights of cooperative game theory that coalition stability is a function of the relative payoffs to different members of the coalition; the payoff to each member must be sufficient to keep them committed to the coalition's aims. In Hamburg, a state-owned development company played a key role in coordinating the actors involved in the development programme. This involved dividing the HafenCity area into a large number of smaller plots, with each developer able to purchase only one. This reduced the power of any single developer within the coalition and encouraged a drip-feeding of development over time. Developers also had to compete with each other for the sites, being judged against prior tight design criteria; this encouraged a high level of compliance with the design criteria. In Lille, the development activities were overseen by an inter-municipality joint authority, which has a long history of coordinating local government in the area. This helped build a consensus on future directions, a consensus maintained by requiring all projects to be collectively agreed by the leaders of the four largest communes. It involved acknowledging that the economic success of the region depended on the ability to establish Lille as a base for international mobile service and knowledge-based industries, and also recognising that the less affluent communes also should have their needs met during this process. Lord and O'Brien suggested a cooperation game can help explain the success of this 'grand coalition', by identifying the 'fair shares' on which the game is predicated, the so-called Shapley value and clarifying the role of 'superadditivity', whereby members of the coalition realise they will get better outcomes inside rather than outside the collectivity.

Adopting a rational choice perspective in this way involves looking for the kinds of behaviour that might fit with the concepts and strategies that the theory proposes. The research may or may not find this, or it may amend the details of the way that the strategies are assumed to work. However, the research task and research questions are centred around the assumed relevance of such strategies to understanding planning situations.

Understanding Lobbying as Rent-Seeking

Rational perspectives can provide insights into the nature of the lobbying that occurs within planning systems. In part this is about applying the collective action problem outlined earlier, but there is also the identification of rent-seeking action by different groups. This concerns the tendency on the part of private sector actors to engage in lobbying activity in relation to the public sector in order to improve their financial situation. This is called rent-seeking since it is not about the private sector engaging in wealth creation but rather involves them in exerting political influence in order to increase their share of wealth. This is typically discussed in terms of attempts to achieve more beneficial regulatory decisions for private sector activities. In the case of planning, this could involve lobbying and other moves to get more, quicker and more lax development consents from the regulatory arm of the planning sector. Where such activities lead to a closer relationship between the regulator and the regulated, the planner and the developer, then this can be described as regulatory capture. But it could also involve lobbying to prevent the grant of development consent where this could otherwise reduce certain actors' share of wealth, as with classic NIMBYism.

Taylor (2016) provides an example of research into rent-seeking by landowners on the urban fringe of Melbourne, Australia. The context here was the expansion of Melbourne's Urban Growth Boundary in 2010, having first been established in 2002. This expansion would have granted considerable development value to the landowners within the expansion zone. As a result, a Growth Areas Infrastructure Contribution (GAIC) was proposed to apply to all sites above one acre brought inside the growth boundary. This was effectively a hypothecated betterment tax on the anticipated new development value. It was proposed to be levied at $95.00 per hectare on landowners selling land or developers already owning land. Taylor examined the lobbying activity by landowners in response to this proposal. The research tested the assumptions that the claims put forward by landowners were, at least in part, rent-seeking, that is motivated by perceived economic self-interest, and that the scale of profits associated with urban expansion could help explain the relatively low level of opposition to the GAIC from residential developers.

Her methodology was based on a content analysis of a sample of public submissions made in response to the growth boundary expansion and the proposed contribution; the first 20% of submissions by individuals and organisations was selected (out of a total of 1411 individual and 503 organisational submissions respectively). The code number for submissions had been randomly assigned by officers, so taking the first 20% produced a random sample of 382 submissions. Some 118 sampled submissions were removed because they exclusively concerned other issues or were confidential, duplicates or content-less. Therefore, 264 submissions were coded by content factors drawn from rent-seeking theory relating to land and housing markets and planning. The research thus investigated perceptions of tax incidence and its policy significance.

The analysis confirmed that landowners were opposed to the new contribution and, further, that they queried both whether the anticipated development value increments would arise and, if they did, whether it was fair to levy the tax on landowners. The morality of the tax was queried. Notably the submissions sought to discredit the argument that the extension of the Urban Growth Boundary would lead to windfall gains. Overall it was found that the opposition was driven by landowners rather than developers. This appears to have legitimised a misinterpretation of the premise of the contribution.

Interestingly, the submissions and associated pressure under the *Taxed Out!* campaign led to a revision to the policy, although it is noted that a version of the contribution was retained. Smaller land sales were exempted, but more significantly, landowners avoided formal liability and, instead, the tax became intended for payment by housebuilders and then passed on to new home-buyers. Taylor argues that this demonstrates the existence of rent-seeking lobbying and, further, its success.

She labels the landowners as 'insiders' to the political process and points out the implications of potential misrepresentation of the development gains that could be expected to arise from the growth expansion policy.

The rational choice framing supported a detailed and hypothesis-based approach to researching lobbying within planning. The starting point was the examination of how economic rent can be appropriated through the development process (here involving a tax) and how this can explain the lobbying that occurred. The self-representation of interests or values is not taken as the explanatory basis of such lobbying but is rather devised from formal modelling of the incentive structures of actors.

A second example concerns the release of rural land for urban development in a paper by Murray and Frijters (2016), again looking at Australia but at the case of Queensland. The context for the research was the well-documented problem of corruption around planning in Queensland at the time and how this related to bargaining between politicians and landowners over rezoning of areas to enable development. The framing of the research is in terms of the extent to which political insiders were maximising economic rents by achieving rezoning in unexpected areas (where the current use value would be low but the value upon development high). As the researchers put it: "the main contribution of this paper is to look at the micro-mechanism of influence by vested interests in rezoning decisions" (p. 101).

The data collection focussed on property ownership just inside and outside the rezoned boundaries for selected areas for the period 2007–2012. This was an interesting period because the Queensland government published plans to rezone for growth, and it also, through the aegis of the Urban Land Development Authority (ULDA), took over planning control from local authorities. Of 17 rezoning areas proposed, the researchers looked at 6 areas that involved privately owned land and where the winners and losers of rezoning could be traced. The data was of two kinds: a database of land, land price and rezoning status information; and a database of measures to determine the political connectivity of corporations, politicians, bureaucrats and—crucially—landowners. The first database collated information on land ownership, sales and sale prices for 1192 land parcels, 274 of which were inside the growth boundaries. The second database was compiled from multiple sources: political donors, clients of lobbyists, membership of industry associations, politicians, ULDA staff and corporate landowning entities. Matching all this data together created a matrix of 13,740 entities connected by over ¼ million links; this was analysed using Social Network Analysis to extract various metrics of connectivity from this database (see Chap. 5). The relationship between landownership, favourable rezoning, the resultant price effect and position within a connected network was formally modelled.

The main finding was claimed as demonstrating that "having many relationships to other well-connected property market participants was highly predictive of political favouritism" (p. 109). This quantitative analysis suggested that landowners found to be 'connected' owned 75% of the land inside the rezoned areas and only 12% of the land outside. The degree of connectedness by landowners was significantly related to reaping the benefits of rezoning. Being well connected led to a 25%

high chance of favourable rezoning; interestingly, employing a lobbyist independently increased the changes by 37%. The researchers, therefore, argued that rent-seeking was significant because the precise boundaries were not important for the growth coalition seeking rezoning as a whole, but it was highly important for individuals who owned an asset in this area. Furthermore, the researchers were able to estimate the development value captured by these politically connected landowners at $410 million out of a total development value created by the rezoning of $710 million. This research thus demonstrated the economic value of such rent-seeking lobbying. As they conclude: "property rezoning is one of the biggest rent-seeking activities for local and State politics in Queensland, with a small set of connected property market participants getting the lion's share of the new property rights from rezoning" (p. 110).

Here the argument about economic rent is taken beyond the conceptual understanding of how the incentives to develop are shared between actors, towards actually costing such rents. This involved quantitative data gathering and analysis. However, the central theme of rent-seeking is addressed by linking this to assessed measures of lobbying, here garnered from a Social Network Analysis (discussed further in Chap. 5).

Planning and Property Rights

A focus on property rights provides a different form of analysis of planning processes. Two examples are discussed here; the first considers the use of the Coase Theorem as a framing device for the research; the second relates to the difference and relationship between formal and informal, state and indigenous property rights systems.

Gurran et al. (2018) looked at the highly topical issue of the growth of online property sharing platforms, specifically Airbnb which allows people to rent out part or all of their home to visitors. They asked whether the Coase Theorem might not suggest an alternative to traditional regulation where the growth of this phenomenon is concerned. This theorem argues, following the rational choice approach, that well-defined property rights can provide the basis of private arbitration and compensation for externalities that are experienced, rendering state intervention through regulation redundant. It seeks to capitalise on the efficiencies and low transaction costs of interactions that approximate to market interactions, as opposed to using bureaucratic decision-making.

The research therefore sought to address two issues. First, it established the scope of the externalities arising from home-sharing. For this, data collection initially focussed on 212 submissions to a government inquiry into regulation for the short-term rental market in the state, using this as evidence of the localised tensions associated with negative externalities. It then supplemented this with knowledge of the geography, scale and location of Airbnb, looking at the two locations of Greater Sydney and the Northern River region of New South Wales, both areas that have seen rapid expansion of online holiday rental platforms. This was achieved through a webscrape of data available on InsideAirbnb.com, supplemented with housing market information including median rents for permanent properties in the area and comparing these with monthly income revenue for the different Airbnb listings. This provided aggregate data and spatial mappings.

The research identified that while there were considerable benefits for the hosts and guests from home-sharing, for those not directly party to the online transactions, there were a range of potential negative externalities including both for neighbours—noise, disruptive behaviour—and the wider local community—traffic congestion, change to character, housing shortages and higher rents. The analysis also suggested that the pattern of costs and benefits varied with urban, suburban and regional contexts, with different housing forms and different home-sharing practices. This suggested that "a one size fits all regulatory framework is likely to be both unnecessary and ineffective in managing externalities arising from online home-sharing" (p. 8). The spatial mapping also identified areas where the pressures on the local housing market from Airbnb rentals were particularly acute.

Second, the research considered the relevance of the Coase Theorem to the particular case of Airbnb in the form of a thought experiment, based on the information about the sector that had been collected. This involved a discussion of the difficulty of monitoring transactions on online platforms and hence regulating them but also the possibility of generating greater clarity around the residential occupancy and tenancy rules for the property right that is being traded on those platforms. It also raised the possibility of incorporating new rights for third parties, so that compensation can be negotiated. Thus, the externality of noise could potentially be managed by communication and bargaining, including over compensation, between neighbours.

While there are constraints placed on traditional regulation by limited information and potential for monitoring in this sector, it was recognised that the more diffuse and difficult-to-value externalities are less likely to be captured by the creation of new property rights. They noted that Airbnb has created an institutional structure through its 'friendly building program' that might provide a framework for such negotiation. But even with neighbour-impacted compensation, monitoring for compliance would be difficult unless the online platform cooperated. It seemed likely that not all neighbour nuisances would be identified by such a regime and further that impact on the wider spatial area would not be suitable for such online negotiation between property rights owners. Thus, traditional regulation may continue to play an important role.

This paper rather refutes the idea that all rational choice approaches necessarily favour market solutions; rather they frame the research in terms of the question of whether state intervention or market-based approaches are more appropriate. This involves conceptualising the way that a market-based approach might work, here using the Coase Theorem. This enabled the basis for identifying property rights, as well as costs and benefits (including externalities) from exercising these rights, to be specified. However, the answer remained an empirically based one.

For a property rights perspective based in the analysis of property regimes, Frimpong Boamah and Amoako (2020) provide an interesting analysis of the interaction of customary and statutory property rights regimes in Ghana and the implications for urban planning. Research into property rights regimes typically draw on statutes and other policy documentation, as well as historical research. In this case, the historical origins of the current Ghanaian property regimes were set out, going back to colonial times and the period of decolonisation. This enabled them to set out the current co-existence of customary and statutory property ownership and the resulting four different pathways to obtaining land ownership and use rights in Ghana involving different roles for the customary institutions based around chiefs, the state and the state-backed private property owners. This set the backdrop to the question they wished to investigate of whether the dual property rights regime was implicated in the misuse or non-use of planning and land rules, or whether they supported compliance.

The researchers used a variety of data to build their analysis. They did a content analysis of documentation including laws and planning documents. A set of criteria were established for this analysis: the landownership and use decisions; the actors responsible for these decisions; deontic modalities related to permissions, obligations, and rights; and sanctions and penalties. The coding was verified independently, and NVivo used to support the qualitative analysis. Second, they did a search for scholarly publications on landownership and planning in Ghana and also an online search of newspaper sources for material on land and planning in the country. These were also coded for conflicts/complementarities within and between land and planning laws and policies, and for examples illustrating the effects and impacts of land and planning laws, practices and discourses. The two sets of content analysis were then compared. Finally they conducted semi-structured interviews with 25 officials in planning and public land agencies in Kumasi and Accra, and five representatives from the customary land secretariats in both cities; two neighbourhoods were selected resulting in further 22 interviews in Accra and 20 in Kumasi together with one focus group in each neighbourhood involving about five residents.

The key finding was that the dual legal system around property rights implicated a planning 'idiom' characterised by misuse of statutory and customary laws. This involved the arbitrary reallocation of land to new owners and new land uses, alteration of land uses in opposition to policy and abusive use of eminent domain or compulsory purchase. The resulting planning system was 'brutal' with regard to some urban residents and ignored the needs of others. The authors then called for a political economy analysis (see Chap. 7) to understand this more fully.

This research is based on an understanding of legal property rights according to two regimes and then the way that these rights were ignored or manipulated for economic gain. It is interesting that to understand such misappropriate or dispossession fully, the researchers recognised the need to go beyond a property rights approach; this enables the situation to be described but not its causal roots to be fully identified.

Conclusions

Rational choice approaches are rather more critical of planning processes than the public administration approach, but they share the focus on what planning actors do in practices. Rather than evaluating this and seeing how new tools could enable better implementation and performance in relation to public interest goals, rational choice approaches seek to understand the way that self-interest drives the dynamics of planning. The rational choice perspective offers a view of planning as a series of competitive games. It is partly a game itself that planners play in order to promote their interests. Partly it is an arena in which private sector interests compete and where planning interventions can shape the nature of that competition.

Research in this approach proceeds through thought experiments or actual experiments with volunteers as well as using the rational choice framework to guide the analysis of interviews and documents. As such, modelling of costs and benefits, incentive structures, economic interests and behaviour is a central part of work within this perspective. Planning is a structured set of interactions between rational actors with interests. And as the rational choice perspective assumes rationality on the part of actors, exploring motivations and values through qualitative research is not really required. While rooted in an apparent critique of the welfare economic case for planning, it is interesting to note that this does not preclude criticism of more market-based approaches as several examples here have shown. This is despite the roots of the approach in neo-classical economics and a focus on the individual, their decision-making and their assumed rationality.

Key Theoretical Readings

Hillier and Healey (2008) Chs. 16 and 17.

Key Research Readings

Chiu, C-P., and S.K. Lai. 2009. An Experimental Comparison of Negotiation Strategies for Siting NIMBY Facilities. *Environment and Planning B: Planning and Design* 36:956–967.

Frimpong Boamah, E., and C. Amoako. 2019. Planning by (Mis)rule of Laws: The Idiom and Dilemma of Planning Within Ghana's Dual Legal Systems. *Politics and Space* 38: 97–115.

Gurran, N., G. Searle, and P. Phibbs. 2018. Urban Planning in the Age of Airbnb: Coase, Property Rights and Spatial Regulation. *Urban Policy and Research* 36: 399–416.

Lord, A., and P. O'Brien. 2017. What Price Planning? Reimagining Planning as "market maker". *Planning Theory and Practice* 18(2): 217–232.
Murray, C., and P. Fritjers. 2016. Clean Money, Dirty System: Connected Landowners Capture Beneficial Land Zoning. *Journal of Urban Economics* 93: 99–114.
Taylor, J. 2016. Urban Growth Boundaries and Betterment: Rent-seeking by Landowners on Melbourne's Expanding Urban Fringe. *Growth and Change* 47(2): 259–275.

Bibliography

Boamah, Emmanuel Frimpong, and Clifford Amoako. 2020. Planning by (Mis)Rule of Laws: The Idiom and Dilemma of Planning within Ghana's Dual Legal Land Systems. *Environment and Planning C: Politics and Space* 38 (1): 97–115.
Chiu, Ching-Pin, and Shih-Kung Lai. 2009. An Experimental Comparison of Negotiation Strategies for Siting NIMBY Facilities. *Environment and Planning: Planning and Design* 36 (6): 956–967.
Dunleavy, Patrick. 1991. *Democracy, Bureaucracy and Public Choice: Economic Explanations in Political Science*. London: Prentice Hall.
Gurran, Nicole, Glen Searle, and Peter Phibbs. 2018. Urban Planning in the Age of Airbnb: Coase, Property Rights, and Spatial Regulation. *Urban Policy and Research* 36 (4): 399–416.
Hartmann, Thomas, and Barrie Needham, eds. 2012. *Planning by Law and Property Rights Reconsidered*. Farnham: Ashgate.
Hillier, Jean, and Patsy Healey, eds. 2008. *Contemporary Movements in Planning Theory*. Aldershot: Ashgate.
Laffin, Martin. 2016. Planning in England: New Public Management, Network Governance or Post-Democracy? *International Review of Administrative Sciences* 82 (2): 354–372.
Lord, Alex. 2012. *The Planning Game: An Information Economics Approach to Understanding Urban and Environmental Management*. London: Routledge.
Lord, Alex, and Philip O'Brien. 2017. What Price Planning? Reimagining Planning as 'Market Maker'. *Planning Theory & Practice* 18 (2): 217–232.
Murray, Cameron K., and Paul Frijters. 2016. Clean Money, Dirty System: Connected Landowners Capture Beneficial Land Rezoning. *Journal of Urban Economics* 93: 99–114.
Pennington, Mark. 2000a. *Planning and the Political Market: Public Choice and the Politics of Government Failure*. London: Athlone Press.
———. 2000b. Public Choice Theory and the Politics of Urban Containment: Voter-Centred Versus Special-Interest Explanations. *Environment and Planning C: Government and Policy* 18 (2): 145–162.
Poulton, Michael C. 1997. Externalities, Transaction Costs, Public Choice and the Appeal of Zoning: A Response to Lai Wai Chung and Sorensen. *Town Planning Review* 68 (1): 81–92.
Reeve, Andrew. 1986. *Property*. London: Macmillan.
Sager, Tore. 2002. *Democratic Planning and Social Choice Dilemmas: Prelude to Institutional Planning Theory*. Aldershot: Ashgate.
Taylor, Elizabeth Jean. 2016. Urban Growth Boundaries and Betterment: Rent-Seeking by Landowners on Melbourne's Expanding Urban Fringe: Urban Growth Boundaries and Betterment. *Growth and Change* 47 (2): 259–275.
Webster, Christopher J., and Lawrence Wai-Chung Lai. 2003. *Property Rights, Planning and Markets: Managing Spontaneous Cities*. Cheltenham: Edward Elgar.

Chapter 4
The Influence of the New Institutionalism: How Culture Shapes Planning

Framing the Research

The questioning of planning as a rational activity—either a rational form of governing (Chap. 2) or the result of rational actors' decision-making (Chap. 3)—has led to a search for alternative conceptual framings, ones that recognise the cultural nature of planning practices and how they are embedded in institutional arrangements. This has gone with a shift away from considering the formal structures of planning organisations and the organisations these are embedded within, to an appreciation of the importance of the informal and the way that organisations are activated through the practices of actors. Thus, it matters the way that actors operate as this gives institutions life. Furthermore, it matters how actors see the world as this influences their activities, practices and behaviour.

Institutions are here defined as not only a particular set of organisational arrangements but also incorporating norms, values and everyday routines (March and Olsen 1989). The theoretical framework that uses this as its departure point has been termed new institutionalism, and it provides a cultural perspective on urban and environmental planning. There are different varieties of such institutionalism. Hall and Taylor (1996) distinguish rational choice, sociological and historical versions, although only the latter two fit within the scope of the discussion here; rational choice perspectives were covered in Chap. 3. Here the focus is on approaches which emphasise the work needed to be done to keep institutions operating and which consider the implications of that work, setting the whole in the context of ways of seeing the world, which may be termed cultures or worldviews or narratives or discourses.

It is the emphasis on such worldviews, narratives and discourses that situates this approach to planning studies within the so-called 'cultural turn' that can be traced back to the 1980s (Rydin 2003). This fitted within a broadly social constructivist paradigm which argued that representation was not neutral or undistorted but carried

© The Author(s), under exclusive license to Springer Nature Singapore Pte Ltd. 2021
Y. Rydin, *Theory in Planning Research*, Planning, Environment, Cities,
https://doi.org/10.1007/978-981-33-6568-1_4

with it its own agency and impacts. At this time, the significance of the way in which the world was perceived was more fully appreciated along with how narratives or images or other carriers of meaning circulated. The idea that 'meaning-making' was an important social activity became appreciated through social constructivism. This is a widely used term with slightly different nuances in different contexts. Here is it used to indicate the need to appreciate how words come to have meaning through the social interaction of people and organisations. It is not just about mapping how the world is talked about; these ways of talking create meaning for actors and this is the link through to their behaviour and action. Institutions, with their emphasis on socially constructed ways of seeing the world and therefore acting on the world, were a ready focus of attention within the cultural turn.

If public administration and rational choice theory understood planning policy development and practice as intentional, motivated, rational actions, new institutionalism offers a perspective in which the influence of culture drove actions in unexpected ways (Taylor 2013). New institutionalism as a theoretical framework describes a body of work that begins with the procedures of organisations within governmental bureaucracies such as planning departments—that is, old institutionalism—but goes further. The new element is to identify the cultural dimension to how those procedures are put into practice. This draws attention to prevailing norms, values and everyday routines within those organisations. These may reinforce and add detail to the stated intention of how procedures are supposed to operate, but closer examination may also reveal tensions and even contradictions. This can help explain why planning actions do not always follow stated intentions.

It may be argued that this book takes an institutionalist approach to considering planning research since it has put considerable emphasis on how a particular theoretical approach 'frames' planning research, directing attention in certain ways. The concept of the 'frame' is central to new institutionalism as will be expanded on later. At the core of new institutionalism is the idea that prevailing norms within an organisation or society more generally shape our behaviour. Not all actions have to be thought out and calculated; in many areas, the almost automatic reaction to prevailing institutional arrangements dominates. Here behaviour tends towards continuing existing ways of being and doing. So, the focus becomes how the organisational and wider culture shape planners' actions.

The value of considering the cultural dimension of urban and environmental planning is more widespread though. Included here is work on how planning problems and solutions are framed, and the role that non-decision-making and the mobilisation of bias may play. Institutionalism is useful for understanding why changes don't happen as well as occasions when they do. The concept of path dependency is often deployed in understanding the tendencies towards the status quo but also explaining what needs to happen in order for a shift from that status quo to happen.

While these can help understand the limitations of how urban and environmental planning operates, there is also a normative version of how cultural processes impact on planning. These relate to how planners as practitioners are cultural actors. They can engage in self-critical reflection, and this can inform learning, itself a way of reframing and improving policy practice. A significant aspect of an institutionalist approach to planning is understanding how learning can occur within planning organisations and by planners, individually but particularly collectively in their institutional setting.

This institutional work has implications for how power operates within such institutions. In discussing this it is useful to make reference to Lukes' well-known account of the three faces of power (Lukes 2005). Lukes identifies the overt face of power—the ability of one actor to make another actor do or not do something—that underpins many pluralist accounts of the policy process. But he also argued there was a second face of power, known as non-decision-making; (the third face will be discussed in Chap. 8 on Foucauldian approaches). Non-decision-making was a term coined by Bachrach and Baratz (1963, 2012; see also Catney and Henneberry 2012) to describe a situation where power is used to keep an issue off the political agenda, thus shaping the terrain on which policy action takes place. While non-decision-making may involve certain people being active in keeping the issue quiet, the impact lies in the way the subsequent agenda (with its silenced elements) influences the policy process.

This idea encourages us to look for the silences in the planning agenda and ask why these issues are not more to the fore. It suggests that the frames within which planning practice operates are as important for what they do not highlight or discuss as for those aspects that they specifically emphasise.

Dynamics of Analysis and Key Concepts

The institutionalist analysis looks in detail at how institutions work and what is necessary to maintain them and how to make them work well. This involves a focus on institutional work, on the discursive framings involved and how to achieve positive change through learning.

Institutional Work and Its Consequences

The chief insight of institutionalism is the stability that is associated with institutional arrangements. The idea of a logic of appropriateness, as identified by March and Olsen (1989), is key here. Those working in organisations decide how to behave using this logic to guide them. They learn to behave and act differently in one setting to another one. Thus, planners learn how to devise a plan, manage an urban regeneration project or run a community engagement exercise not just from their education and training but also from existing professionals who convey—explicitly and implicitly—what is the 'right way' to do these activities. This suggests that ways of doing things within institutions get stabilised by a logic of appropriateness.

They become embedded so that they are difficult to change (Booth 2011; Bunker 2012; Sorensen 2014). Sometimes even the reasons for doing things in a certain way within an organisation get lost, and the institution and its constituent actors will be running almost on automatic. Repetition over time of certain working practices reinforces this so that change becomes not only difficult to achieve but almost impossible to contemplate. Planning practitioners can be very self-aware of the existence of such path dependencies. Filion et al. (2015) showed that awareness of two types of path dependency was particularly identified by Canadian planners in Toronto: that arising from relationships between local governments, developers and consumers; and those associated with the outcomes of interactions between transportation and land use. While the latter focusses on the urban system itself, the former is concerned with governing processes, and the consequences of path dependency here include a lack of coordination, jurisdictional silos, inadequate policy tools and a lack of fit to local circumstances.

However, such institutional work does not have to lead to complete stasis. Bisschops and Beunen (2018) studied an attempt by a citizens' group known as GOUDasfalt in Gouda, the Netherlands, to redevelop a brownfield site previously used as an asphalt plant into an area for small craft businesses, urban farming, public events, a city beach, restaurants and micro-houses. They found evidence of how new norms, rules and regulations had been institutionalised. By careful dating of interactions, they traced how one action could be linked back to earlier ones or to past events or existing rules. "We looked for recurring patterns to explain the path of development of this specific urban planning process and the outcome" (2018: 6). This showed that the uncertainties involved in creating a new institution tended to reinforce the maintenance of existing institutions, but, nevertheless, new ideas on the role of citizens' initiatives were also institutionalised, even though it was difficult to create new rules and practices. Thus, it was possible to generate institutional change but by reinterpreting existing rules rather than replacing them.

The ability to act in the context of path dependencies is related to the capacities of the institution, that is institutional capacity. This is quite a slippery term but generally covers all the 'soft' skills and resources that those working within an institution have to hand, as opposed to the 'hard' resources of finances, regulation and hierarchical authority. Softer skills relate to the ability to manipulate frames, discourses and worldviews in order to achieve new ways of doing planning. The next section discusses these aspects in more detail.

Discourses, Frames and Worldviews

New Institutionalism as an approach falls broadly within the social constructivist tradition. This means that it does not take for granted the terms within which planning discussions occur but rather seeks to uncover the cultural implications of the way that issues, problems and solutions are discussed. There is a close link here to discourse studies which show how cultural framings and forms of talking and writing about issues can influence planning in urban and environmental domains; there is a particularly rich set of work on environmental discourses (Dryzek 2005). The term 'discourse' is used here to denote a set of ideas, representations and modes of talking/writing that form a coherent way of enabling communication on a particular issue or topic.

Identifying such discourses provides the opportunity to analyse how societal assumptions, say about the environment, shape the potential for planning practice and may—in detail—lead to particular language being adopted. But new institutionalism does not stop at deconstructing the discourses of planning practice. The key theoretical point is that these discourses get transmitted within planning institutions to significant effect. The institutionalist perspective combines a concern with the framing qualities of language together with an analysis of the implications of how the relevant organisations are structured and operate (Martínez et al. 2016). It makes a difference to planning practice how various discourses are constructed and circulate among planning actors within their institutional settings: the planning office, the public inquiry, the consultation arenas and so on.

For example, Krueger et al. (2018) use an interpretive institutionalist approach to understand how urban policy responses are framed and the implications for regional competitiveness. They see this as an integral part of "the way institutions are created, sustained or modified through the ideas and actions of individuals" (2018: 4). They draw on three key concepts of interpretive institutionalism: dilemmas or the perceived paradoxes of existing policy, traditions or the wider web of social meaning within which actors operate and beliefs or the way that individuals construct their world. Looking at three case studies in Lincolnshire, London/South East of England and the Duchy of Luxembourg, they were able to identify three very different framings to a similar problem or dilemma.

In Boston, Lincolnshire, the framing was strongly influenced by themes of economic development and affordable housing, and policy ideas around smart growth only gained traction after they had become more prominent at national and local levels. These were then incorporated by an organisation called MetroFuture, which put considerable effort into enrolling the business community into the smart growth framing, but they did not penetrate out into the wider local community. In London and the South East, central government influence was a major factor in the framing of the local situation. Before 2010, New Labour framed policy in terms of creating development markets but also monitoring externalities due to the tradition of a concern with fairness; after 2010, the Coalition Government prioritised the speed of development and downplayed the significance of affordable housing targets. Across both periods, the efficiency of the planning system was emphasised as implicated in adequate housing provision. In Luxembourg, there was a tradition of protecting private property at the same time as protecting centralised regulation leading to an initial emphasis on new spatial planning laws alongside a broad goal of sustainable development; however, when these failed to deliver, there was a reversion to market-based approaches.

Krueger et al. conclude that the dilemmas in the three cases share many common features, but they are managed differently because the pre-existing traditions are significant in shaping policy responses. The implication is that a policy is more likely to be successful if it takes account of these traditions.

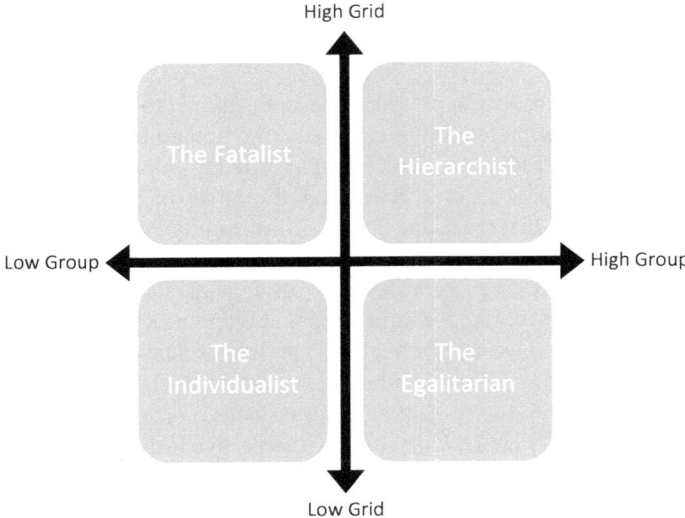

Fig. 4.1 Douglas' grid-group theory

One influential account of how frames are established and structured comes from Mary Douglas' work and its applications (Gosden 2004). Douglas is an anthropologist known for many ethnographic studies but also for an account of how pollution is framed (as 'matter out of place'). She developed a cultural theory that can provide a framework for suggesting how different worldviews are differentiated from each other. Known as the grid-group framework it provides a fourfold typology as illustrated in Fig. 4.1.

On the vertical axis, there is a differentiation between whether behaviour is rulebound (high grid) or not (low grid); and on the other axis the distinction is between whether individual (low group) or collective (high group) decision-making dominates. This produces four distinct worldviews: the individualist (low grid, low group), the egalitarian (low grid, high group), the hierarchist (high grid, high group) and the fatalistic (high grid, low group). The individualist frame favours market-led approaches where individuals are in competition with each other and 'anything goes'. By contrast, the hierarchist is more aligned with traditional bureaucratic approaches in which behaviour is guided by rules, policies, organisational guidance and protocols and the goals are in the collective, group or public interest. The egalitarian worldview seeks to achieve common goals but through individual actions, not necessarily aligned with each other through the operation of rules. Finally there is the fatalist frame in which there is no allegiance to a collective group but a strong adherence to common guidelines for behaviour. This cultural theory can be used to characterise particular institutions and can help describe how they operate; it provides an added richness of detail to institutional accounts.

For example, Jayne (2003) used grid-group theory to organise and understand the multiple responses to local economic development strategies, as part of an unpacking of the dominant representation of locality, place and community in terms of tropes such as the post-industrial or postmodern city. In the case of Jayne's chosen case study of Stoke-on-Trent, England, framing had very real impacts, which Jayne describes as industrial inertia and a "seemingly obsessive internal focus" (2003: 961). Jayne tried to allocate local actors to the different categories of grid-group theory, but he noted that this was not always easy; the messiness of real life meant that there were hybrid sociocultural positions that spanned different grid-group categories, and actors also espoused internally inconsistent positions. The result of the analysis was a visual representation (using the 2 × 2 matrix) of the variety of positions within Stoke-on-Trent on local economic development. The majority were clustered in the fatalist category, following by hierarchical and then egalitarian and individualistic. More important, perhaps, were the types of actors in the different categories. Jayne identified the local evening newspaper *The Sentinel* as fatalistic, clearly important in terms of any media influence; many local individuals also fell into this category as did the City Council. Councillors were spread across the fatalistic, hierarchical and egalitarian categories, but council officials tended towards the egalitarian label. The creative industry practitioners were more likely to be egalitarian or individualistic, while the voluntary sector and private sector companies were widely spread. And so on. The complexity of local framing of economic development was evident from this cultural analysis.

Social Learning and Communities of Practice

While the institutionalist approach is best at considering stabilised processes—perhaps over-stabilised processes that entrench old and ineffective ways of doing things and keep important issues off the policy agenda—it can also support analysis of change. Here the key term is 'learning'; change occurs through policy actors thinking, reflecting and learning. This is not just about how individuals enhance their knowledge and understanding. Such learning is more collective and affects how institutions approach policy work. Planning as a professional practice is thus learned collectively within planning institutions. Planners learn from each other and also from actively noticing and reflecting on live examples of planning practice. Again the logic of appropriateness is at work, as planners learn 'on the job' what is the right and wrong way to 'do' planning.

Schon (2008) has provided a dynamic version of this idea through his work on the reflective practitioner. While communities of practice may be seen to convey and embed established ways of working (see below), Schon considers that a reflective practitioner may look back at the impacts of these working methods and learn to practise differently. This is unlikely to cause wholesale change in working practices, but rather incremental change may be possible in response to persistent problems that arise during the course of established institutional practices. Closely allied with this is the idea of single-, double- and triple-loop learning (discussed further below). Single-loop learning is just about garnering knowledge to aid the implementation of chosen pathways; double-loop learning questions those pathways and suggests alternatives; while triple-loop learning questions the very policy goals, impelling more fundamental revision of that policy approach.

The concept of communities of practice has also been used to explain the way that actors learn from each other in institutional settings (Wenger 1998). They identify the transmission mechanism by which practices persist within an organisation and become stable and accepted ways of doing things. A community of practice encompasses a group of practitioners—perhaps inside one organisation but also, as with professional groupings, operating across organisations. They undertake the same kind of work and collectively engage in passing on knowledge about how to do that work. The key point is that practitioners learn to become proficient practitioners by working together and learning from each other during that work. Together they constitute what counts as proficiency in that institutional context. The informal conversations, the copying of one another and the joint problem-solving of working together transmit the norms of what appropriate working practices are. In one of the examples of research discussed later, this idea of a community of practice is supplemented with that of a community of inquirers, suggesting more of a focus on innovative ways of doing things rather than embedded established practices. This tension between the status quo, embedded practices and path dependencies and change, innovation and learning new practices is typical of work in the institutionalist approach.

Nilsson (2005) uses social learning to understand how policy integration can be fostered. He focusses on social learning through an institution rather than the individual policy actor. He argues that such learning occurs through reframing and changed discursive practices pervading policy institutions. This involves changes in the patterns that have limited practitioners' thinking about problems and solutions. In this way, new patterns of thinking enable new issues—such as climate change, say—to be taken into account and, through mutual reframing, policy integration to occur. This is discussed further later in one of the research themes.

Research Themes in Practice

Three themes will be discussed in relation to examples of institutionalist research in practice; these are the role of path dependency, the use of the single-double-triple-loop learning model and explorations of the broader idea of social learning.

Path Dependency in Practice

One particular strength of new institutionalism is that it can provide explanations of why change is difficult to achieve and what might be required for that change. A key concept here is that of path dependency.

Imran and Low (2007) provide an example of examining path dependency in their study of transport planning in Pakistan. Focussing on why the initial path taken towards transport planning has persisted to the present day, they set themselves three research questions focussing on: institutional relationships, power and finance; methods for analysing transport problems and generating solutions; and the definition of transport problems by decision makers locally and internationally. To support their research, they distinguished three categories of path dependence: institutional, technical and discursive. The empirical basis for the analysis was a review of transport and planning policy documents together with 30 semi-structured interviews of key actors involved in transport decision-making, that is local and international bureaucrats, politicians and professionals. The data analysis proceeded in three steps based on the categories of path dependence set out earlier.

First, the way in which transport decisions were made was mapped. This identified the capacity of different institutions involved through looking at budgetary and human resources and policy documents since 1947; this was used to identify institutional path dependence. Second, the methods for analysing transport problems and identifying solutions were examined, largely using the review of policy documents. This helped pinpoint technical path dependence. And third, policy discourses were explored, understanding this term as "a specific ensemble of ideas, concepts and categories that are produced, reproduced and transformed in a particular set of practices" (p. 322). Hajer's work (see also Chap. 8) was used here to clarify the importance of storylines as "the linguistic representations of issues that provide ways of holding ideas together and enable arguments to be transmitted among stakeholders or key institutions" (p. 323). Using policy documentation and the semi-structured interviews, these storylines supported the analysis of discursive path dependence.

The researchers undertook an initial mapping of the formal institutional arrangements for transport planning in Pakistan, which identified 9 federal ministries and 22 different departments across the governmental levels of the federal, provincial and local government. The decision-making process was also mapped, showing the formal lines-of-dependency relationships. This confirmed that transport planning was heavily centralised in Pakistan at the federal level, that there was limited research funding for sustainable aspects of transport and that the federal government controlled access to local and international financial resources for this sector; the federal government acts simultaneously as financier, executor and regulator. The research then sought to identify the capacities of transport institutions. These 'capacities' were subdivided into substantive and support categories: the former covered policy formulation, institutional capacity, human resources and finance; the latter covered research and information.

The research found that there was substantial reference to sustainability in relation to transport across legislation and policy. However, looking at institutional capacity, they found a lack of coordination among different transport institutions and a strong presence of departmental and professional boundaries. In addition, there was a prevailing 'elitist growth model' which projected a narrow vision of transport goals in terms of better and wider roads, largely ignoring other modes of transport. Because of a lack of financial support, transport institutions were heavily dependent on international development institutions and associated foreign consultants, which had grown over time. This has led to an emphasis on hard infrastructure and a failure to build localised capacities. A serious deficiency of institutional human resource capacity at the national level was noted, and this was amplified by a lack of education, training and research into public transport, non-motorised transport planning and sustainable transport.

The analysis explained this institutional path dependence and the associated power of international and national transport institutions in terms of the technical and financial reliance on international development institutions, which meant that most transport projects were donor driven and aligned with the norms and established expertise of those international organisations. Furthermore, transport policies and solutions became technically path dependent through adopting a 'decide and provide' approach to road development and investment, with inbuilt assumptions about the 'necessary' length of road per land area. This prevented more innovative ways of thinking about transport planning that would have disrupted the path dependency.

This was reinforced by a storyline of transport development that foregrounded economic development, with road construction assumed to lead to economic growth. This had four sub-storylines: motorisation will bring more economic well-being, poverty reduction will occur through road development, there is a technical fix to environmental problems, and road accidents are a major economic cost. These different dimensions of path dependence reinforced each other, the implication being that all need to be tackled for a change in transport planning.

This comprehensive analysis built on the mapping of formal structures and procedures (which one would focus on in a public administration approach) but then supplemented this with an analysis of the way transport problems and solutions were constructed and the terms in which transport planning was discussed. This considerably deepens the analysis and pinpoints the dynamics behind path dependency.

A second example of research on path dependency comes from water planning in Montana, USA, as studied by Anderson et al. (2018). They looked at the Yellowstone Basin, a large arid and rural area where 80% of the surface water goes to irrigation of agriculture and where climate-induced drought is increasingly a threat to both urban and rural residents. This analysis was derived from data collected from close observation of the workings of the Yellowstone Basin Advisory Council (YBAC), one of four citizen councils established in 2013 to develop recommendations for an updated state water plan together with two specific measures: a water-use measuring mandate and a 'shared sacrifice' programme of water sharing for short-term management of drought.

The Council met 18 times over 18 months to engage in (a) a scoping exercise, (b) technical presentations and (c) deliberation and adoption of recommendations. The research team was commissioned to facilitate the first phase but was permitted to attend and record the other phases as well. All meetings were video-recorded and transcribed; documents prepared in the third phase were also studied. Analysis proceeded by discourse analysis, seeing the policy measures as a constructed narrative and drawing on a systematic content analysis of video-recording transcripts, meeting notes and recorded observations of key interactions between state officials, YBAC members and the research team.

The analysis highlighted the influence of the established legal doctrine of prior appropriation—'first in time, first in right'—whereby those legally using water over the long term—usually the private agricultural property owners—could deny use of water to others in case of short-term needs during droughts. This doctrine was seen to constrain the attempt to introduce more participatory forms of planning via the Advisory Councils, redirecting deliberations back to the status quo rather than towards other alternatives that wider participation favoured. It further prevented the adoption of the mandate to measure individual water usage.

This did not mean that no change occurred. Rather change was shaped by the path dependencies established by the prior appropriation doctrine, and this meant that consensus could be generated for the alternative water-sharing programme known as 'shared sacrifice'. This was seen as a pragmatic response to drought conditions and not threatening the fundamental principle of prior appropriation. The analysis showed that the prior appropriation doctrine was not just a legal doctrine but "an institutional manifestation of a deeply entrenched cultural landscape" (Anderson et al. 2018: 2), linked to libertarian principles such as individual freedom, private property rights and distrust of government. Change was able to occur but within certain institutional constraints.

The researchers supplemented the reliance on path dependency to explain their case by also framing the prior appropriation doctrine as a 'boundary object' enabling discussion across institutional boundaries or borders on the basis of certain shared meanings (see also Chap. 8). In this way a measure was agreed that met with the core assumptions of prior appropriation but also recognised the threat of drought. The voluntary and temporary aspects of the adopted measure were stressed as was the sense of control that water rights owners felt they retained. Interestingly, the 'shared sacrifice' measure still involved measurement of usage!

This example highlights how an established legal doctrine carries significant cultural resonance when it is seen in the context of a broader analysis of how problems and solutions of water management are framed. It also shows that path dependency does not have to lead to stasis but rather can shape change.

Loops of Learning

As emphasised above, learning as a means of achieving change in the context of institutional pressures towards the status quo is a key concern of this approach. Such learning may be conceived narrowly or more widely. In this section, two papers that use the single-double-triple loop model of learning are discussed.

Willems et al. (2018) studied water infrastructure renewal in the Netherlands. Their research was framed by a focus on organisational learning, understood as a change in the shared understanding of the problem to be addressed. Learning is here shared meaning-making and is "contingent on how water authorities frame the issue at stake" (p. 1090). To research this, the single and double-loop model of learning was used, positing that if water renewal was framed as an operational issue this might promote single-loop learning, whereas if it was framed as a strategic issue, this would lead to more reflexive, double-loop learning.

The case study was the Dutch agency Rijkswaterstaat, which is charged with renewing Dutch waterways, a massive challenge in this watery country. This agency had its origins in water engineering and was more recently repositioned as an executive agency with responsibility for implementing programmes formulated at the ministerial level. Three exploratory interviews with senior officials of the agency resulted in the Program on Navigation Locks and its six subsidiary projects being chosen as a key example of waterway renewal for study.

Data collection proceeded by way of in-depth interviews, participatory observation and analysis of secondary documents. Two periods were distinguished. For the first period of 2004–2012, 11 interviews with key actors in the Dutch water infrastructure sector were undertaken; for the subsequent period, another 11 interviews with officials on the Navigation Locks Program were conducted. All interviews were recorded, transcribed and sent to interviewees for verification. Thirteen meetings of the Program were attended, and one researcher was involved in biweekly programme team meetings and meetings with private companies. Observations on these meetings were recorded in a digital diary.

Analysis proceeded by looking for key concepts for each frame; two main families of codes were identified—central concepts and action strategies. Central concepts described terms relating to mission, ambitions and aim; strategies were coded by looking at the operationalisation of these central concepts. In addition, interviewees were asked to reflect on their belief systems and practices and to identify barriers to putting a frame into practice. This was done within each time period identified above. Secondary data in the form of policy documents and newspaper articles were used to triangulate the results.

The researchers found that waterway renewal is typically framed from a new public management perspective (see also Chaps. 3 and 8), particularly during 2004–2012, with reliability and cost-effectiveness prioritised. Rijkswaterstaat sought to operate as a compact and flexible agency to achieve this. This involved narrowing down the scope of the agency's work to clear targets and measurable outputs; several areas of work within the programme were outsourced such as design, construction and maintenance. Stakeholder involvement was limited to reduce disruption, and the work was broken down into distinct projects. The focus was less on the renewal of the waterways per se and more on the procedural and contractual issues involved in the public-private partnerships. In the second phase, the research found the emergence of distrust between public and private partners. As a result, the agency emphasised uniformity and predictability in its projects, establishing a limited partnership of projects with an aligned philosophy or worldview. It also sought more openness and flexibility between partners to promote exchange of knowledge.

However, the researchers concluded that these framings led to a rather pragmatic approach in which existing practices were refined and the agency's mission was protected. The learning that occurred was largely single loop, aiming at more efficient implementation of existing projects. Higher-level learning did not occur here because it was considered too disruptive. More positively, there was reflection on existing dominant frames, and new concepts were considered, but further institutional work would be needed to overcome the inherent uncertainties involved in change and to embed these concepts within existing institutional practices.

This research project operates with a strong understanding of the different dimensions of water infrastructure planning in cultural terms, exploring the framing and joint meaning-making that shapes the nature of learning. This enables the researchers to identify both the learning that does occur and the limits to learning.

Henly-Shepard et al. (2015) used the full range of the single-double-triple-loop learning model in their practice-driven research seeking to establish a social learning framework based on stakeholder participation to facilitate community disaster planning. Their geographical context was the north shore of O'ahu, Hawai'I, an area vulnerable to natural hazards but where the collective social memory of past disasters and how to cope with them had been affected by fragmentation, tourism and globalisation. Hence the researchers sought to develop a planning methodology that "standardizes diverse stakeholder knowledge and management strategies in a form that maintains the integrity of complex human understanding and is useful to analysing a community's dynamics in relation to natural hazards" (p. 110). The idea behind the research was that adapting to change and being resilient in the face of natural hazards involves communities anticipating a problem, collecting and sharing knowledge, reflecting and then developing a shared vision for action. Changing people's mental maps to enable this was a form of learning and sharing ideas through a deliberative process facilitated social learning. The most thorough form of learning within such deliberation would be triple-loop learning.

The methodology was action based and involved the use of a computer-based fuzzy cognitive mapping tool, Mental Modeler. This iteratively constructed and revised visual models of stakeholders' mental maps, as well as defining desired targets for resilience. It also helped the researchers understand how communities were anticipating impacts from hazards and modelled the effects of different adaptation strategies. This was executed in a semi-rural tourist area of about 25,000 residents (long and short term), visitors and employees, with a pre-existing community-based disaster preparedness committee, representing residents, businesses and various local, county and state organisations and institutions.

Four participatory mental modelling workshops were held with 6–15 participants drawn from the committee. The three phases of the research were designed to move from single- up to triple-loop learning. Phase I developed two small-group shared models of the community; Phase II merged these, ran iterative scenarios and sought to build consensus on the structure and dynamics of the community and how a tsunami might impact it; and Phase III challenged local to state-level plans and protocols. Four resulting strategies were then examined more fully by the Committee, and an implementation plan was developed. The researchers not only developed this planning methodology but used the learning model to analyse their participant observation of its deployment and to compare the outputs from the three difference phases of the project; networks were used to visualise these outputs.

The research concluded that, as the discussion moved into more collective settings and involved more iterative discussion, there was a move from single to double to triple learning. It also indicated some of the conditions that needed attention to ensure that this happened. It required diverse expertise, attention to existing power dynamics and careful facilitation as well as a willingness to adapt the template when needed.

This paper provides an interesting contrast to some of the work reviewed in Chap. 2, where tools to support planning were also developed. Whereas the research there sought to use such stakeholder involvement to test and refine these tools, here the focus is on identifying cultural dimensions that might impact on that decision-making. This helps identify the institutional work required to promote learning beyond the change in planning procedures that the public administration approach stresses.

Social Learning Explored

The final set of papers discussed take the broader social learning frame for their research.

The first example of research into learning concerns the development of a four-step methodology to guide case study fieldwork by Holden (2008) in Seattle, Washington, USA. Seattle's sustainability initiatives included the development of a suite of sustainability indicators, which were widely considered to be world-leading when they were first initiated; Holden studied whether they instigated social learning. She used the organisational learning literature alongside that from pragmatism and communicative action (see Chap. 5) to identify different communities of learning: the functional group within an organisation, the community of practice (see above), and the community of inquirers (defined by common processes of knowledge coding and codes of practice). On this basis, Holden identified her four-step fieldwork methodology. These steps were identifying the communities as a unit of analysis, investigating tacit knowledge by studying group routines, studying processes of change within communities and the knowledge codebooks (that guided the indicator development), and searching for the diffusion of knowledge out to policy practice.

Holden applied this to investigate a particular example of innovation in Seattle—the sustainable community indicators project created by the NGO Sustainable Seattle. The fieldwork was undertaken in 2002 and comprised a systematic review of sustainability-related policy documents, internal files for Sustainable Seattle and interviews with 71 policy actors involved with the NGO network or other aspects of sustainability policy. This was described as a mixed-methods, in-depth case study approach. The material was used to provide a chronological narrative of the sustainability indicators project.

The analysis found that the NGO Sustainable Seattle or S2 did approximate to a community of inquirers and thus was potentially capable of transformative social learning. A number of features described this NGO: enduring personal and professional attachment to the organisation, a strong common purpose, mutual respect, willingness to re-engage after absences, an ability to recruit new members, and a sense of simultaneously working with a 'big picture' and targeted actions. There were tacit community priorities of collaboration and recognising linkages between public issues (i.e. a holistic approach). These helped cement the NGO but made it less accessible to outsiders. The codebooks were successfully completed but were then significantly revised over time, partly due to changes in local political and institutional context, turnover in NGO members and a general maturing of the concept of sustainable development. Finally, in terms of the four-step framework for analysis, while some diffusion of knowledge had occurred, funding shortfalls and staff constraints limited this; some felt that the social justice dimension of sustainability was under-represented and that this showed a lack of innovation. It seemed that it had not been possible "to move clearly beyond engaging the 'like-minded'" in the indicator project (p. 31).

The analysis looked specifically at evidence of forward and backward adaptation in the knowledge codebook for the Sustainable Seattle project. The indicators were adopted by opinion leaders, diffused through a range of professional networks and led to the rapid reinvention of existing projects. These were all examples of positive forward adaptation, promoting the sustainability goal. Backward adaptation (negative change) was represented here by lack of financial and organisational commitment and trade-offs with an equality agenda. Turning to tacit knowledge, again examples of forward adaptation or positive change could be identified: the emphasis on widespread citizen engagement and even empowerment, the testing of the limits with regard to the sustainability agenda and the improving of local government accountability. Negative or backward adaptation was seen in the risks of confusion due to lack of precision in goals, a focus on dissemination (and nothing more) and turning indicator organisations into unique advisors.

Holden, thus, concluded—taking all the evidence together—that social learning had occurred but was limited. The indicator project was remarkable for its collaborative efforts and was effective in diffusing knowledge internationally. But diffusion was much less obvious across the city and its diverse stakeholders, calling "into question the effectiveness of S2's work to diffuse outwards to create a new system of policy practice" (p. 35).

Social learning can be quite a slippery concept, and Holden here managed to identify how different stakeholders came together to learn and the limits on that learning through detailed study of a specific initiative and associated documents. A tight focus supported the wide-ranging analysis of the extent of the changes associated with indicator development.

An example of research on social learning operating across very different geographical contexts is provided by Fisher et al. (2018), who looked at the usability of climate change information in sub-national planning in three countries: India, Kenya and Uganda. The framing was in terms of the social learning supports that existed and the impact they and intermediary organisations had. In this context, new information was judged in terms of its fit with the context and how it interacted with existing knowledge. Here users' behaviour, experience and cultures all had an influence. In their research they looked for social learning in terms of a change in understanding that had taken place in individuals but also went beyond the individual to social units or communities of practice; they particularly looked at the role that social interactions between actors played.

On the basis of this discussion, they developed a number of categories to guide their empirical work. They identified the following dimensions of social learning: stakeholder engagement/participation, building capacity and understanding, and using iterative processes for reflection, with challenging institutions as a cross-cutting theme. They moved from examination of the process of social learning to consider the outcomes in terms of: factual information (cognitive); values and beliefs (normative); and trust, networks and relationships (relational). The whole analysis was placed within a multi-scalar understanding based on a three-level framework of the individual (micro), the organisation (meso) and the institution (macro); this not only enabled the differentiation of the role of information but also pointed to the role of boundary organisations in bridging changes of level.

Three case studies of sub-national planning in different counties were chosen: shared learning dialogues in Gorakhpur, India; district climate planning in Bundibugyo District, Uganda; and devolved climate change planning in Isiolo County, Kenya. The data collection methods were semi-structured interviews with key stakeholders (13 in Gorakhpur, 23 in Bundibugyo, 16 in Isiolo), document and policy analysis, observation and focus groups with local communities engaged in the activity in question (three, two and two focus groups respectively). Local intermediary organisations were gatekeepers to the research field and became partners in discussing, reflecting on, understanding and analysing the emerging evidence. Stakeholders for interview were selected on the basis of being active and representing the diversity of all groups. The interview schedule was based on the above dimensions of social learning and the specific characteristics of climate change information (long-time horizons, uncertain evidence, multi-sectoral issue). These dimensions and characteristics guided the coding of transcripts.

Their findings were threefold. First, they argued that intermediaries often prioritise commitment to project goals rather than using climate change information to act on climate change measures; they tend to use a simple framing of climate change to introduce the issue before moving on to introducing new information. Second, they pointed out the barriers to critical reflection arising from iterative processes that exist for government stakeholders, barriers that can be somewhat overcome by using monitoring and evaluation frameworks. Third, where it worked, social learning could broaden the framing from a single-sector issue to one that covers multiple sectors, but uncertain aspects were often ignored. The latter is important as climate change is an example of an issue that requires significant shifts in institutional norms and practices in multiple locations.

This research highlights the importance in some projects of involving local stakeholders to get access for institutional research and also to fully understand the details of learning processes. Again there is a nuanced account of the extent of social learning emphasising successes and limitations.

Koontz (2013) looked at two collaborative watershed partnerships involving multiple stakeholders in Ohio, USA, and Niedersachsen, Germany, from a social learning perspective. The research questions focussed on identifying the individual and group components of social learning, comparing the extent of such learning across the cases and analysing which factors had promoted or inhibited social learning. The precise definition of social learning adopted used this emphasis on the individual and the group: "individual cognitive gain related to the resource, what other stakeholders want, what solutions are politically feasible, and the process of multi-scale planning; plus relational elements of trust-building, network connections and development of group agreement" (p. 1574). Drawing on previous literature on the use of collaborative and deliberative processes to enhance social learning, the researchers identified six factors as important: inclusiveness, extended engagement, information exchange, opportunities for interaction, process control and process equity. This framework guided the data collection and analysis.

The Ohio and Niedersachsen cases were alike with regard to the physical nature of the current water problems and solutions, their economic structure in terms of growth and important sectors (agriculture and food production), their federal political structures and the existence of national water quality statutes. The differences included the electoral system (winner-takes-all versus proportional representation), the tradition of corporatism within Germany compared to that of pluralism in the USA and the role of the land-use planning system. In Germany, this occurred through vertically integrated, consensus-oriented institutions, whereas in the USA there was less vertical integration; in the former there has been a trend towards regionalism and in the latter towards state institutional structures. Watershed planning in Ohio was typically bottom-up; in Niedersachsen, top-down. Nevertheless, both have sought greater stakeholder involvement.

The data collection involved two different approaches to gathering information from interviewees. First, interviews asked participants to describe how processes of collaboration unfolded and triangulated these to develop a unified account of these processes. Interviewees were identified by a snowballing method and followed a protocol, with notes written up and corroborated afterwards. About 19 interviews were undertaken in Niedersachsen (11 face-to-face; 8 by telephone); 21 interviews (all by telephone) were conducted in Ohio. This was supplemented with document analysis including meeting minutes, attendance lists, policy documents and various reports. Analysis proceeded by summarising, coding and pattern searching, focussing on aspects of social learning.

In addition, the researchers used perceptual questions in a survey asking for levels of agreement with statements about social learning and the factors expected to affect it; this is because the researchers considered that actors often underestimated the impact of their own involvement in social learning. These surveys were conducted by telephone. In Niedersachsen, members of three area cooperation groups were identified; of 55 active participants who had attended at least three meetings, the researchers were able to contact 39 and 31 agreed to participate. In Ohio, members of three collaborative watershed partnerships were contacted with a focus again on 'active' members attending at least three meetings. About 37 met this criterion and 30 could be reached, all of whom agreed to be surveyed. Questions covered the following topics: cognitive knowledge gain, trust, group agreement and networks (following the definition of social learning outlined above). Answers were coded on a five-point Likert scale.

The research found that four of the six factors involved in enabling social learning were similar—inclusiveness, extended engagement, information exchange and opportunities for interaction—but that process control and process equity varied. Process control was much stronger in the Ohio case due to the bottom-up nature of the process. The data on process equity was more mixed, but the survey data indicated that one factor—individual efficacy—was perceived to be significantly higher in Ohio; the other factor—being taken seriously—was not significantly different. So Ohio was distinguished by strong control of the process and a perception of individual efficacy by stakeholders.

These results were cross-referenced against evidence for social learning, largely from the survey results. In Ohio, the most knowledge gain was about what others wanted followed by watershed planning, watershed processes and ecology, and finally political feasibility; in Niedersachsen, the knowledge gains were about basin scale water planning and the EU directive that drives watershed planning, followed by watershed planning, watershed processes and ecology and political feasibility in the same order as in Ohio. Comparing across the case studies, cognitive gain was higher in Ohio in three of the four types of knowledge, and two of the relational factors—trust and agreement—were also higher there.

Control and a perspective of individual efficacy were linked to the level of learning. This led to the conclusion that the level of local process control was key for enabling social learning and that it was, therefore, important to give stakeholders opportunities to develop and shape the processes that they are engaging in if learning is the goal. The terms of the analysis here were quite disaggregated to identify different aspects of the institutional processes and perceptions and to try and pinpoint which aspects had the most impact on social learning. This is less of a story of institutional change and stasis, and more of an attempt to find a causal link through a focus on a number of institutional dimensions.

Conclusions

New institutionalism provides a more forgiving approach to the work of planners. It helps explain why planning practice takes the forms that it does and hence why this practice may diverge from expectations and stated intentions. It sees planning activity as a culturally shaped set of actions in which behaviour is driven by a logic of appropriateness. Planners learn from each other, in communities of practice, how to plan and thus they follow the pathways of behaviour that have already been established and considered suitable for professional practice. Norms and values of planning practice develop over time within institutions, both the wider planning profession and specific planning organisations at all governmental scales. Specific planning organisations may be found to have very specific organisational cultures that help explain the behaviours that are seen as appropriate in that context.

The research focus within new institutionalism is likely to be on a specific planning institution, and this needs careful defining. It could be as broad as the American or British planning profession. It could be as narrow as a specific neighbourhood planning forum. The scale and extent of that institution needs to be clarified along with the actors that can be considered members of that institution. Identification with the institution is important as the theoretical dynamics depend on the norms, values and routines of that institution having purchase on the member. If that person does not 'buy in' to the institution, then there is unlikely to be much impact from these cultural aspects; the actor will just ignore them. It should also be recognised that actors may simultaneously be members of multiple institutions (a local authority, a profession, another work-based affiliation), and these will all impact how they behave.

The institutionalist approach provides detailed analyses of how planning organisations work based, in part, on understanding how they see the world. This highlights the constraints on achieving change and why path dependencies often limit new ways of doing things. In so far as planning research identifies deficiencies in how planning operates with respect to its public interest goals, such institutional work can also suggest where significant constraints should be targeted in to order to offer improved planning practice. The framework also puts a lot of emphasis on learning and on understanding—again in detail—how learning occurs.

Key Theoretical Readings

Hillier and Metzger (2015), Chs. 18 and 25.
    Gunder et al. (2018), Chs. 19 and 20.

Key Research Readings

Anderson, M.B., L.C. Ward, S.J. Gilbertz, J. McEvoy, and D.M. Hall. 2018. Prior Appropriation and Water Planning Reform in Montana's Yellowstone River Basin: Path Dependency or Boundary Object? *Journal of Environmental Policy and Planning* 20: 198–213.
Fisher, S., D. Dodman, M. van Epp, and B. Garside. 2018. The Usability of Climate Information in Sub-national Planning in India, Kenya and Uganda: The Role of Social Learning and Intermediary Organisations. *Climatic Change* 151: 219–245.
Henly-Shepard, S., S.A. Gray, and L.J. Cox. 2015. The Use of Participatory Modeling to Promote Social Learning and Facilitate Community Disaster Planning. *Environmental Science and Policy* 45: 109–122.

Holden, M. 2008. Social Learning in Planning: Seattle's Sustainable Development codebooks. *Progress in Planning* 69: 1–40.

Imran, M., and N. Low. 2007. Institutional, technical and discursive path dependence in transport planning in Pakistan. *International Development Planning Review* 29(3): 319–352.

Koontz, T. 2014. Social Learning in Collaborative Watershed Planning: The Importance of Process Control and Efficacy. *Journal of Environmental Planning and Management* 57(10): 1572–1593.

Willems, J. J., T. Busscher, M. van den Brink, and J. Arts. 2017. Anticipating Water Infrastructure Renewal: A Framing Perspective on Organizational Learning in Public Agencies. *Environment and Planning C: Politics and Space* 36(6): 1088–1108.

Bibliography

Anderson, Matthew B., et al. 2018. Prior Appropriation and Water Planning Reform in Montana's Yellowstone River Basin: Path Dependency or Boundary Object? *Journal of Environmental Policy & Planning* 20 (2): 198–213.

Bachrach, Peter, and Morton S. Baratz. 1963. Decisions and Nondecisions: An Analytical Framework. *The American Political Science Review* 57 (3): 632–642.

———. 2012. Two Faces of Power. *The American Political Science Review* 56 (4): 947–952.

Bisschops, Saskia, and Raoul Beunen. 2018. A New Role for Citizens' Initiatives: The Difficulties in Co-Creating Institutional Change in Urban Planning. *Journal of Environmental Planning and Management* 62 (1): 72–87.

Booth, Philip. 2011. Culture, Planning and Path Dependence: Some Reflections on the Problems of Comparison. *Town Planning Review* 82 (1): 13–28.

Bunker, Raymond. 2012. Reviewing the Path Dependency in Australian Metropolitan Planning. *Urban Policy and Research* 30 (4): 443–452.

Catney, Philip, and John Henneberry. 2012. (Not) Exercising Discretion: Environmental Planning and the Politics of Blame-Avoidance. *Planning Theory & Practice* 13 (4): 549–568.

Dryzek, John S. 2005. *The Politics of the Earth: Environmental Discourses*. 2nd ed. Oxford: Oxford University Press.

Filion, Pierre, Michelle Lee, Neluka Leanage, and Kent Hakull. 2015. Planners' Perspectives on Obstacles to Sustainable Urban Development: Implications for Transformative Planning Strategies. *Planning Practice and Research* 30 (2): 202–221.

Fisher, Susannah, David Dodman, Marissa Van Epp, and Ben Garside. 2018. The Usability of Climate Information in Sub-National Planning in India, Kenya and Uganda: The Role of Social Learning and Intermediary Organisations. *Climatic Change* 151 (2): 219–245.

Gosden, Chris. 2004. Grid and Group: An Interview with Mary Douglas. *Journal of Social Archaeology* 4 (3): 275–287.

Gunder, Michael, Ali Madanipour, and Vanessa Watson, eds. 2018. *The Routledge Handbook of Planning Theory*. London: Routledge.

Hall, Peter A., and Rosemary C.R. Taylor. 1996. Political Science and the Three New Institutionalisms. *Political Studies* 44 (5): 936–957.

Henly-Shepard, Sarah, Steven A. Gray, and Linda J. Cox. 2015. The Use of Participatory Modeling to Promote Social Learning and Facilitate Community Disaster Planning. *Environmental Science & Policy* 45: 109–122.

Hillier, Jean, and Jonathan Metzger, eds. 2015. *Connections: Exploring Contemporary Planning Theory and Practice with Patsy Healey*. Farnham: Ashgate.

Holden, Meg. 2008. Social Learning in Planning: Seattle's Sustainable Development Codebooks. *Progress in Planning* 69 (1): 1–40.

Imran, Muhammad, and Nicholas Low. 2007. Institutional, Technical and Discursive Path Dependence in Transport Planning in Pakistan. *International Development Planning Review* 29 (3): 319–352.

Jayne, Mark. 2003. Too Many Voices, 'Too Problematic to Be Plausible': Representing Multiple Responses to Local Economic Development Strategies? *Environment and Planning A* 35 (6): 959–981.

Koontz, Tomas M. 2013. Social Learning in Collaborative Watershed Planning: The Importance of Process Control and Efficacy. *Journal of Environmental Planning and Management* 57 (10): 1572–1593.

Krueger, Rob, David Gibbs, and Constance Carr. 2018. Examining Regional Competitiveness and the Pressures of Rapid Growth: An Interpretive Institutionalist Account of Policy Responses in Three City Regions. *Environment and Planning C: Politics and Space* 36 (6): 965–986.

Lukes, Steven. 2005. *Power: A Radical View*. 2nd ed. Basingstoke: Palgrave Macmillan.

March, James G., and Johan P. Olsen. 1989. *Rediscovering Institutions: The Organizational Basis of Politics*. New York; London: Free Press.

Martínez, Joyde Giacomini, Ingrid Boas, Jennifer Lenhart, and Arthur P.J. Mol. 2016. Revealing Curitiba's Flawed Sustainability: How Discourse Can Prevent Institutional Change. *Habitat International* 53: 350–359.

Nilsson, Måns. 2005. Learning, Frames, and Environmental Policy Integration: The Case of Swedish Energy Policy. *Environment and Planning C: Government and Policy* 23 (2): 207–226.

Rydin, Yvonne. 2003. *Conflict, Consensus, and Rationality in Environmental Planning: An Institutional Discourse Approach*. Oxford: Oxford University Press.

Schon, Donald A. 2008. *Reflective Practitioner How Professionals Think In Action*. New York: Basic Books.

Sorensen, Andre. 2014. Taking Path Dependence Seriously: An Historical Institutionalist Research Agenda in Planning History. *Planning Perspectives* 30 (1): 17–38.

Taylor, Zack. 2013. Rethinking Planning Culture: A New Institutionalist Approach. *Town Planning Review* 84 (6): 683–702.

Wenger, Etienne. 1998. *Communities of Practice: Learning, Meaning, and Identity*. Cambridge: Cambridge University Press.

Willems, Jannes, Tim Busscher, Margaretha van den Brink, and Eric Arts. 2018. Anticipating Water Infrastructure Renewal: A Framing Perspective on Organizational Learning in Public Agencies. *Environment and Planning C: Politics and Space* 36 (6): 1088–1108.

Chapter 5
Governance Theories: Stakeholders, Networks and Collaboration

Framing the Research

Governance theories were widespread within theorising about planning processes in the later twentieth century and continue to have resonance today. They principally arose from a dissatisfaction with the kinds of approaches that were discussed in Chap. 2 and the view of state action that they promoted. By the later twentieth century, notably in North America and Europe, there was a major crisis of confidence in state-led planning occurring in countries with established planning systems. The post-war promises of buoyant cities, affordable and plentiful housing and better environments were not being delivered on. The 1973–1974 oil crisis arising from war in the Middle East triggered a global recession that dramatically affected economic activity in many regions and cities.

This—combined with, in some cases, significant social unrest—led to a rediscovery of the 'urban problem'. Cities were sites of poverty, discrimination and lack of opportunity for many. The hope of providing adequate housing for all faltered on the experience of the public housing projects and estates that had been built and were demonstrating a wide variety of problems, including structural issues and a lack of services. Private sector housing developments were also subject to criticism due to dull design and low densities that inhibited social contact and made them highly car dependent. At the same time, environmentalists were pointing to the inability of planning to protect cherished landscapes and key natural habitats, or to tackle problems such as air pollution.

This all led to a collapse of confidence in the ability of the state to plan, to take the lead and to deliver a better environment, both built and natural. The broader political response to this was the swing to the right with the rise of Thatcherism, Reaganism and associated variants, characterised by the rhetoric of 'rolling back the state'. In the domain of planning, this led to policy measures curtailing the freedom

© The Author(s), under exclusive license to Springer Nature Singapore Pte Ltd., 2021
Y. Rydin, *Theory in Planning Research*, Planning, Environment, Cities,
https://doi.org/10.1007/978-981-33-6568-1_5

of planning authorities to regulate and take direct action on their own and resulting in a search for new ways of thinking about policy and planning processes.

Rather than just a negative commentary on how governmental processes are often presented, the governance concept suggests more positively that new forms of governing have emerged to take account of complexity, uncertainty and contested decision-making and to enable learning. This approach is built upon a recognition that policy making is not a linear process but rather recursive as interventions led to unintended consequences, implementation gaps and a general 'policy mess' (Rhodes 1997: 3). Success centrally depended on building new alliances and connections (Fairbrass and Jordan 2004).

This has prompted governance theorists to look outside the public sector for an understanding of how policy processes work in practice. As a term, 'governance' is used in many different ways, but it can be seen as an attempt at reframing formal and informal aspects of governing. It can be a concept for analysing state action, for analysing societal capacities beyond the state and, even more broadly, for analysing the social order of economic systems (Salet et al. 2003). Here, with the concern over how planning processes work, the focus is more on the first two of these uses of 'governance'. Stoker defines it as: "a concern with governing, achieving collective action in the realm of public affairs, in conditions where it is not possible to rest on recourse to the authority of the state" (Stoker 2000: 93).

The reaction of planning authorities (and many other public sector actors) was to build partnerships with other actors in the private sectors and within civil society. Planning was no longer something that the state did on its own. Rather it was an activity that involved multiple actors, partners or stakeholders working together. This wider involvement of different actors was not a form of enhanced consultation. Rather such actors were jointly involved in making policy, in the policy formulation stage. They were legitimate policy makers in conjunction with others, and such legitimacy was no longer the preserve of state bodies. Such arrangements were reinforced by the spread of privatisation and outsourcing programmes within government that brought private sector actors into the policy process.

One example of how governance structures could incorporate civil society can be found in the sustainability arena. The Brundtland Report *Our Common Future* (World Commission on Environment and Development 1987) had called for a new era of development that supported the economic, social and environmental sustainability of societies. This was followed up by the World Conference on Environmental and Development held in Rio, Brazil, in 1992. A mix of organisations got together to produce a manifesto for sustainable development—Agenda 21—and within this Chapter 28 set out the role that local communities could play. This gave rise to the Local Agenda 21 movement, which sought to find new ways to embed sustainability at the community scale (Lafferty and Eckerberg 1998). The distinctive feature of Local Agenda 21 was that it was based on building networks and partnerships between different actors and organisations, across the different sectors. Local businesses, local communities, local government and local representatives of governmental bodies and agencies would work together to achieve change.

It has been noted that this ability to involve actors across the state, the economy *and* civil society seems easier to develop at the local or urban scale. It seems that institutions at this scale are 'softer' and more permeable, with perhaps less at stake due to the limited resources available and the lower levels of professionalisation (Pierre 1998: 1). There is also the immediacy that comes from the lesser distance between institutions and the targets of policy. The advantages of being able to internalise dissent and capitalise on local knowledge through such decentralised governance structures are seen as a particular advantage of urban governance.

It should also be recognised that there is a normative dimension to the development of governance approaches in that many researchers and theorists were looking for a more democratic as well as effective way to do planning. Hence there was an engagement with political scientists looking at means of deliberation understood as reasoning together among equals (Heinelt 2015), particularly within urban policy but also planning more widely. Thus, the rise of governance perspectives on planning in the latter twentieth century reflected both a recognition of a shift that was occurring in how planning was practised and also a new sense of how planners could achieve their goals, both a positive and normative impetus.

Dynamics of Analysis and Key Concepts

The analysis of dynamics within governance processes centres around the way that actors are brought together into networks and how resources are then exchanged between actors to achieve policy goals, with the suggestion that strengthening those relationships through building a form of social capital is important. It should be noted at the outset that the way the term 'network' is used here is quite different from that encountered in Chap. 9, when Actor-Network Theory is discussed.

Governance Structures: Forms and Operationalisation

Instead of looking inside the state at the structures of governmental organisations— central government departments, agencies, local councils—governance studies examine the range of *ad hoc* structures that arise to build new networks of connections between actors inside and outside the state. Rhodes, a key governance theorist, identifies five such network structures: policy communities which are tightly integrated around a policy theme, professional networks using professional identity to work across boundaries, intergovernmental networks that often link different scales of governmental organisation, producer networks focussed more on how specific goods and services are delivered and issue networks which are more loosely integrated around aspects of policy agendas (Rhodes 1997: 9).

These can be grouped under the general term 'policy network'. Such networks are important for a number of reasons. While they open up involvement to a range of stakeholders, networks are not boundless, and thus they also limit participation to manageable levels. They help define the nature and role of the policy action and how the policy agenda should be shaped, including some aspects and excluding others. Such networks are also institutions (see Chap. 4) and thus have 'rules of the game' which shape actors' behaviour. Inevitably, networks are not equitable, and thus certain actors will be privileged in terms of access and outcomes; this is a key issue for empirical inquiry. Finally, these governance approaches involve a degree of outsourcing of government, and while they may be seen as more democratic by some for involving a wider range of stakeholders, they are substituting for democratically controlled government where public accountability is concerned.

Judith Innes is one of the best-known planning researchers working within a governance frame. Among her many publications, an article undertaken with her oft-collaborator David Booher and also Sarah Di Vittorio provides a strong account of governance (Innes et al. 2010: 62):

> They [the networks] seek to fill the interstitial spaces where public agencies lack authority or where they have conflicting mandates. While much of the work is done informally without legislative or bureaucratic authority, the practices, which typically involve collaboration and the building of networks among diverse actors, are tolerated and often encourage by formal government. They are largely self-organizing once set in motion; they are task oriented and often place based; they are made up of interdependent agents who recognize the possibility of joint gain from working together.

It is worth noting that many commentators argue that such new governance structures continue to co-exist with traditional governmental arrangements. For example, Han (2019) shows how governance structures continue to operate in the 'shadow of hierarchy'. In his study of green building certification in Singapore, he emphasises the role of legal and regulatory mechanisms in supporting the local Green Mark Scheme, as well as financial incentives, means of sharing the risk of adopting the scheme and specific rewards, all these more typical governmental mechanisms. In another example, Brownill (2009) emphasises that "networked and participatory governance" (p. 360) opens up a "potential"; it remains the task of research to see to what extent that potential is fulfilled or not. Her specific case study was the participation exercise associated with a central government-funded project redesigning a two-mile stretch of Cowley Road in Oxford, England, which acts as a major access road, a local shopping centre (particularly for student and ethnic minority communities) and an entertainment area. This showed the tensions between representative (governmental) democracy and a more participatory mode involving networks of local actors, with more formal modes of community representation re-emerging.

This shift towards engagement with actors across different sectors suggested the scope for planners to operate in a new and better way, operating collaboratively. Thus, the focus of urban governance is twofold. First it seeks to understand how the capacity of planning authorities to act is built by engaging with other actors and also how collaboration within networks is created. Second, rather than just analysing planning practice in terms of such network-based collaboration, influential planning theorists such as Patsy Healy and Judith Innes suggest ways of improving planning by encouraging such collaboration. Thus, governance comes to be identified with certain normative characteristics such as openness, accessibility, the quality of deliberation and links to the public sphere, as well as policy effectiveness (Heinelt 2015). It also became rationalised in terms of democratic ideals such as the right to involvement in policy processes by those likely to be affected.

The step from analysis to normative prescription was influenced by the theory of communicative action propounded by the German social theorist Jürgen Habermas and adopted by political scientists such as John Dryzek (2000) and David Schlosberg (1999). At the core of this theory was the distinction between the kinds of action occurring within the public sphere, the private sphere and the economy and the concern that the public sphere—where public policy and state actions should be debated—were being colonised by the rationality of the market-place—based on self-interest and instrumental rationality. Instead, Habermas argued for the rationality of the private sphere to act as the model, a rationality based on communicative action. Such action was not only intrinsically interpersonal but also oriented towards mutual understanding and seeking consensus, rather than private interests and negotiation to promote those interests. While accepting that this was not automatically likely to happen, Habermas considered that if discussions within the public sphere could approximate to the 'ideal speech situation'—in which each actor was aware of their own interests and oriented towards understanding others'—this would promote communicative action and act as a defence against the encroachment of market rationality into political debate and public policy.

These ideas provided an intellectual context within which collaborative planning has grown as a normative planning theory (Healey 1997). They have also informed those interested in environmental policy, suggesting that collaboration and deliberation can be ways of promoting environmental protection and preventing environmental injustice. The emphasis here is on creating the conditions for communicative action including arenas for deliberation where communicative, as opposed to interest-based strategic rationality, will hold sway. The hope was that better planning outcomes and greater sustainability would result. As will be seen later, there is a strand of research that has based itself within this theoretical approach but focussed more on the extent to which the conditions for communicative action, deliberation and collaboration are not achieved in practice. This will be picked up further in the discussion of environmental justice in Chap. 6, alongside consideration of how some governance networks, such as urban regimes, embed inequality in their operation. For now, it can be noted that governance theories involve a tension, at times a creative tension between understanding how governance and collaborative arrangements work in practice and seeking to show how they might work better, given different actions on the part of the planner.

Resource Exchanges Within Networks

A key aspect of governance structures is that the diverse actors involved are sharing responsibility for implementing policy as well as formulating it. This is a response to the perceived 'lack of capacity to act' that had been revealed by the policy world of the late 1970s onwards. This phrase is particularly associated with the key analysis of urban policy in Atlanta, Georgia, USA, provided by Clarence Stone (1989). This highlighted how, over an extended period of time, an 'urban regime' was developed that brought business and local governments together to shape the city. While Stone's urban regime analysis suggested a rather limited and skewed form of joint working (see Chap. 6 for further discussion), this idea of a lack of capacity of act underpins the wider shifts towards governance operating across business, governmental and civil society sectors. It prompted a focus on structures such as public-private partnerships, bringing together actors from across the state-economy divide (Pierre 1998).

A particularly useful definition of governance comes from Rob Rhodes, who has defined governance networks as being "self-organizing, interorganisational networks characterised by interdependence, resource exchange, rules of the game and significant autonomy from the state" (Rhodes 1997: 15). He also emphasises these are mutually dependent systems of resource exchange. All of these terms are important. Governance networks are semi-autonomous in that they involve state actors and are involved in public sector work (here, planning processes), but they are delinked from the public sector to some extent, so that they have their own distinctive existence. This is connected to the idea that such networks are also self-regulating and self-organising in that the state does not direct how they work. Governance approaches have been linked to the idea of new public management (see also Chaps. 3, 4 and 8). This is a mode of arm's-length monitoring that involves setting up targets and indicators of performance against those targets and requiring regular reporting by organisations within governance structures. Central steering functions are strengthened so that policy strategy can be set within the core of the state, while delivery is shifted to a mix of organisations inside and outside the state, including partnership bodies and even the private sectors (Laffin 2016). This links with the self-regulating nature of such governance structures, but the idea that new public management methods can *in themselves* have an impact on planning actors seems to require a different form of explanation than that offered by network governance (see Chap. 8).

The key focus of governance approaches tends to be on the way that governance networks are involved in exchanging different kinds of resources in order to achieve an outcome that the network collectively desires. For one of the key claims of governance approaches is that they release resources that would otherwise not be available for implementing policy, and this develops the capacity to act. These resources encompass not only the more obvious financial resources but also a wider variety of capacities that actors may bring to the planning process: for example, legitimacy, political capital and regulatory powers. These can also be 'negative resources' as where an actor potentially may lobby and protest against a given planning policy or project; even if ultimately unsuccessful, such conflict is time-consuming and requires a response and is therefore expensive. Partnership structures, for example, can lead to less conflict at implementation stages (Bache and Flinders 2004). Involving actors with such 'negative resources' is helpful to the planning effort, according to the urban governance approach, as it reduces the costs of conflict.

There has also been a particular emphasis in the urban governance literature on so-called soft resources, contrasting these with monetary and more formal political resources that actors may control. Such soft resources involve the ability to persuade and to create consensus, compromise and agreement through ways of interacting and setting the right context for interaction. The involvement of actors with these resources is also relevant to the way that urban governance networks work. For such resource exchange to occur successfully, the network members need to recognise that they are mutually dependent. If I wish to achieve a particular outcome, then I need your (another network member's) agreement to use the resources they control to this end. And this applies to all the network members. They are not just in contact with each other, they are dependent on each other to fulfil their needs, wants and interests; and a governance network recognises this dependence.

While there is a distinctive set of work on local or urban governance (Stoker 2000), much research has also emphasised how, in many policy domains, networks are not limited to the local scale. Rather the idea of multi-level governance has been put forward to suggest that policy processes usually involve cross-scalar relationships between actors and organisations. Thus, actors concerned with planning at the urban scale often have connections to the regional, national and even international scale, and these are increasingly important in achieving urban planning goals through mobilising resources at different scales. This involves not just resource flows between scales (including finance and knowledge) but also negotiation: "a system of continuous negotiation among nested governments at several territorial tiers" (Bache and Flinders 2004: 3).

Urban regeneration within one city, for example, may be promoted by links to central government and even further afield to the international scale, in the case of countries within the European Union particularly to the European Commission. Similarly, action for sustainability at the local scale, while involving the localised networks of Local Agenda 21, has also been supported by national and international networks of sustainability activists and city governments keen to promote sustainable development. Within urban climate protection policy (seeking to reduce carbon emissions that cities are responsible for and mitigating the impacts of climate change) Bulkeley and Betsill have shown how much such multi-level governance connections are relied upon (2003). These multi-level networks have repeatedly been shown to be important in terms of resource flows, including soft resources, but they are less able to demonstrate their democratic credentials in terms of promoting active deliberation.

Hooghe and Marks have put forward a widely used typology of two kinds of multi-level governance (2001). Type I are those networks with general-purpose jurisdiction and non-intersecting membership; here there are jurisdictions at a limited number of levels, and a system-wide architecture is in place. This could describe, for example, the formal structures of the European Union. Type II is focussed on task-specific jurisdictions and comprises intersecting memberships interacting in a flexible structure with no limits to the number of levels. This is better used to discuss the networks around specific policies such as climate protection or transport. Thus,

Bulkeley et al. (2015) list no fewer than ten international and regional networks involving cities which are engaged in transnational climate governance activities including membership and tailored support, networking and showcasing of activities, and enforcing collective commitments made within a network. These networks take a variety of forms such independent bodies, coordination of local governments and sub-sections of an existing NGO. The key characteristic is their operation across scales of government.

Social Capital Operating Within Networks

Beyond exploring the resources flow within networks and the way that communication occurs among network members, some governance theorists have focussed on the extent of social capital generated by network relations in explaining governance outcomes. Social capital is a concept much used in community studies to describe how a community functions as a collective, but it can also be applied in policy contexts, indeed, to any network context where social actors are involved.

Social capital is defined as comprising the relationships between actors in a network together with the norms that apply to all the actors. The relationships concern the connections between different actors, namely their social contact. Such relationships can be more or less frequent and also more or less significant. Two policy actors—say a local planner and a local landowner—may be in contact. They may meet frequently in various policy meetings but not have much in the way of interchange. Or they can have frequent contact not only in these meetings but also in personal telephone conversations and email threads when they discuss policy issues in some depth. Or they may only meet occasionally, but those meetings may be weighted with considerable significance concerning the policy issue at hand.

The norms that are associated with social capital are threefold: mutuality, reciprocity and trust. Mutuality refers to the idea that the network has a common goal, a goal that the actors have a mutual interest in pursuing. Reciprocity is about one actor doing something that will benefit another within the network, in the reasonable expectation that this favour will be returned or reciprocated at another time. Such reciprocity can be specific, in that if A does something to benefit B, then the expectation is that B will do something to benefit A. But it can also be general so that if A does something that benefits B, it may be someone else in the network that returns the favour. The network may be generally engaged in undertaking actions that benefit network members.

Finally, there is trust, although some may consider trust not to be a norm strictly speaking. Nevertheless, the expectation of trustful relations may be considered a norm. A network with high social capital has a high expectation that members of the network will trust and may be trusted by each other. They will deliver on their promises, be open and honest and not seek to undermine other network members.

Together with reciprocity and mutuality, trust makes a powerful combination. It can be expected that a network with social capital in these terms will be much more effective in negotiating and delivering mutual exchanges of resources.

It is standard to recognise that social capital can take different forms (Rydin and Holman 2004). The kind of social capital that is associated with, say, a closely knit local community is termed bonding social capital. This involves many dense connections and common norms among a bounded group of relatively homogeneous actors. This is often contrasted with the 'weak links' provided by bridging social capital, which links heterogeneous actors and usually comprises less dense bonds. Since bridging social capital is often assumed to be horizontal, connecting actors at the same level (local, regional, national), a further category of linking social capital has been coined which is a form of social capital that comprises vertical links across these levels. Finally there is bracing social capital which has been suggested to comprise a rather specific combination of bonding social capital linking some actors within a network and bridging (or linking) social capital forming other connections; it relates to a rather specific form of network, the hub-and-spoke form.

From the point of view of understanding the dynamics of urban governance, the value of such social capital existing within networks is that it changes the incentive structures facing actors within the network. The existence of social capital means that it is much more beneficial to engage in mutual cooperation within the network. The norms support this, and the links between actors reinforce those norms. If someone acts contrary to the norms—by reneging on a reciprocal arrangement or acting in an untrustworthy manner or rejecting the sense of mutuality—then the contacts can become a way of exercising 'soft sanctions'. Blame, 'naming and shaming' and other forms of social opprobrium can be exercised to try and bring the actor back into conforming behaviour. It is possible to link this kind of analysis within governance theory to the rational choice perspective as this focus on individuals' incentive structure is very much the key dynamic that rational choice theorists focus on (see Chap. 3). However, governance theorists see this as only part of the analysis and that the way individual actors behave must be seen in the context of the operation of the overall network or set of networks.

Research Themes in Practice

The examples of planning research that will be discussed here look at how governance works in practice and also consider at how Social Network Analysis (SNA) can help deepen the understanding of how these networks work. Given that governance is used as both an analytic and normative term, the last set of papers look at how far the cases researched live up to the promises of what governance will deliver, looking specifically as the hopes of collaboration and deliberation within planning.

Governance in Practice

Governance frameworks support research into planning processes, which provides detailed accounts of how different actors are involved, both critical accounts of how far community groups or business groups (or others) were able to dominate proceedings, and also more normative accounts of how planning practice would benefit from collaborative networks of different actors working together.

Elander and Gustavsson (2019) firmly set their empirical analysis of the Swedish sustainable urban development programme—Delegation for Sustainable Cities 2008–2012 (DCS)—in the context of a narrative about the shift from government to governance. Their aim was "to position and examine the implementation of DSC projects in relation to this narrative" (p. 2). They supplemented this research focus with an interest in how social sustainability had been interpreted within this process. The methods adopted were based around analysis of the documents produced by the DSC and team members, interviews and in situ observations. For this, they focussed on nine projects funded by the DSC for detailed study. In addition, academics (including the authors) had been involved in shadowing and evaluating the programme (as is common practice in Sweden); the authors' experience of this involvement and the reports from such activities were also used to build the overall picture. They paid careful attention to the implications of their positionality, seeking to be neither "naively uncritical or overly critical" (p. 9) and relying on their self-awareness and each individual researcher acting as a check on the others.

They narrated how the Swedish Popular Government Model that drove policy processes closely approximated to the governmental model and how this was undermined by concerns of excessive demands on the public sector, a fiscal crisis and claims of ungovernability, as well as the growing complexity of society. This, it was argued, pushed Sweden towards governance modes, with greater flexibility, more openness and deliberation in policy processes and greater networking for implementation. They distinguished the different forms that governance networks could take from highly integrated policy communities to looser issue networks. The former is characterised by functional interests being represented within government organisations, extensive memberships, vertical interdependence for policy delivery and a compartmentalised horizontal structure, insulating one policy community from conflict with others. In Sweden, particularly where housing was concerned, this corporatist network dominated in the 1980s with a tight governance network of central government, local authorities and their housing companies (providing a form of social housing) and other major interest groups in housing.

The DSC was developed in a context of reduced state subsidies and fragmentation of the national housing department, largely a result of a programme by the centre-right government to weaken the tight housing policy network; nevertheless, the state's regulatory powers over planning and construction persisted as did a commitment to widespread consultation. The DSC sat at the meso implementation level between national policy making and local implementation. In terms of actors, it comprised a politician as chairman, consultants from the private building sector, representatives of municipal housing companies, local politicians, a head of a local authority and two professors. During 2008–2012, it awarded 357 million SEK to nine major investment projects and 89 small ones, with Boverket, the governmental housing agency, responsible for steering and monitoring the projects.

The researchers then undertook a comparison of how the DSC programme worked as against the previous corporatist and governmental models. They noted that many "initiatives taken under the flag of participation have a strong flavour of deliberative planning" (p. 13), but the DSC as a whole was a form of hybrid between government and governance, rather than the latter replacing the former. They note that central government still took a leading role by controlling finances and exercising regulatory power while at the same time trying to steer implementation and fragmenting the established policy community into issue networks. Sustainability turned out to be "a perfect umbrella" for this fragmented implementation structure (p. 15) with its multiple interpretation possibilities. Thus, the sustainability agenda did not simply support more participatory, collaborative or deliberative policy processes but rather cloaked the co-existance of a mix of governmental and governance approaches.

Such research is situated within the argument that governance structures have superseded governmental ones (as in Chap. 2) and then uses empirical data to assess the strength of this argument. Thus Elander and Gustavsson's research found that the shift to governance was only partial, producing a more complicated, overlaid pattern of governing.

Another example of using the governance narrative as a starting point for a more nuanced analysis of planning in practice is provided by Gualini and Fricke (2019). The case study was local economic development policy in the city-state of Berlin and the state of Brandenburg, which surrounds it. As well as discussing how the idea of scale was differentially constructed over time, the paper focusses on the "practices of policy-driven governance and cooperation" (p. 60). It considers how these practices themselves challenged "established territorial articulations of government" and helped create new ones (p. 61). This, therefore, extended some of the traditional governance references by considering how scale and territory are active elements of governance practices. The authors described the empirical work implied by this framing as challenging: "this poses the challenge of turning meso-level theorizations on scalar processes into empirical, contextually specific inquiries on how these unfold in concrete-complex situations" (p. 64). The methods they deployed primarily involved working with policy documents, focussing on "programmatic statements and on form analysis of processes, arenas and modes of interactions" (p. 76). They explicitly said that an analysis of concrete processes or outcomes was beyond their scope.

The analysis proceeded through several thematic accounts but also a history of economic planning in the region. The starting point was the proposal in the 1990s for a territorial merger of the states (or Länder) of Berlin and Brandenburg, a proposal that was rejected by referendum in 1996. Joint planning and governance mechanisms had been put in place in anticipation of the merger, but these too were rejected by Brandenburg's government. However, initiatives called 'small mergers', 'partial mergers' or forms of 'cohabitation' survived the rejection of any merger, resulting in ad hoc inter-state contracts. This consolidated cooperation between Berlin and Brandenburg, and joint initiatives in spatial planning were pushed further by strategic projects such as airport development.

From the mid-1990s onwards cooperation in spatial planning developed by being embedded in organisational arrangements such as inter-municipality associations for regional planning and an inter-municipality neighbourhood forum coordinating more localised planning in the Berlin fringe. An intergovernmental agreement established a joint Berlin-Brandenburg spatial planning department, with a joint commission on planning at ministerial level. The researchers described this as: "creating cooperation initiatives between existing territorial units in a less intensive and institutionalized, but more flexible and targeted fashion, within a joint territorial planning framework" (p. 66). Federal-level spatial planning in the form of European Metropolitan Regions reinforced this, given that bottom-up definitions of such regions were allowed. Under this, Berlin and Brandenburg jointly designated themselves as a 'capital region'.

The authors concluded that "Intergovernmental cooperation in spatial planning and regional policy have barely affected the statutory competences of Berlin and Brandenburg governmental actors, rather constituting a general framework for flexible, ad-hoc forms of cooperative governance in several policy areas" (p. 67). However, in 2005, a new coalition government in Brandenburg reformulated its regional policy, leading to a greater concentration on growth centres. This policy was implemented through further governance structures, relying on decentralisation and cooperation with micro-regions as ad hoc arenas for involving key stakeholders. The outcome was a joint innovation strategy for Berlin-Brandenburg in 2011, which "formalized the outcomes of informal initiatives by actors involved in specific economic networks" (p. 71). The result was a classic set of collaborative forums including stakeholders across the public and private sectors in developing local economic development strategy, with the concepts of the 'cluster' and 'cluster dialogues' being central.

Thus, the research told of how governance arrangements evolved over time, implicating scale in different ways with consequences for how the state governments individually and jointly developed and pursued local economic development. This is a case where the governance idea was combined with key concerns from economic geography about the roles of space, territory and scale. Much of the language of this paper also draws from relational approaches discussed in Chap. 9, and there were references to political economic (see Chap. 7), Foucault (see Chap. 8) and Actor-Network Theory (see Chap. 9 again). However, it is relevant to discuss here as an example of how the governance concept can be re-examined, combined with other insights and critiqued through an empirical case study. Throughout there was an emphasis on how governing evolved in response to failures of traditional government, how different actors in different sectors and at different scales interacted with each other and the consequences of those interactions for the process of governing.

Using Network Analysis

There has been a recent growth in research that uses more formal Social Network Analysis (SNA) to investigate how governance works in practice. Rather than telling narratives of the differential involvement of various actors within governance networks, this kind of research focusses on the structure of the network and what analysis of that structure can tell us about planning as a process.

An example is provided by Holman's study of the partnerships involved in economic regeneration under the English City Growth policy, launched in 2001 (Holman 2013). This initiative created 17 partnerships across the country, each of which was charged with creating a local strategic plan. As Holman pointed out "what stands out is the sheer number of schemes that introduce new 'specialist' partnerships with their accompanying strategic plans into what many have described as an already congested policy field" (p. 83), creating multi-stakeholder strategies in response to 'wicked' problems. Rather than follow other research that had looked at the internal functioning of these partnerships, Holman considered the form of the networks that were created by cross-board membership of City Growth Partnerships with other similar bodies existing at the local level. The hypothesis was that "strong levels of partnership interconnectivity … is directly related to well-integrated local strategic planning documents", and this reflected mutual priorities (p. 83). The result could, therefore, be more integrated problem-solving based on shared knowledge and better buy-in by business stakeholders, staving off partnership fatigue.

The methodology was twofold. First, Holman created an affiliation matrix of cross-organisation membership in ten English cities involved in the City Growth programme, using lists of board memberships for this programme and for Local Strategic Partnerships (another local economic governance network), Chambers of Commerce and Industry (representing local businesses) and other local economic development organisations and regeneration partnerships. She used this to generate two-mode networks or graphs for analysis showing the number of tied memberships shared across organisations in each city. This enabled Holman to distinguish between the cities in terms of the spread of the networks, how dense and how well connected they are and the nature of the ties specifically to the City Growth Partnerships from the other governance organisations. Thus, cities such as St. Helens and Derby, which had graphs approaching a small world structure were contrasted with Manchester and Luton, which were much more disconnected in terms of their networks.

In a second stage, Holman then supplemented this with a document analysis of key strategies produced by the City Growth Partnerships for these four cities. The documents included the Corporate Plan for the local authority (more of an overarching business plan), the Community Strategy/Plan (the core strategy document) and the Local Area Agreement (setting out priorities agreed between central and local governments with a strong economic development focus) and some associated documents. The analysis focussed on the policy goals, language and project-level alignment, considering overlap and common aims. From this, Holman concluded that a well-connected local network of governance organisations enabled specific partnerships such as City Growth Partnerships to be better embedded in local governance structures, and this resulted in their goals being better reflected in key local policy documentation.

Formal SNA allows networks of governance to be specified, visualised and measured. However, in undertaking such research, Holman cautioned against reading off any form of governance practice, such as achieving synergies, from the network form. How the network is operationalised in practice remains a recommended next stage of network-based governance analysis (see also Rydin 2013). It was suggested that her research identified the need for further research, considering how various governance partnerships are networked together if the assumed benefits of governance structures (knowledge sharing, policy innovation, resource efficiency, social cohesion and competitive advantage) are to result.

Again, looking at local economic planning in England, Deas et al. (2013) provided a network analysis of four Local Enterprise Partnerships (LEPs). They set this in a framing of change in local government towards 'scalar multiplicity' associated with diversity, flexibility and the impermanence of arrangements. Their aim was to "understand actor interrelationships and institutional dynamics associated with subnational territorial governance" (pp. 719–720). LEPs were chosen as they were partly defined by bottom-up preferences and sought to involve a wide range of stakeholders from civil society and business. They were also interested in how LEPs fitted into formal governmental structures such as being a mayor-led local authority or a combined authority of multiple local councils.

Social Network Analysis was used "to develop an objective and systematic means of describing governance networks" (p. 723), although they recognised (and cautioned against) the dangers of downplaying wider socio-economic and political influences and over-emphasising micro-level aspects of relationships between actors. They saw networks as useful heuristic tools for exposing structural aspects of governance arrangements. A particular benefit was the highlighting of the importance of actors as information brokers, bridges, early adopters and boundary spanners. They also pointed to the potential of a classification of networks into scattered fragments, hub and spoke (organised around a single broker), small worlds (fractal patterns of hubs and spokes) and core/periphery divisions.

Using board membership data, they looked at LEPs in Birmingham, Bristol, Leeds and Liverpool to create affiliation matrices and associated graphs. The cities were chosen to reflect the different possible city-regional governance structures. Links between actors were inferred from geographical location, membership of sub-groups, thematic or policy areas and other LEP sub-structures. As the researchers pointed out, this excluded informal relationships or connections made outside the LEP arrangements. yEd software was used to generate maps and to calculate the level of centrality of each node (actor) in the network (via the Kamada-Kawai algorithm which ascertains the shortest distance of each node from the centre of the network). In addition, yEd was used to configure the representation of the network for easier interpretation.

The graphs generated by this Social Network Analysis enabled Deas et al. to show how the network in each city varied, both from other cities and from the idealised model that LEPs are meant to embody, potentially reducing the transaction costs across a network. Birmingham was considered close to the hub-and-spoke model, but others, to varying extents, approximated to the 'small world' model. The researchers saw part of the reason for the variation between cities in the historical experience of building governance structures at a city-regional scale that existed in some places. However, in each case, there was evidence that of "a very clear tension between the rhetorically permissive standpoint underlying the LEPs' establishment, and the practical need, for political reasons, for central government to retain control and scrutiny" (p. 734). This was again governance operating within the shadow of government.

These papers suggested that there are new insights that may be gained from formal SNA, but they do put particular demands on the researcher, including collecting data in the form that can be entered into SNA software and fully understanding what the metrics that the software offers may and may not tell us about the actual practices of governance. Any formal structure revealed by SNA has to be operationalised by actors, and this involves choices and discretion that ultimately shape outcomes; this may need to be researched by other means.

The Failures of Collaboration and Deliberation

Finally, we turn to some examples of the literature which has sought to understand why governance approaches have often not delivered the kinds of collaboration that more normative versions have envisaged. This involves considering how communication occurs within those networks, and it is here that there is the strongest link between the analytic and normative dimensions. Analytically, research can investigate how such communication occurs; normatively, suggestions can be made for improving that communication against an ideal benchmark. In particular, these papers have explored the failures of collaboration and deliberation, often looking to see if the Habermasian conditions for communicative action are present or not. The requirements are stringent. Communicative rationality presupposes an orientation on the part of the participating actors towards mutual understanding rather than just seeking to game-play in order to achieve strategic advancement in negotiations. This further means that actors should be able to understand their own interests and position; they should not be misled by any prevailing ideologies. The ideal speech situation should prevail in which communication is open and not skewed in a way that benefits certain participants.

There has been considerable consideration of how to promote real communicative action through different participatory practices. It has been suggested that for this to be achieved, the discussions have to be open to different kinds of speech act, including storytelling and dramatic monologues rather than just dry, neutral expositions of an actor's position and views. Particular institutional arrangements that may help promote communicative action and innovations such as citizens' juries and deliberative cells have been devised and investigated with this in mind.

Bickerstaff and Walker (2005) looked at two examples of deliberative exercises used by English local authorities in the development of their Local Transport Plans. They situated these within a broader opening up of policy processes that had involved experimentation by local authorities with new means of stakeholder and public engagement. They defined deliberation as "the process by which participants interact, engage in considered debate and modify their views based on information, shared views and respect for different perspectives" (p. 2124). They then asked: what are the participatory initiatives actually delivering, has there been a change and is this change an improvement? Using the Habermasian framework—but critically—they set out the key elements of the ideal speech situation and the central principles of comprehensibility, integrity, legitimacy and truth/accuracy. Rather than concentrating on detailing the processes of attempted deliberation, they looked at the outcomes also; in studying the latter they distinguished policy impacts, relational changes and institutional constraints affecting outcomes.

The methodology deployed was a two-stage one. First, Bickerstaff and Walker used a survey of English highway authorities and content analysis of draft Local Transport Planning documents to establish the broad background. Then, they moved to two case studies of local authorities (Warrington Borough Council and Warwickshire County Council) that had emerged from the survey as having tried a range of different and innovative stakeholder engagement methods. These cases were also chosen as they reflected variation in organisational structure and culture. As well as building up a chronology of all the elements of the participatory exercises in both authorities, the researchers undertook some 42 semi-structured and extensive (1.5–2 hours long) interviews. Analysis was based on coding of transcribed interviews, the codes derived iteratively from themes emerging from the data but also drawing on theoretical ideas associated with communicative rationality and its critiques.

Criticising some research for using a 'checklist approach' to understanding Habermasian communicative action, Bickerstaff and Walker instead used the interview material to understand how power relations were involved in the various participatory activities. They situated themselves not as Habermasians but as influenced by the theoretical and practical criticisms made of collaborative and deliberative planning. This involved careful attention to how interviewees spoke about both the process and outcomes of participation. This was necessary to produce, they argued, "a more sophisticated and reflexive understanding of the manifestations and dynamics of power in the implementation of the current participatory agenda in the UK" (p. 2138).

The analysis produced insights into the tensions inherent in these participation exercises around "issues of inclusion, consultation fatigue, power inequalities and the dearth of practical outcomes" (p. 2138). The interviews and textual analyses showed how technical language and the existing frameworks used by local authority officers tended to filter the way that the materials were used in deliberation. There were general perceptions revealed by interviewees of "participation initiatives as dominated by particular and forceful interests (civic, business or institutional) or that these interests served to co-opt and neuter any dissenting or oppositional voices—reinforcing a distinctly unequal set of power relations" (p. 2138). Strategies and tactics used to influence or bypass the "so-called consensus position" (p. 2138) were highlighted.

Many interviewees recognised the relationship-building and learning aspects of the participatory exercises but felt that they were being emphasised because of the lack of any more direct impacts. Furthermore, the acquisition of knowledge remained largely confined to the "elite citizenry" rather than being more broadly spread or concentrated on conveying local people's knowledge to the planning officers.

The example shows how communicative action and deliberation can be used as a benchmark for actual practice, using the clearly specified prerequisites for ideal communication and deliberation within the theoretical framework. However, here the conclusions suggested the need for a different way of theorising planning, on the basis that the governance frameworks were too far removed from practice to offer a reasonable model although they could—as Bickerstaff and Walker and others show—offer a way into critiquing the kinds of participation and engagement that governance structures imply.

While many examples of research into deliberative practices and innovations highlight the limitations of these approaches, Quick (2018) provided an interesting example of a failed process that was turned around into a success. She took a very detailed approach to investigating the narrative work implied by stakeholder engagement, going beyond the focus on talk through framing and storytelling to consider how enactment works, that is the narrative construction of reality. Narrative work here was the work involved in narration but also the work that narration did. It could be argued that the research framing here overlaps with that discussed in Chap. 8 around the role of discourses; this points to the absence of firm borders between theoretical approaches as they are operationalised through empirical research. Using this combination of conceptual thinking, Quick focussed on three aspects in the analysis of her data: narrative as talk (framing, storytelling, persuasion, interpretation, imagination), master narratives structuring expectations about participation, and narrative logics which drive the engagement process forward.

The research methodology adopted centred on an ethnographic study of the process involved in creating a land-use plan for Belknap, a neighbourhood in Grand Rapids, Michigan, USA. Quick had been alerted to this case study by interviewees for a longitudinal study of participation in Michigan and paid close attention during the Belknap process to try and understand how participants were making sense of plan-making. Data sources included interviews, observations and public materials. Central were the set of 63 confidential, unstructured, active interviews, most of which were recorded and transcribed. The first stage in the analysis was to organise this into a chronology of events, producing an 80,000-word document. This was then used for the analysis, identifying episodes, junctures, momentum and disruptions in the flow of action, divergent and convergent interpretations, and conflicts between expectations and perceived outcomes. Quick argued that her methods "allow scholars and practitioners to observe and reshape important features of participation in public engagement, mediation, deliberative democracy, or collaborative governance that they might not otherwise observe" (p. 5).

The interesting feature of this case study was that a failed participation exercise—that ended with a 'shouting meeting'—became a successful exercise in community planning. Belknap was a centrally located but physically isolated area, one of the most diverse neighbourhoods in the city but facing mounting gentrification pressure. The area immediately adjacent was redeveloped as a major medical service, research and education centre, creating the anticipation (and hope for some) that higher-income employees would wish to move into Belknap next door. Quick related the chronology of the community participation in some detail from 2000 to 2010. The analysis of this detail drew out how competing and implicit master narratives of what constituted a public participation exercises contributed to the breakdown of the first plan-making attempt: "conflict ensued less from ill intent and intentional abuse of participation than from unresolved, divergent interpretations of the master narratives about how a 'participatory process' should be enacted" (p. 7).

The second phase of the analysis showed how community members found a narrative logic that would then enable them to proceed with the outcome of an agreed plan for the neighbourhood. The story itself was very rich, but it focussed on how stakeholders worked together to create a shared narrative logic, and how they engaged in imaginative storytelling of possible planning solutions co-generating the concept of 'cottage retail' to define an acceptable form of commercial development for the neighbourhood. In this analysis, Quick used on the concept of agonism, discussed more fully in Chap. 6, to suggest how allowing for conflict and negotiation across conflict may be more productive than searching for a consensus, another common finding from research on deliberation in practice.

In the final example discussed under this heading, Beaumont and Loopmans (2008) drew on research into the involvement of local residential communities in Rotterdam and Antwerp in the Netherlands. Again, the turn to governance, the Habermasian framework and the ideal of deliberation was the starting point for a critical examination of communicative rationality in practice. The empirical work was based on a mix of data collected from document analysis, in-depth interviews and focus groups, resulting in—in total—some 140 discussions from at least a year's fieldwork in a neighbourhood in each city. The two neighbourhoods were chosen for comparability in terms of social and ethnic composition, history of urban change, issues for consideration and the pursuit of decentralisation within local government. However, the policy framework differed in that the local authority in Rotterdam had favoured a structure whereby municipal departments acted as quasi-companies with considerable autonomy, whereas Antwerp had been evolving much more slowly in this direction. Rotterdam also had a tradition of top-down corporatist elitism and the culture of a working-class city; it had adopted a technocratic approach and been labelled as a bureaucratic municipality. By contrast, Antwerp was more mixed in terms of economic structure (encompassing the diamond trade, fashion and tourism) and had operated with a more pluralist democratic model, ruled by a 'rainbow coalition'. It also had a frail bureaucracy with politicians holding more influence.

The deliberative initiative involved the creation of residents' boards according to Habermasian ideal speech principles in response to grassroots protest. Even though in Rotterdam there was a strong attempt not to privilege any one social group over another, there were failures in reaching certain minority groups. In addition, the ideal speech principles soon came into conflict with the corporatist decision-making of the local governmental system, so that the city attempted to incorporate the residents' boards into their bureaucratic and technocratic structures. Antwerp had a more fragmented governmental system, and residents were more able to exploit the opportunities this offered for permeating the pluralist politics of the city. However, this meant that there was a more instrumental approach and more of a focus on specific projects. There was less emphasis on seeking to represent all residents. This eventually led to more grassroots activism by residents outside the governance structure of residents' boards.

These findings enabled a commentary on the assumptions of Habermasian governance: "Our two case studies suggest that … the idealized Habermasian communicative rationality and ideal speech situation … [is not] sufficient for ensuring a deepening of democratic engagement and pluralist radical governance" (p. 110). In coming to this conclusion, Beaumont and Loopmans chose to contrast the conceptual framing of deliberative democracy with the ideas about 'agonism' discussed further in Chap. 6, which suggested that a greater emphasis should be given to conflict rather than the search for agreement and consensus.

Conclusions

The governance framework has provided a very useful and widely used basis for considering the new forms of governing found in planning systems in the late twentieth and early twenty-first centuries. Its key focus on the relationships between actors results in research exploring these relationships, largely in qualitative but also (through SNA) quantitative terms. Part of its strength lies in its link through to the broader theoretical frameworks of collaborative planning and deliberative democracy, although research guided by these often seems to highlight the deficiencies of how planning is currently conducted. In doing so it offers the potential for practical guidance on how to improve the collaborative and deliberative dimensions of planning practice and thus fulfil the normative aspirations of planning as governance.

But this association also brings with it limitations. The conditions for real deliberation rarely exist in practice, and many argue that there is inadequate attention to the relative power of the stakeholders within the networks. The ability of planners and others managing these networks to control interactions and outcomes so as to prevent inequalities emerging has been commented on (Tewdwr-Jones and Allmendinger 2016). Some question the extent to which power is adequately conceptualised within governance approaches since it tends to focus on resource flows,

flows which are assumed to be eased and negotiated over by interactions within the network. Thus, Gualini and Bianchi raise the following pertinent questions (Gualini and Bianchi 2015: 44):

- Are collaborative resolution strategies viable?
- Do they really resolve conflicts, or do they only provide compromise solutions?
- Is it possible to overcome power differentials through dialogue?
- Who has the right to take decisions when policies and measures affect also non-directly involved stakeholders?
- Is collaborative planning possible in an uncollaborative world?

This has led to the greater interest in agonism and a more overt focus on conflict, power and interests, moving the accounts more into the field of urban politics, discussed in Chap. 6.

Key Theoretical Readings

Campbell and Fainstein (2003), Ch. 13.
Hillier and Healey (2008), Chs. 5, 6, 7 and 13.
Hillier and Metzger (2015), Chs. 3, 13, 23 and 24.
Gunder et al. (2018), Ch. 8.

Key Research Readings

Beaumont, J., and M. Loopmans. 2008. Towards Radicalized Communicative Rationality: Resident Involvement and Urban Democracy in Rotterdam and Antwerp. *International Journal of Urban and Regional Research* 32(1): 95–113.

Bickerstaff, K., and G. Walker. 2005. Shared Visions, unholy alliances: Power, Governance and Deliberative Processes in local transport planning. *Urban Studies* 42(12): 2123–2144.

Deas, I., S. Hincks, and N. Headlam. 2013. Explicitly Permissive? Understanding Actor Interrelationships in the Governance of Economic Development: The Experience of England's Local Enterprise Partnerships. *Local Economy* 28(7–8): 718–737.

Elander, I., and E. Gustavsson. 2019. From Policy Community to Issue Networks: Implementing Social Sustainability in a Swedish Urban Development Programme. *Environment and Planning C: Politics and Space* 37(6): 1082–1101.

Gualini, E., & C. Fricke. 2019. "Who governs" Berlin's Metropolitan Region? The Strategic-Relational Construction of Metropolitan Scale in Berlin-Brandenburg's Economic Development Policies. *Environment and Planning C: Politics and Space* 37(1): 59–80.

Holman, N. 2013. Effective Strategy Implementation: Why Partnership Interconnectivity Matters. *Environment and Planning C: Government and Policy* 31: 82–101.

Quick, K.S. 2018. The Narrative Production of Stakeholder Engagement Processes. *Journal of Planning Education and Research.* https://doi.org/10.117 7/0739456X18791716

Bibliography

Bache, Ian, and Matthew Flinders, eds. 2004. *Multi-Level Governance.* Oxford: Oxford University Press.

Beaumont, Justin, and Maarten Loopmans. 2008. Towards Radicalized Communicative Rationality: Resident Involvement and Urban Democracy in Rotterdam and Antwerp. *International Journal of Urban and Regional Research* 32 (1): 95–113.

Bickerstaff, Karen, and Gordon Walker. 2005. Shared Visions, Unholy Alliances: Power, Governance and Deliberative Processes in Local Transport Planning. *Urban Studies* 42 (12): 2123–2144.

Brownill, Sue. 2009. The Dynamics of Participation: Modes of Governance and Increasing Participation in Planning. *Urban Policy and Research* 27 (4): 357–375.

Bulkeley, Harriet, and Michele Betsill. 2003. *Cities and Climate Change: Urban Sustainability and Global Environmental Governance.* London; New York: Routledge.

Bulkeley, Harriet, Vanesa Castán Broto, and Gareth A.S. Edwards. 2015. *An Urban Politics of Climate Change: Experimentation and the Governing of Socio-Technical Transitions.* London: Routledge.

Campbell, Scott, and Susan Fainstein, eds. 2003. *Readings in Planning Theory.* 2nd ed. Oxford: Blackwell.

Deas, Iain, Stephen Hincks, and Nicola Headlam. 2013. Explicitly Permissive? Understanding Actor Interrelationships in the Governance of Economic Development: The Experience of England's Local Enterprise Partnerships. *Local Economy* 28 (7–8): 718–737.

Dryzek, John S. 2000. *Deliberative Democracy and Beyond: Liberals, Critics, Contestations.* Oxford: Oxford University Press.

Elander, Ingemar, and Eva Gustavsson. 2019. From Policy Community to Issue Networks: Implementing Social Sustainability in a Swedish Urban Development Programme. *Environment and Planning C: Politics and Space* 37 (6): 1082–1101.

Fairbrass, J., and A. Jordan. 2004. *Multi-Level Governance.* In *Multi-Level Governance*, ed. I. Bache and M. Flinders. Oxford: Oxford University Press.

Gualini, Enrico, and Irene Bianchi. 2015. Space, Politics and Conflicts: A Review of Contemporary Debates in Urban Research and Planning Theory. In *Planning and Conflict: Critical Perspectives on Contentious Urban Developments*, ed. Enrico Gualini. New York: Routledge.

Gualini, Enrico, and Carola Fricke. 2019. 'Who Governs' Berlin's Metropolitan Region? The Strategic-Relational Construction of Metropolitan Scale in Berlin–Brandenburg's Economic Development Policies. *Environment and Planning C: Politics and Space* 37 (1): 59–80.

Gunder, Michael, Ali Madanipour, and Vanessa Watson, eds. 2018. *The Routledge Handbook of Planning Theory.* London: Routledge.

Han, Heejin. 2019. Governance for Green Urbanisation: Lessons from Singapore's Green Building Certification Scheme. *Environment and Planning C: Politics and Space* 37 (1): 137–156.

Healey, Patsy. 1997. *Collaborative Planning: Shaping Places in Fragmented Societies.* Basingstoke: Macmillan.

Heinelt, H. Local Democracy and Citizenship. In *The Oxford Handbook of Urban Politics*, ed. K. Mossberger, S. Clarke, and P. John. Oxford: OUP.

Hillier, Jean, and Patsy Healey, eds. 2008. *Contemporary Movements in Planning Theory*. Aldershot: Ashgate.

Hillier, Jean, and Jonathan Metzger, eds. 2015. *Connections: Exploring Contemporary Planning Theory and Practice with Patsy Healey*. Farnham: Ashgate.

Holman, Nancy. 2013. Effective Strategy Implementation: Why Partnership Interconnectivity Matters. *Environment and Planning C: Government and Policy* 31 (1): 82–101.

Hooghe, Liesbet, and Gary Marks. 2001. *Multi-Level Governance and European Integration*. Lanham, MD: Rowman & Littlefield Publishers.

Innes, Judith E., David E. Booher, and Sarah Di Vittorio. 2010. Strategies for Megaregion Governance. *Journal of the American Planning Association* 77 (1): 55–67.

Lafferty, William M., and Katarina Eckerberg. 1998. *From the Earth Summit to Local Agenda 21: Working towards Sustainable Development*. London: Earthscan.

Laffin, Martin. 2016. Planning in England: New Public Management, Network Governance or Post-Democracy? *International Review of Administrative Sciences* 82 (2): 354–372.

Pierre, Jon, ed. 1998. *Partnerships in Urban Governance: European and American Experience*. Basingstoke: Palgrave.

Quick, Kathryn S. 2018. The Narrative Production of Stakeholder Engagement Processes. *Journal of Planning Education and Research*. https://doi.org/10.1177/0739456X18791716.

Rhodes, Rob. 1997. *Understanding Governance: Policy Networks, Governance, Reflexivity and Accountability*. Maidenhead: Open University Press.

Rydin, Yvonne. 2013. The Issue Network of Zero-Carbon Built Environments: A Quantitative and Qualitative Analysis. *Environmental Politics* 22 (3): 496–517.

Rydin, Yvonne, and Nancy Holman. 2004. Re-Evaluating the Contribution of Social Capital in Achieving Sustainable Development. *Local Environment* 9 (2): 117–133.

Salet, Willem, Andy Thornley, and Anton Kruekels, eds. 2003. *Metropolitan Governance and Spatial Planning: Comparative Case Studies of European City-Regions*. London: Spon Press.

Schlosberg, David. 1999. *Environmental Justice and the New Pluralism: The Challenge of Difference for Environmentalism*. Oxford: Oxford University Press.

Stoker, Gerry, ed. 2000. *The New Politics of British Local Governance*. Basingstoke: Macmillan Press.

Stone, Clarence N. 1989. *Regime Politics: Governing Atlanta, 1946–1988*. Lawrence, KS; London: University Press of Kansas.

Tewdwr-Jones, Mark, and Phil Allmendinger. 2016. Deconstructing Communicative Rationality: A Critique of Habermasian Collaborative Planning. *Environment and Planning A* 30 (11): 1975–1989.

World Commission on Environment and Development. 1987. *Our Common Future*. Oxford: Oxford University Press.

Chapter 6
Urban Politics: Conflict, Power and Justice

Framing the Research

An urban politics perspective starts from the insight that conflicts are unavoidable in planning: "Turbulent debates between politically divergent actors are part of the fiber of planning" (Trapenberg Frick 2018: 1). But rather than following the governance framework in assuming there is the potential to handle these in a way that delivers effective and even agreed outcomes, the urban politics perspective sees power at play within planning processes and inequality in the outcomes. This is not to suggest that the results of planning research are predetermined by adopting this framework, but rather every framework has some issues that it focusses on and, in the case of urban politics, these are equity, equality and power in terms of how planning processes handle conflict.

This provides a challenging and potentially normative perspective on urban planning and urban planners. Planners cannot be neutral in this conceptual context. Seeing planning processes as potentially disadvantaging the dispossessed and disempowered means that planners cannot be neutral technocrats or bureaucrats but need to behave more like advocates. Thus, issues of justice are centrally linked to the urban politics perspective, and the task for the planner (and the planning researcher) is to consider how to plan justly. Increasingly it is recognised that this involves working with conflict rather than wishing away conflict through the lens of assumed agreement or even consensus. This is the case whether one is considering conflicts between different groups in society, between communities and developers or between various groups and the state.

It is important to note here that the urban politics perspective looks at both elite and non-elite actors and the power relationships between them. The position of those who seem to receive little from planning activity can only be understood by considering the position, tactics and resources of those who receive the most. Thus, this approach considers both how more economically resourced and privileged

Y. Rydin, *Theory in Planning Research*, Planning, Environment, Cities, https://doi.org/10.1007/978-981-33-6568-1_6

groups—both within the private sector and in civil society—are able to exercise power to achieve their goals, and the mobilisation of social groups in response to that. It encompasses the way that key proponents of urban growth and development seek to gain traction within the planning system and the activism that occurs around planning issues such as zoning on the basis of colour or ethnicity, the spatial segregation that reinforces such racialised divides and the impact of gentrification on lower-income communities.

A key focus is the emphasis on how social groups are formed and how they campaign to achieve their agendas. This shines a spotlight on a wide range and number of urban campaigns including protests against development, loss of key community assets such as open space, demands for better quality urban services and concerns over recognition of diverse identities. The urban political perspective goes beyond the pluralist idea of groups forming when there is a demand to address a specific issue. Under pluralism, social action was a case of supply—through pressure group activism—following demand (Dahl 1998). A theory widely promulgated in the USA in the nineteenth century, by the late twentieth century pluralism was widely regarded as naïve. There were clear inequalities in power and resources between different groups that could not be explained by differences in the demand for activism. There were also issues that never became the focal point of urban activism. In effect, the pluralist perspective on urban activism legitimated a focus on middle-class pressure groups.

Urban politics, by contrast, looks to forms of political activism outside of middle-class pressure group politics and particularly emphasises the ways in which disempowered and ignored groups seek to make a political mark. This involves acknowledging and supporting a wider variety of urban political activities than the more institutionalised public participation of petitions, attending meetings and lobbying. Non-violent occupations and violence against property are seen not only as an expression of frustration by the urban disempowered but as a legitimate form of social protest. Sometimes these political activities range across local concerns and global agendas. This has particularly been the case with environmental protests where the awareness of global interconnectedness is strong.

Across all the urban politics work on such politically active groups and how they mobilise runs a strong concern with justice. While such a concern is evident in different domains of planning, it has been particularly clearly articulated with regard to the environment. This is often referenced back to the growth of the environmental justice movement in the USA arising from toxic waste sites being located close to the residences of communities of colour. The Love Canal development was a trigger case where a low-income development was built on top of an old landfill site, where harmful leachates were found and high levels of childhood illness were recorded (Blum 2008). But the idea of environmental justice can be found worldwide associated with industrial activities and infrastructure investment.

Agyeman identifies a number of different aspects of justice. First, there is the recognition of all groups within the planning process, which goes beyond simply giving voice to a group (Agyeman 2005). It is about recognising their claims as a self-determined group and engaging with them on this basis. He gives the example of the Black American community and planning in USA. Second, it is about process and ensuring that the processes of planning, particularly the more open-ended processes of visioning, are fair in the treatment of different groups. Third, justice involves the just exercise of procedures, such as those concerned with regulation and the implementation of planning decisions. Finally, justice involves fair outcomes, ensuring that the urban environment that planning helps to shape meets the needs of different social groups in a just way. This framework has been used to study social justice in the city but also widely applied to the impact of environmental 'bads' and the inequitable way that the natural environmental supports different social groups.

Another justice-related theme is associated with the Right to the City movement, identified with protest actions across the world in response to both limitations on access to the city and its resources and also the way that the city's assets are being used inequitably to the benefit of different social groups (Butler 2012). In the wake of the 2008 financial crisis, for example, the Occupy Movement became a focal point for calls to a 'Right to the City'. Not only do such protests and campaigns deserve attention in their own right as notable actions, they raise important questions about how planning as a political and professional activity should respond. What is distinctive about the urban politics approach to such questions is that not only does it take a more critical angle on the prospects of even-handed governance but it sees these conflicts as, to some extent, related to broader issues of power and inequality within society. There are often strong links to the structuralist approach discussed further in Chap. 7. This means that the views on what planning systems on their own can achieve is more nuanced, and there is a greater emphasis on how social and environmental justice more broadly can only be fostered through wider political change.

Dynamics of Analysis and Key Concepts

Planning is caught up—through its shaping of urban areas—in these socially based and politically-exercised protests and demands. The urban politics perspective asks the question of whether local planning processes are supporting capitalist interests—say in facilitating urban development—or middle-class interests—say in protecting certain urban areas from such development—and whether they are failing to meet the needs of other social groups and the demands of associated urban social movements. Given that the emphasis here is on researching planning processes rather than cities and urban societies, the task is not a sociological one of understanding the conflicts between different actors but rather in understanding the response of planners, planning organisations and planning systems to the conflicts that exist within society. There are different ways of developing this understanding depending on how one understands these underlying conflicts. The following looks at the dynamics involved in growth coalitions and urban regimes, in the role of urban social movements and in agonistic processes.

Coalitions and Regimes

Growth coalitions were first proposed as a concept by Molotch in the 1970s (Molotch 1993), and as their name implies, the focus was on how a coalition comes together to pursue a pro-growth agenda at the urban scale. The purpose of identifying such growth coalitions was in response to what was seen as a rather technocratic approach to planning and thus involved a call to emphasise power relations, social class and the role of local elites in local planning processes. Such growth coalitions were closely tied to the perceived benefits and indeed profits to be made from land ownership and the development of property, and hence the control of such land and development was pinpointed as a key factor shaping urban politics. The coalition itself was formed from those actors who had the most to win in decisions about land and development (Lauermann and Vogelpohl 2017). These actors came together and coalesced to secure the conditions (particularly political conditions) for property-led growth; this included key links to local government and could even evolve into partnership with more entrepreneurial local governments.

There were a number of critiques made of the growth coalition concept. Some of these were from the political economy perspective (see Chap. 7), favouring a more structuralist approach and thus seeing the coalition approach as too agent-based. However, there was also a push to nuance the growth coalition idea, arguing that it had identified something important but was too simplistic. The coalitions that formed in cities were often fragmented, not always stable and not limited to the urban locality. In addition, they were not always growth dominated; other priorities sometimes dominated urban politics. From this critique, the urban regime concept emerged.

The urban regime concept was introduced by Stone in his study of urban politics in Atlanta, Georgia, USA (Stone 1989). The essence of the urban regime is that it emerges in order to generate the capacity to act, based on the failure of local government and other state agencies to achieve the implementation of their agendas. Such capacity to act can be achieved only by combining resources of all kinds and is thus a consequence of recognising the interdependency of actors in achieving their individual goals. Urban regimes are about generating power, but this is 'power to' achieve change in line with certain goals rather than 'power over' (i.e. by one actor over another). "Regime analysis views power as fragmented and regimes as the collaborative arrangements through which local government and private actors assemble the capacity to govern" (Mossberger and Stoker 2016: 812). This power is not always visible and operates outside or rather alongside the formal processes of urban politics and planning apparent within local government. As Holman puts it, "regime analysis is interested in the less visible connections between actors that empower them to act collectively and 'crowd out' other ways of acting" (Holman 2007: 437).

Stone defined an urban regime as "an informal yet relatively stable group *with access to institutional resources* that enable it to have a sustained role in making governing decisions" (Stone 1989: 4). Subsequent literature on urban regimes has produced several lists of characteristics that define a regime or, rather, demonstrate when one has developed. An urban regime is defined as stable, having congruent goals, informal in nature, based on resource interdependency and exchange, and involving cooperation across various organisational, sectoral or even territorial boundaries. Dowding et al. (Dowding et al. 1999) provide a set of eight criteria for identifying a regime in empirical research: the existence of a distinctive agenda, the agenda being long-lived, the agenda sustained by a coalition of actors, the coalition crossing boundaries, the ability to survive changes in personnel, the mobilisation of external resources, the presence of strong leadership and the creation of public/private partnerships.

The key insight though is that cooperation between actors cannot be taken as a given but has to be achieved, and this may involve going across state, economy, civil society boundaries (building on governance theory). Distinctive policy agendas may be identified in localities as a result, and an urban regime may focus on very different goals in different places. Stone identified four such regimes: maintenance or caretaker, development, middle-class progressive and lower-class opportunity expansion. This has been amplified or varied since (Mossberger and Stoker 2016).

However, there remains—as with growth coalitions—a bias towards corporate interests in many cases. Pierre sees an important strength of urban regime theory that it is based upon "the logic of overcoming an insufficient institutional capacity to govern by forging alliances with resourceful but politically weak society actors" (Pierre 2014: 867). This often means that to "gain access to the 'systemic power' of the corporate sector, the political leadership must be willing to cater to corporate interests" (p. 872). This dynamic was particularly apparent in the USA cases, where urban regime analysis was originally applied but later commentators have situated this in the specific character of USA local government, including its reliance on local property taxes and its relative autonomy from central government. Others have queried the transferability of the concept to other geographical contexts. Holman (2007) identifies four aspects of urban politics that tend to reduce the capacity of the urban regime as a comparative framework: increasing diversity of actors in urban politics; cross-national difference in local autonomy; differences in the institutional configuration of the economy and the incentives that it offers businesses to engage with city politics; and the impact of globalisation. Indeed, research has often focussed on interrogating the ways in which the urban regime concept has to be amended or added to if it is to be useful in these other contexts.

Urban Social Movements

For many theorists who saw themselves on the progressive left of urban politics but were disheartened by the stark message of political economy—that structural change came about through crisis and revolution (see Chap. 7)—a more incremental approach was sought by focussing on the nature of urban politics itself. This drew attention to the way that different social groups formed and mobilised in order to achieve political goals. The idea of endemic conflict between different social groups remained within a broad analysis of society and the economy as shaped by capitalist dynamics. However, politics was not reduced to being a handmaiden of these socio-economic structures. Rather, in a more hopeful move, it was seen as having a degree of autonomy and able to develop an agenda outside of capitalism and in pursuit of progressive goals.

The theorist that was often cited as driving this urban political focus in the 1980s was Gramsci, a left-wing theorist and political prisoner of the early twentieth century. Immured in a fascist gaol, Antonio Gramsci developed an alternative to mainstream Marxist political economy in his prison notebooks. These opened up the possibility that political action would be able to achieve change short of a wholesale revolution. The key social groups—the working class, the disempowered—were conceptualised as having a degree of autonomy from the prevailing socio-economic structures so that they were able to perceive their interests and also develop programmes of action to promote them. No longer was there a need to rely on a vanguard to recognise the interests of the oppressed, as was intrinsic to classical political economy.

It is telling that the word 'movement' has been attached to these political activities. Urban politics is seen as the realm of social movements, which are socially more significant than individual pressure groups. They represent something more profound in terms of a social cleavage that is being represented, a fundamental aspect of how society is structured rather than a particular issue that concerns a group of people. This raises the issue of how such social cleavages and their associated social movements are constructed.

Manual Castells in the 1980s sought to theorise urban social movements as associated with conflicts and activism around 'the means of collective consumption' (Castells 1977). In this way he made a link back to the neo-Marxist understanding of capitalist dynamics (see Chap. 7 for more details). Collective consumption referred to the means by which the reproduction of labour was enabled. The phrase recognised that the labour force could not be reproduced by private means, within the family or household alone. Some collective means were required which typically meant the involvement of the public sector. Thus, disputes around public services and the extent to which they met the needs of all social groups are at issue in the formation of social movements. Such movements are resisting, on the one hand, the appropriation of urban public services by middle-class groups and, on the other, the limitation of such services to the needs of capitalist interests. Instead urban social movements protest for the right to have adequate urban public services to meet their needs (Castells 1983).

But urban social movements have been identified with other sources of organisation and mobilisation based on the insight that cities are not just concentrations of labour but also spaces of difference, alterity and freedom (Nicholls 2008: 843). This links the growth of urban social movements with the rise of identity politics. It has delinked Castell's first formulations from the more structuralist forms of political economy and drawn attention to political mobilisations around defending cultural and social identities in relation to a particular place and seeking to achieve control and management of local spaces, institutions or assets in that place (Gualini and Bianchi 2015: 46). Mayer sees urban social movements in terms of four phases; the first two relate to the crisis in industrial production of 1960–1980 and then the erosion of the welfare state giving rise to the focus on collective consumption in 1980–1990; however the next two phases concern campaigns around gentrification and urban regeneration in 1990–2000 and then the response to globalisation and financialisation since 2000 (Mayer 2010).

In this way, the bases of urban social movements have been expanded further. However, they have still been open to critique for ignoring key social dimensions such as gender (Beebeejaun 2017; Levy et al. 2017). They also have drawn heavily on political activity in North America and Northern Europe, leading to a call for research to investigate their relevance in other geographical contexts (Leontidou 2010). The distinctive feature of an urban social movement remains its physical base in a specific location, differentiating it from other NGOs. Beyond that attention is concentrated on understanding the stakes at issue in the social movement's actions, its social base, the demands it makes and the way that it mobilises, always situating this local action in the context of broader changes that would affect society more fundamentally.

Agonism and the Persistence of Conflict

Civil society is diverse. It comprises people of different kinds and with different values and interests. Is the heterogeneity and fragmentation of civil society so extensive that the public or community can be represented by a limited number of people who can pragmatically be involved in the activities of urban governance networks? Planners have long sought ways of representing a diverse and heterogeneous civil society in manageable ways. There is a tendency to include those who emerge through self-organised community organisations as key representatives. There are a number of problems here though. What of the sectors of society that do not self-organise? These sectors are described as 'hard to reach' or 'silent', language which suggests that they are being recalcitrant in the face of offers of involvement in key networks. And how to handle the disagreements between such groups?

The key issue that urban politics raises as a perspective for planning research is this: what determines the social groups that are involved in conflict, protest and activism? What counts as a group, class or community? There are a variety of bases that can be used to classify such entities. Traditional classes are based on economic interests. The working class, the middle class, capitalist classes are all determined by their relationship to the economic processes they are involved in: ownership of capital, receipt of a salary, selling of labour power. But this may not coincide with perceptions. So self-identity may be a basis for group formation. This could include different grounds of identity: ethnicity, sexuality, status, political alignment. Groups may be formed out of identities that are imposed on them and then taken back and owned for political mobilisation. Thus, many ethnic groupings are a mixture of both self-expressed and owned identity and the legacy of racist political and social systems that only saw people in terms of their colour or race (Beebeejaun 2006). And, given the place-based nature of planning, there are identities and interests linked to locality, some of which are captured in the idea of place attachment; the use of this term has been an attempt to resist the pejorative connotations of the label NIMBY (not in my back yard) (Devine-Wright 2009).

More recently attention has focussed on putting conflict between these groups centre-stage in a positive way. Drawing on the work of Mouffe on agonism (Mouffe 2013) this approach dismisses the claims of the governance approaches about being able to move towards agreement and even consensus, arguing that this is misleading about the potential for policy and planning action. The approach of agonism still looks at how different groups exist in opposition with each other and how they come to work together, but it does so on the basis of neither an immanent tendency towards consensus (see Chap. 5) nor overt negotiation between sectoral interests. Rather it operates with a normative framework that sees conflict as inevitable and further as productive. The us-and-them articulation of different groups in relation to each other still remains, but the aim of engaging with these different groups—in planning situations, say—is to enable them to co-exist with respect. In essence, agonism involves a willingness to agree to disagree. This, it is argued, would enable actors to shift from being opponents in relation to each other towards being adversaries, who can recognise each other's point of view and work with it towards a potential agreement. Mouffe sees this as fundamentally more democratic than the false promises of deliberation.

This approach has received much attention within planning theory (as a potential new normative theory after collaborative planning) but also within planning research interested in how opposing actors and groups engage with each other. It is attractive that conflict, change and uncertainty are not treated as traits of planning failure but rather can be accepted within planning practice. Some see this as part of a resistance to the silencing of conflict within planning disputes and to the broader silencing of conflict within a post-political society (Raco 2014). However, some have questioned the extent to which a focus on agonism leads to an acceptance of existing power dynamics and inequalities (Yamamoto 2017). This has spurred much research into how conflicts are handled in practice within planning situations and with what consequences.

Research Themes in Practice

The papers reviewed here address the urban regime concept, but in a critical way, as well as research into how planning practices have addressed racism and tackled conflicts.

Revisiting the Urban Regime Concept

There is a range of work that not only applies the urban regime concept in a variety of contexts but also uses this work to interrogate the concept and, particularly, consider its transferability to other national contexts than the USA where it originated.

Ravazzi and Belligni (2016) considered the relevance of the concept to the case of Turin, Italy, using it to understand the governing coalition that led the city and guided it towards a post-industrial future in which the local economy was diversified. They were particularly interested in how 'power to' was manifested through the actions of this coalition and led to the emergence of a new agenda. They looked at the incubation phase in which "a common frame is shaped by the local élite" (p. 325) and then how this emerged as an agenda, considering whether sectoral policy negotiations or a collective effort was involved. In this, they linked the work of Stone (referenced above) with that of Kingdon (2003) on political agendas. They asked the question: "how do issue concerns come to be specified as purposes, and how are they linked, enlarged and refined for action?" (p. 327). This question was set in the context of the informal relations, repeated interactions and resource-based negotiations that are typical of an urban regime.

Their methodology used an in-depth case study followed over seven years during which data was collected from documentary sources and 50 semi-structured interviews with key actors. Network analysis was undertaken together with process-sequencing, the former to consider the links between actors and the latter to clarify the chronology of events and associated actions.

The resulting analysis was a detailed history of changing policy for the city of Turin from the mid-1990s. The policy package that emerged comprised housing development, city centre renovation and significant infrastructure, particularly transport; creating an urban district for the knowledge industry; and profiling tourism, entertainment and leisure through activities and projects. While social and environmental policies were not completely side-lined, they were not resourced sufficiently to address the scale of the problems in Turin. Considering the categorisation of urban regimes as pro-welfare or market-centred, the authors considered that this was a clear shift from the former towards the latter.

The coalition associated with this shift was formed of a 'great alliance' between Centre-Left politicians, liberal elements of the business class organised within the Group of 70 and led by a powerful banker, and a group of academics from the Politecnico di Torino, bringing their urban design and planning expertise to bear on the problems facing the city. This coalition agreed on a pro-growth effort to drive change. The researchers then traced how the detailed agenda emerged through processes of naming (the formation of a common perception of the main problems in the city), blaming (the construction of a narrative about the path-not-taken in the past towards modernisation) and claiming (setting out core beliefs and key purposes for the city's common goal).

The detailed account showed how the coalition became consolidated and institutionalised. It also pinpointed how a small number of key organisations led the coalition and constituted the regime: the local authority, the regional authority, two universities, two bank foundations and (early on) the key local industry of FIAT. However, this coalition was then opened up to involve a wider range of civil society leaders after a narrow election victory by the incumbent mayor suggested a lack of electoral support. A so-called city dialogue resulted, which created more of a sense of collective effort rather than just negotiation between a limited set of sectoral interests. There were conflicts, but these were overcome by internal management, and also a more purposive and open approach. The multi-vocal nature of the process opened up new 'windows of opportunity'. The research is interesting in identifying the combination of public, informal and structured processes of discussion that enabled the regime to resolve conflicts and go beyond negotiation within an urban regime purely on the basis of self-interest.

Such research goes beyond the more open framework of governance to consider how a set of actors consolidate their influence, to specify those actors and to link their power to aspects of urban change.

Turning to research in China, Li and Liu (2018) similarly used and amplified the urban regime concept to make it relevant to their context and specific research problematic. They studied regeneration in Guangzhou and the 'Three Old Redevelopment' (TOR) policy, which covered old towns, old villages and old factories. They were attracted by the urban regime concept for its focus on informal coalitions, resource exchange and cross-boundary cooperation of different kinds. They considered this more relevant than the growth coalition model because the latter assumes conflict between residents and a pro-growth coalition, and between use and exchange value. With the TOR policy, this was a case study of top-down institutional change, promoted by the state but stimulating the creation of cross-boundary cooperation typical of an urban regime. It depended centrally on a 'shared interests mechanism' bringing stakeholders together across the local state, the market and communities.

However, the researchers saw a need to supplement the urban regime concept in order to fully understand the Chinese situation and its TOR policy. In particular, they saw the private sector as relatively less influential than in the USA and civil society as rather weak. They, therefore, chose to use ideas of 'fragmented authoritarianism' and 'strategic selectivity'. The former idea pointed to the origins of an urban regime in the use of an authoritarian policy style to overcome the fragmentation of resources among a variety of actors, although this authoritarian power was also used to grant autonomy for reform at the local level. The latter concept looked at how a policy may selectively benefit certain groups, interests and strategies due to the history of the state's role. Nevertheless, they kept the urban regime's emphasis on key aspects of policy work such as small opportunities which require cooperation among interdependent actors, selective incentives and working across boundaries.

To investigate these sets of ideas in Guangzhou, Li and Liu conducted two periods of fieldwork, in both cases undertaking semi-structured interviews (35 in total). This was supplemented by participant observation based on their prior work as planners in the city. Secondary data was collected from governmental documents, media reports and research reports. Additional online interviews were subsequently used to fill in details.

The research found that the core 'shared interests mechanism' was based in the fragmented authoritarian environment and the four institutional innovations that the state had promoted: the relaxing of land management regulation with regard to the legal status of land, the sharing out of local authorities' fiscal income from land transactions, the distribution of resources to communities, and urban planning relaxations around density and land use. These underpinned the emergence of urban regimes and created 'power to'.

However, the authors also identified interesting differences in how the TOR policy worked with regard to towns, villages and factory sites. They found that the redevelopment of old towns did not fit with a regime-building process because of the formality of the relationship between the community through its committees and the government; there was little need to create a regime. By contrast in the old villages there was some evidence of regime building. In Pazhou a win-win coalition was built among government, village volunteers and an enterprise implementing the redevelopment. The deployment of selective incentives, creation of long-term trust, informal links and cooperation were all found to be present in the context of empowered villagers. This was not necessarily the case in other villages, where some but not all elements of a full urban regime were found; typically long-term trust was missing. Similarly, with regard to old factories, most of the elements were found but not this long-term trust.

These patterns were, it was argued, based in the pattern of strategic selectivity that differentiated resources between towns and villages, and between different villages in China. These concerned a range of resources including land ownership, connections to the state and the media, and the existence of social capital. Strategic selectivity was found to differentiate the Three Olds but also actors within regimes and the projects that were pursued. This added a layer of detail to the application of the urban regime concept in this research.

Thus the urban regime concept was adapted for the Chinese context by adding regionally relevant ideas about governing and considering the influence of historical patterns. However, the core elements of the urban regime concept remained useful in highlighting how actors across sectors came together to achieve shared aims.

Challenging Racism in Urban Planning and Politics

A key focus of the urban politics approach is the inequalities affecting community engagement with planning policy and practice. Racism is an invidious aspect that emerges from much empirical work into the urban politics of planning, including— but not only—as framed by environmental justice concerns. Two examples are considered here, from Turkey and USA.

A classic example of conflict around an urban regeneration scheme and the further marginalisation of a disadvantaged community is provided by Evrim Uysal

(2012), who looked at the planning of the area of Sulukule in Istanbul, an area inhabited by a largely Romani community. The research focussed on the question of how the activists in the Sulukule Platform gained the capacity to resist the state-led urban regeneration of the area based around promoting tourism. It specifically considered how the activists presented their demands and how the Platform contributed to the struggles around urban regeneration and influenced urban change.

The research was conducted in two periods before and after the large-scale demolitions had occurred. As well as site visits, the analysis was based on eight interviews with activists, professionals and local residents. The interviews with activists and professionals concentrated on the oppositional activities of the Sulukule Platform; those with Sulukule residents looked at the problems generated by ambiguous property rights and displacement; and another set with residents of the adjacent neighbourhood of Çarşamba documented the prejudice against the Roma. This was supplemented with other data sources such as newspapers, petitions, court documents, statistics, surveys, reports and websites.

Evrim Uysal framed the activities of the local community as an urban social movement (USM), following Castell's alignment of a USM with the articulation of the three goals of collective consumption demands, community culture and political self-management; his USMs were connected to both society and the state and were self-conscious of their political role. However, Evrim Uysal noted that USMs have changed over time and become more organised and more globally connected. The important point was that they emerged in response to a particular stake, had a specific social base and mobilised around specific demands in a way that then created action and made them a social force. They typically still focussed on a specific neighbourhood, emerged in the presence of poverty and concerned an oppressed minority, all aspects that applied in Sulukule.

The Sulukule area had a long historical connection with the Roma people and their economic base in the entertainment industry. This community had suffered centuries of prejudice; most recently, the sites for their entertainment activities had been closed down and access to basic municipal services had been denied. Thus, they were in a weak position when the regeneration of the area was announced in 2006 by the Istanbul Metropolitan Municipality, the local municipality of Fatih and the Mass Housing Administration. The plan involved extensive demolition to make way for new development across a large area which would "protect cultural heritage and … promote tourism" (p. 15). Given the high cost of acquiring property in the area and in order to receive full compensation, most Roma residents were displaced to housing on the outskirts of Istanbul.

The Sulukule Platform was developed in response to this threat. It was described as an urban coalition comprising NGOs, locals organised by the Association of Advancement of Romani Culture and Solidarity, and a mix of independent activists including professionals, artists, academic and researchers, largely from outside the area. This coalition campaigned against the regeneration project, including the planned demolition of much of the built stock and for a proposal that instead met local needs. Their demands centred on recognition that the regeneration project was actually about gentrification, and instead of meeting local needs and stopping the demolitions.

They mobilised using a mix of meetings, demonstrations, gatherings, festivals and exhibitions to raise public awareness. Connecting with the concept of social capital (discussed in Chap. 5), the research found both weak and strong ties involved in the operation of the Platform. It also found different roles for the different actors with NGOs focussed on public opinion, and activists providing a variety of activities to enhance locals' capacities but also taking the campaign out to different sites; local residents, meanwhile, were increasingly taking the main role, defending their claims forcibly. The Platform also inspired an academic-based initiative called STOP, with academic planners preparing an alternative plan for the area. The paper identified several distinctive features of the Platform as a social movement: it emerged in opposition to gentrification and was based on long-established locals not incomers; it had a distinctive ethnic and cultural identity based in the Roma community; it attracted considerable national and international attention and support; and it played a part in refreshing political debates on community participation.

Nevertheless, it failed to halt the demolition programme. The research suggests three reasons for this. First, property rights were unclear in the area reducing the formal legal stake of local residents. Second, this fostered land speculation and increased the benefits of allowing the demolition for developers. Third, the Sulukule Platform was unable to mobilise widespread public support, due to an unwillingness to be aligned with the Romani population. Fourth, the local Romani community were lacking resources and already politically marginalised. Fifth, the Sulukule Platform experienced fragmentation which undermined its efficacy. Finally, there was strong counter-pressure from the actors involved in the regeneration project, which included the local council. The powerful retained power and were able to control urban change to the disadvantage of the local community, a marginalised social group. Some hope remained in that the coalition, at the time of writing, was still in negotiation for future concessions, linked back to the wider political impact of the Platform's activities.

This research uses a wide conceptual repertoire—including aspects of USMs, actors' differential resources, often based in institutional arrangements, and the strength of social capital—to tell a powerful story of discrimination within urban planning. However, this still leaves scope for identifying ways in which the USM had an influence and how it might enlarge that influence.

A study within the environmental justice frame is provided by Miller Cantzler and Huynh (2015) looking at the position of Native Americans in the disputes around salmon fisheries in the Pacific Northwest. They supplemented this approach by 'taking history seriously' and setting current conflicts over environmental assets and rights in the context of the long-term racialisation of the Native Americans and (de)colonisation processes. They sought to link the current racial stratifications in society and politics to their historical roots. But their research also highlighted the agency of groups fighting for their civil rights, in this case the recognition of fishing rights that underpinned Native American culture and livelihoods. The research methods for data collection relied on archival and interview data, setting these within the richly theorised literature on racial formation, environmental justice and (de)colonisation. Their focus was on the strategies used by Native Americans to assert their fishing rights.

The historically framed analysis pointed to the way that acknowledgement of indigenous people's natural resource rights—as with the significant Boldt legal decision of 1974—had wider significance in that it "validates Indigenous groups' governmental autonomy over their territories and legitimates such rights based on alternative cultural and political logics" (p. 209). The researchers thus looked at the struggles around Native American fishing rights in the 40 years since Boldt, using the environmental justice framing of distributive justice, procedural justice and recognition. They showed how distributive justice was enhanced by an approach that interpreted Boldt flexibly to meet the evolving social, culture and economic needs of the tribes. Procedurally the tribes have followed a two-fold approach, both building partnerships with other local communities but also using the courts to produce judicially enforceable positions that require local communities to engage with the tribes. Finally, the research pointed to the important shift towards incorporating and recognising local knowledge as a basis of environmental resource management.

They concluded that the strategies used to fight for fishing rights had been part of a struggle to decolonise state institutions and to undo discriminatory colonial logics that were still used to legitimate laws, policies and practice concerning these environmental assets. This highlighted "the role of Indigenous agency in successfully challenging long-standing legal and cultural foundations of racial inequality" (p. 221). This should not be overstated; there remained challenges as with ongoing habitat destruction, the conflicts with tourism and the complexity of resource management regimes. But set in the context of the long history of colonisation and decolonisation, these strategies suggested the potential of "human agency in episodes of contention between civil rights activists and the state" (p. 221).

This again points to the potential emancipatory stories that research undertaken within the urban politics frame can tell. This relates to the framework's emphasis on actors' agency achieved through a variety of means including resource use but also modes of mobilisation.

Managing Conflicts in Practice

The greatest recent growth in urban politics research has been concerned with the theme of agonism and the extent to which this is present or not within the interactions of planning and the implications for the treatment of different social groups. The next group of papers look at how conflicts are managed in specific examples of practice.

Trapenberg Frick (2018) provided an analysis looking at how groups in the USA that would typically be in opposition to each other formed tactical coalitions around the issue of sustainable infrastructure. In particular she looked at the alliances that were built between progressive groups and activists from the Tea Party, a conservative movement based on protecting property rights and individual liberties, and other groups opposed to such infrastructure. Frick situated this research firmly within the framework of agonism but also drew on ideas from research into social movements and coalitions to identify the importance of repertoires of contention (meaning the range of social movement activity including the importance of internet communications), the role of a triggering event or threat, and the development of storylines or narratives and the discourse coalition they support (see Chap. 8 for further discussion of the last aspect). The analysis concentrated on how areas of convergence could be located even where the different parties agreed to disagree on other (often fundamental) issues.

She selected three case studies and used the same methodology in each. This methodology comprised document review (including policy documentation, news media reports and online material) together with 39 semi-structured interviews, 35 being case-related and 4 with experts on the Tea Party movement. The case interviews were with Tea Party and property rights affiliates (12), progressive activists including environmental and social justice groups (9) and public agency and planning staff (14), all selected for their knowledge of or involvement in the case studies' planning and participation activities. The interviews were in-depth (1–3 hours in length) and were structured around the nature of the planning issue, the interviewees' interpretation of the process and outcomes, and—where relevant—coalition formation, the motivations for participating and the modes of participation. The researcher also drew on her own participant observation for three years as a planner providing support to another coalition on a contentious infrastructure policy intervention.

The first case was the Columbia River Crossing in Washington-Oregon, replacing a 1917 vintage bridge with one of almost two-times the capacity and at a height to permit tall ships to pass underneath. Here a free-market think tank and an environmental/sustainable land-use non-profit organisation came together to argue for retrofitting the existing bridge and blocking the new construction, managing to agree because they set to one side the role of public transit in the area that they fundamentally disagreed on. The second case was again opposition to a transport scheme, that is bus rapid transit in Florida funded by an increase in sales tax. Here the coalition was between Tea Party and conservative activists, on the one hand, and the lower-income African America community of East Gainesville who argued that resources for services would be diverted from their neighbourhood. These groups had previously worked together to oppose a local biomass fuel plant, and this underpinned ongoing co-working, not only to oppose the rapid transit scheme but also to support conventional bus service improvements in the East Gainesville area. Finally, in Georgia, a Green Tea Coalition was formed from a mix of conservative (Tea Party) and progressive elements, the latter including a chapter of the environmental group, the Sierra Club. Again, they were working together to oppose a sales tax for transportation. At a later stage, the National Association for the Advancement of Colored People (a well-established racial justice movement) joined the coalition to argue against bus rapid transit and in favour of a rail line to a disadvantaged community.

This coalition then moved into support for solar power, but on the basis of not discussing (and thus disagreeing on) climate change itself.

All three cases were analysed to support the argument that radically polarised citizens can come together to influence planning decision-making on the basis of a degree of agonism. She further argued that these coalitions can be different in kind, producing a typology of ephemeral, emergent and established coalitions, each with different characteristics. The Columbia River Crossing involved an ephemeral coalition; the Florida bus rapid transport campaign was an emergent coalition; and the Green Tea Coalition in Georgia had the features of an established coalition, allowing it to shift scales and sectors in its activities. Participants in these coalitions were able to retain their core identities in public while at the same time "forging articulations of equivalence and [setting] aside areas of disagreement" (p. 12).

This somewhat surprising research highlights how conflict and agreement can be made to co-exist within coalitions addressing planning issues and encourages questioning of the assumption that such coalitions are highly cohesive entities. Rather these coalitions can be very pragmatic in their espousal of joint working under conditions of agonism.

The study by Rogers (2016) looked at an example of an informal community-driven engagement strategy sitting outside formal participatory planning. Starting from a critique of governance-inspired modes of planning for participation (see Chap. 5), the research situated itself within the shift towards recognising and striving for agonism. However, it also drew on ideas of monitoring democracy, which involves extra-parliamentary or informal modes of representation in order to exercise but also challenge power. Rogers used this idea to reject the search for consensus and instead focus on monitoring the formal actions of powerful actors through informal spaces in the name of greater transparency and accountability and to foster new forms of political power.

This theoretical discussion framed his research into REDWatch, a local community organisation based in an area south of Sydney's CBD with a significant indigenous population and low-income, public housing stock. REDWatch emerged in 2004 as a response to government plans for the area to reframe it as part of Global Sydney and then developed as a formal organisation with events, activities and—centrally—a well-used website. Given the prevailing plans to redevelop the area in order to release land value through public-private partnerships, REDWatch decided to act as a monitory civil society collective, monitoring government policy and campaigning to try and ensure that outcomes would benefit the local community.

The data for the analysis came from 10 semi-structured interviews with local and state government bureaucrats, senior government planners and REDWatch members, together with extensive participant observation of community organisation over five years and analysis of 31 policy texts. The research questions focussed on the formal planning governance mechanisms and the formal and informal tools of civic action that local residents had gained access to, created or deployed in response to plans for change in the area. In particular, there was an interest in how REDWatch handled the agnostic tensions between the state and private sector stakeholders, on the one hand, and local residents and NGOs on the other.

Rogers showed how REDWatch identified the limitations to the state-run community participation exercises and instead decided to create their own informal civic space to keep an eye on what the public sector, in conjunction with the private sector, was planning for their area. This was an approach that foregrounded conflict and the need to challenge the currently powerful actors in the locality. In particular, they used the website to lodge and make public documents which disappeared from the state websites, acting as "an inconvenient 'corporate memory'" (p. 233). The website became a repository for local knowledge of the area, government plans for the area and the history of planning and consultation commitments that were made to local residents. This website developed a high profile.

Thus, REDWatch was involved in encouraging difference, disagreement and debate. It did not seek negotiated or consensual outcomes. While some concerns were expressed about the extent to which REDWatch was representative of the local area, Rogers' research shows that the "government planners did use the monitory status of REDWatch to internally advocate for different planning outcomes" for the area (p. 236). Thus, the agonistic position of REDWatch enabled it to have some influence, more than it would have had as an interest group incorporated into the state-led consultation activities. Rogers acknowledges that these two means of representation worked alongside each other; agonism did not replace conventional participation: "their monitory civic actions are not framed by, but rather worked alongside of, the rules of political engagement that guide the government's strategic and regulatory planning frameworks" (p. 234).

Thus an agonism frame enables aspects of a civil society group's action that might otherwise escape attention—here monitoring—to become the focus of research and used to identify how that group had impact within local planning processes. The importance of knowledge within these interactions looks ahead to the discussion in Chap. 8 and indeed is replicated in the next paper considered.

One of the themes running through the use of agonism to frame analysis of planning processes is that we are living in post-political times and that planning often works to annul dissent and silence overt political conflicts. Fougère and Bond (2018) studied this in a case of the consenting of a proposed coal mine on the east coast of Aotearoa New Zealand. The context is the operation of the Resource Management Act 1991, which established a procedure by which a panel of independent Counsellors or Commissioners heard submissions on a proposed development and then decided on whether consent should be granted. This provided a number of formal opportunities for community involvement, but in the case of the specific coal mine proposal, community activists also undertook public protests and a 'Bioblitz', a community-based exercise in collecting ecological data in the area of the Denniston Plateau, where the mine was to be located.

The researchers looked at how the formal regulatory process interfaced with activist engagement and what scope resulted for contestatory or dissenting democratic involvement in planning decision-making. The data was gathered from 16 in-depth qualitative interviews with environmentalists, council staff and a commission, all involved in this case, together with documentary secondary sources (decision reports, application documents, media material).

They considered how the generation of discourses, and indeed of hegemony as the construction of a particular stable order through meanings, was related to the balance between antagonism and agonism. On this basis, they mapped the way in which the discourses deployed by different actors largely formed two conflicting narratives: 'save the Denniston Plateau' or 'mine the plateau'. They considered how and to what extent this dissent between the parties espousing these narratives was annulled or delegitimised, so that the space of disagreement was narrowed to one that did not fundamentally challenge the status quo in favour of growth. What they were looking for was where antagonisms (rather than agonisms) could "rupture postpoliticisations" (p. 147).

They showed that "power relations beyond the planning frameworks (in the form of hegemonic practices in particular) and agents operating within them shape the nature of dissent irrespective of what form that dissent takes—agonistic or antagonistic or indeed some other forms of politics" (p. 152). They pointed out that the most antagonistic moments occurred within the formal processes of council and Environment Court hearings. But the research also showed that there were areas where discussion was between adversaries rather than enemies; these were around the agreed need for some element of conservation and the knowledge-generating activities of the Bioblitz. At the moments when these areas came to the fore, the engagement of community and planning system approached agonism rather than the conflict that was apparent both in the public protests and in the formal hearing proceedings. They also acknowledged that antagonistic and agonistic engagements were inter-related and, to an extent, dependent on each other: antagonism created the conditions of possibility for agonistic spaces (p. 162). The formal processes generated the possibility of agonism but also forced it into informal spaces; as in the REDWatch case, these processes can co-exist.

In the event, though, the institutionalised prioritisation of expert and technocratic knowledge meant that the influence of these agonistic moments was limited and the more antagonistic conflict between pro- and anti-development positions dominated. The prioritisation of this knowledge also contributed to a post-political positioning of the interactions in this case. Such knowledge always appeared beyond the scope for discussion or annulled more emotive representations within the discussions. They concluded that while agonism might be a goal, there was a place for antagonism in creating space for agonism and, further, that activism was an essential form of disagreement to prevent dissensus being silenced, for example, by recourse to accredited expertise and knowledge.

Here the research used the agonism framework to show how actors shifted between enemies and adversaries and how antagonistic conflict fostered by formal processes and agonisms fostered through different relationships were inter-related. Again the central role of knowledge within these interactions was emphasised (see Chap. 8 for more on this).

Conclusions

The strength of the urban politics approach is that it brings issues of inequality, conflict and power to the fore in planning research, alongside a focus on examples of resistance to prevailing unjust planning practices. It has a strong community focus and suggests the potential for planning research to support communities which find themselves disadvantaged by urban change. Indeed, some planning research moves into the action research mode (McNiff 2013) where such links with communities are integral to the research activity. But even outside action research, this is work that may inform both planners and communities about the more negative ways that planning operates and thus offers, perhaps, a more critical perspective than the frameworks reviewed so far.

Research within the urban politics perspective tends to operate primarily with qualitative research methods to try and understand how groups form, engage in activism, perceived their activities and understand the justice of the planning system. This does not mean that quantitative material may not be used to support analysis of how different groups fare; for example, statistical detail can be extremely useful in generating a clear picture of inequalities. However, the strong normative dimension of urban politics research often leads the qualitative research beyond the external perspective of an analyst into the more involved perspective of the action researcher. The value commitments of those working with the urban politics paradigm can mitigate against the apparently neutral stance of a social science researcher. Rather the researcher wishes also to support the groups being studied. It will be a key aspect of any urban politics research that it highlighted social groups' own perspectives of the planning situation, how it has progressed and how it has been handled by the planners. This so-called emic perspective is essential to urban politics research as it operates from the perspective of the disempowered and marginalised groups. It thus needs to understand that perspective whether through interviews, focus groups, non-participant observation or more involved action research.

Key Theoretical Readings

Campbell and Fainstein (2003) Chs 11 and 18.
Hillier and Healey (2008) Chs 9, 19 and 20.
Hillier and Metzger (2015) Ch. 17.
Gunder et al. (2018) Chs 9, 12, 13, 21 and 23.

Key Research Readings

Uysal, Ü Evrim. 2012. An Urban Social Movement Challenging Urban Regeneration: The Case of Sulukule, Istanbul. *Cities* 29: 12–22.

Fougère, L., and S. Bond. 2018. Legitimising Activism in Democracy: A Place for Antagonism in Environmental Governance. *Planning Theory* 17 (2): 143–169.

Li, B., and C. Liu. 2018. Emerging Selective Regimes in a Fragmented Authoritarian Environment: The "Three Old Redevelopment" Policy in Gaungzhou, China from 2009 to 2014. *Urban Studies* 55 (7): 1400–1419.

Miller Cantzler, J., and M. Huynh. 2016. Native American Environmental Justice as Decolonization. *American Behavioral Scientist* 60 2: 203–223.

Ravazzi, S., and S. Belligni. 2016. Explaining "Power To": Incubation and Agenda Building in an Urban Regime. *Urban Affairs Review* 52 (3): 323–347.

Rogers, D. 2016. Monitory Democracy as Citizen-Driven Participatory Planning: The Urban Politics of Redwatch in Sydney. *Urban Policy and Research* 34 (3): 225–239.

Trapenberg Frick, K. 2018. No Permanent Friends, No Permanent Enemies: Agonistic Ethos, Tactical Coalitions, and Sustainable Infrastructure. *Journal of Planning Education and Research*.

Bibliography

Agyeman, Julian. 2005. *Sustainable Communities and the Challenge of Environmental Justice*. New York: New York University Press.

Beebeejaun, Yasminah. 2006. The Participation Trap: The Limitations of Participation for Ethnic and Racial Groups. *International Planning Studies* 11 (1): 3–18.

———. 2017. Gender, Urban Space, and the Right to Everyday Life. *Journal of Urban Affairs* 39 (3): 323–334.

Blum, Elizabeth D. 2008. *Love Canal Revisited: Race, Class, and Gender in Environmental Activism*. Lawrence, KS: University Press of Kansas.

Butler, Chris. 2012. *Henri Lefebvre Spatial Politics, Everyday Life and the Right to the City*. New York: Routledge.

Campbell, Scott, and Susan Fainstein, eds. 2003. *Readings in Planning Theory*. 2nd ed. Oxford: Blackwell.

Cantzler, Julia Miller, and Megan Huynh. 2015. Native American Environmental Justice as Decolonization. *The American Behavioral Scientist* 60 (2): 203–223.

Castells, Manuel. 1977. *The Urban Question: a Marxist Approach, translated by Alan Sheridan*. London: Edward Arnold.

———. 1983. *The City and the Grassroots: a Cross-Cultural Theory of Urban Social Movements*. London: Edward Arnold.

Dahl, Robert Alan. 1998. *On Democracy*. New Haven; London: Yale UP.

Devine-Wright, Patrick. 2009. Rethinking NIMBYism: The Role of Place Attachment and Place Identity in Explaining Place-Protective Action. *Journal of Community & Applied Social Psychology* 19 (6): 426–441.

Dowding, Keith, Patrick Dunleavy, Desmond King, Helen Margetts, and Yvonne Rydin. 1999. Regime Politics in London Local Government. *Urban Affairs Review* 34 (4): 515–545.

Gualini, Enrico, and Irene Bianchi. 2015. Space, Politics and Conflicts: A Review of Contemporary Debates in Urban Research and Planning Theory. In *Planning and Conflict: Critical Perspectives on Contentious Urban Developments*, ed. Enrico Gualini. New York: Routledge.

Gunder, Michael, Ali Madanipour, and Vanessa Watson, eds. 2018. *The Routledge Handbook of Planning Theory*. London: Routledge.

Hillier, Jean, and Patsy Healey, eds. 2008. *Contemporary Movements in Planning Theory*. Aldershot: Ashgate.

Hillier, Jean, and Jonathan Metzger, eds. 2015. *Connections: Exploring Contemporary Planning Theory and Practice with Patsy Healey*. Farnham: Ashgate.

Holman, Nancy. 2007. Following the Signs: Applying Urban Regime Analysis to a UK Case Study. *Journal of Urban Affairs* 29 (5): 435–453.

Kingdon, John. 2003. *Agendas, Alternatives, and Public Policies*. 2nd ed. New York: Longman.

Lauermann, John, and Anne Vogelpohl. 2017. Fragile Growth Coalitions or Powerful Contestations? Cancelled Olympic Bids in Boston and Hamburg. *Environment and Planning A* 49 (8): 1887–1904.

Leontidou, Lila. 2010. Urban Social Movements in 'Weak' Civil Societies: The Right to the City and Cosmopolitan Activism in Southern Europe. *Urban Studies* 47 (6): 1179–1203.

Levy, Charmain, Anne Latendresse, and Marianne Carle-Marsan. 2017. Gendering the Urban Social Movement and Public Housing Policy in São Paulo. *Latin American Perspectives* 44 (3): 9–27.

Li, Bin, and Chaoqun Liu. 2018. Emerging Selective Regimes in a Fragmented Authoritarian Environment: The 'Three Old Redevelopment' Policy in Guangzhou, China from 2009 to 2014. *Urban Studies* 55 (7): 1400–1419.

Mayer, Margit. 2010. The 'Right to the City' in the Context of Shifting Mottos of Urban Social Movements. *City* 13 (2–3): 362–374.

McNiff, Jean. 2013. *Action Research Principles and Practice*. 3rd ed. Hoboken: Taylor and Francis.

Molotch, Harvey. 1993. The Political Economy of Growth Machines. *Journal of Urban Affairs* 15 (1): 29–53.

Mossberger, Karen, and Gerry Stoker. 2016. The Evolution of Urban Regime Theory. *Urban Affairs Review* 36 (6): 810–835.

Mouffe, Chantal. 2013. *Agonistics: Thinking the World Politically*. London: Verso.

Nicholls, Walter J. 2008. The Urban Question Revisited: The Importance of Cities for Social Movements. *International Journal of Urban and Regional Research* 32 (4): 841–859.

Pierre, Jon. 2014. Can Urban Regimes Travel in Time and Space? Urban Regime Theory, Urban Governance Theory, and Comparative Urban Politics. *Urban Affairs Review* 50 (6): 864–889.

Raco, Mike. 2014. The Post-Politics of Sustainability Planning. In *The Post-Political and Its Discontents: Spaces of De-politicisation, Spectres of Radical Politics*, ed. Japhy Wilson and Eric Swyngedouw. Edinburgh: Edinburgh University Press.

Ravazzi, Stefania, and Silvano Belligni. 2016. Explaining 'Power To': Incubation and Agenda Building in an Urban Regime. *Urban Affairs Review* 52 (3): 323–347.

Rogers, Dallas. 2016. Monitory Democracy as Citizen-Driven Participatory Planning: The Urban Politics of Redwatch in Sydney. *Urban Policy and Research* 34 (3): 225–239.

Stone, Clarence N. 1989. *Regime Politics: Governing Atlanta, 1946–1988*. Lawrence, KS; London: University Press of Kansas.

Trapenberg Frick, Karen. 2018. No Permanent Friends, No Permanent Enemies: Agonistic Ethos, Tactical Coalitions, and Sustainable Infrastructure. *Journal of Planning Education and Research*. https://doi.org/10.1177/0739456X18773491.

Uysal, Ülke Evrim. 2012. An Urban Social Movement Challenging Urban Regeneration: The Case of Sulukule, Istanbul. *Cities* 29 (1): 12–22.

Yamamoto, Arata D. 2017. Why Agonistic Planning? Questioning Chantal Mouffe's Thesis of the Ontological Primacy of the Political. *Planning Theory* 16 (4): 384–403.

Chapter 7
Political Economy: Crisis and Response

Framing the Research

Planning systems generally present themselves as operating for the general good, in the public interest. This may be presented differently, emphasising environmental, social or economic benefits or a mixture or balance between these dimensions. However, the highly politicised 1960s saw the start of a considerable body of work that questioned the impartial or even benevolent nature of state planning. Chapter 6 outlined how this led to a focus on active protest, social movements and action for the 'right to the city' (and to the environment). However, the work reviewed in this chapter is rather different. It looks at how capitalism as a system is implicated in these uneven outcomes of planning as well as other state activity and questions what roles the built environment and planning for the environment play within the maintenance of the capitalist system.

Central to this perspective is an interest in the interplay between crisis and stability in capitalism. The use of the term 'capitalism' highlights that this approach derives from the challenge that Karl Marx posed to conventional understandings of economic systems (and continues to do). There were specific historical roots to this resurgence of interest in classical Marxism. On the one hand, social commentators and theorists found themselves interested in the crisis precipitated in early 1970s by the Arab-Israeli war, the associated embargo on oil sales and increase in oil prices and the impact of the subsequent recession on a highly indebted property sector. On the other, they also questioned how the capitalist system had managed to avoid such crises during the many decades since the Second World War, during which the living standards of the working class had seemed to improve. What was the role of the state? And, as a state activity, what was the role of a planning system?

In posing these questions, the political economy approach takes as given a set of inter-related working hypotheses, first, that ultimately the state operates in the interests of the capitalist system and, second, that this system is inherently prone to crisis

Y. Rydin, *Theory in Planning Research*, Planning, Environment, Cities, https://doi.org/10.1007/978-981-33-6568-1_7

tendencies. It framed planning as part of the activities of a capitalist state, a state that necessarily ultimately worked in the interests of the capitalist system, but this might not mean that it always operated in the interest of capitalists. For example, there might be situations in which the long-term stability of capitalism was secured by making concessions to non-capitalist interests, notably labour. This involved looking at planning activities anew and asking a fresh set of questions about activities, such as providing public housing, investing in infrastructure, rezoning areas for new urban development or permitting environmental resource exploitation.

But to avoid too simplistic a perspective, this approach also developed arguments about how the interests of the capitalist system might not align with the interests of any particular capitalist or 'fraction' of capital. It also began to debate how necessary it was to adopt a structuralist approach in which the workings of the capitalist economy were the predominant driver for change; this led to debates about the relative importance of and the inter-relationships between structure and agency in determining outcomes; Giddens' structuration approach was an attempt to resolve this dilemma of accounting for structural influences as well as the agency of social groups (Giddens 1986).

This was a radical re-reading of the social democratic argument for planning. It saw many of the benefits of planning as nothing more than buying off the working class or promising them concessions so as to prevent political action for more radical change. In the end, though the structural dimensions of a capitalist economy and society were seen as responsible for the continued persistence of inequalities and disadvantage.

Political economy is a structuralist approach to understanding how planning works. This means that structures at the level of the society as a whole have the greatest influence on how planning works in specific cases. Furthermore, society is understood not as something distinct from the economy but rather encompassing it. The economic processes of capital accumulation are at the core of how society operates and, therefore, what planning does.

The key analytic and normative idea behind the political economy framework is that the contribution of the working class to creating value and profit is not recognised. Rather societal structures allow that value—termed labour value—to be expropriated by capitalist classes. The profits of such expropriation go to the owners of capital, with different types of capital owner represented by landowners, owners of finance capital and others who own and control other types of capital, such as manufacturing equipment. These profits can also be redistributed to a certain extent, say through the state and by giving a disproportionate (unfair) share to the middle classes. It might be asked why capital owners would willingly give a share of the financial returns coming to them under capitalism to the state or the middle classes. The key issue here is whether the continuity of capitalism as a system is being threatened. If this is occurring, then it may make sense for some redistribution of the appropriated labour value to occur.

The state's role in relation to capitalism can take a number of forms. It can become an avenue for giving concessions to the working class in response to struggles that they engage in, struggles which might be termed revolutionary. The state can also play a role in 'the social reproduction of labour', that is of meeting the costs involved in creating the kind of workforce that a continually evolving capitalism requires. This could involve supporting a healthier and better educated workforce as capitalist enterprises are no longer able to deliver profit accumulation with the kind of workforce that is supported only by its wages.

It could be that working-class resistance to their exploitation results in the state providing benefits to 'buy off' that resistance. It can sometimes be difficult to distinguish between, say, the provision of good quality council housing as a response to specific struggles and demands by the working class and that provision as a way of ensuring a better quality and hence more profitable workforce. Thus analyses in the later twentieth century emphasised the growing public sector support of working class housing as an important way of improving the conditions of the working class (to borrow Engels' phrase), without having to increase the wages paid to labour. The origins of urban planning is intrinsically linked to the planning, provision and even management of housing by the public sector, and thus the planning system becomes seen as part of the social reproduction of labour power. It enables capitalism to operate more effectively by creating a more productive working class without affecting the profitability of capitalist activity directly.

Another strategy is not to give concessions to the working class, say through the state, but rather focus on the middle classes. Giving the middle classes a greater share of the expropriated labour value can be seen as a way to create a social class with a firm stake in capitalism as a functioning system. If the middle classes see their position as being underpinned by capitalism, then they will be allies of fractions of capital in any struggles that might occur when the working class realise that they are being exploited and resist.

Thus, a political economy analysis of planning is centrally concerned with how the state operates, to ensure the continuity and profitability of the capitalist system and the way that planning activity in relation to the built and natural environment promotes this. While much political economy work has focussed on how the planning of the built environment affects its role within capitalism, there is the cognate area of political ecology which asks similar questions with regard to the natural environment, including particularly key natural resources required for capital accumulation (Robbins 2012). Such resource exploitation is often associated with the penetration of capitalism into lower-income countries and with the growth of colonialism and the economic dependency of poorer countries on richer ones.

However, political economy also looks at how land, as implicated in urban growth and development as well as in natural resource extraction, is a key aspect of the operation of capitalism and how profits are generated. The Marxist theory of land rent has sought to identify how land ownership and particularly transformation through resource extraction or development generates a source of profit that powers capital accumulation. This is part of the way that a political economy approach has put more emphasis onto the economic processes that planning systems have to engage with and has raised the central question of how planning activity itself supports the generation of profit, capital accumulation and the avoidance of threats to the smooth continuity of capitalism as a system.

Dynamics of Analysis and Key Concepts

The dynamics that will be outlined here pertain to the importance of understanding capital accumulation and the role of the built environment within this, the repeated emergence of crises within the economy and the state response to that, and the importance of key global trends and how these are shaping the role of the state.

Capital Accumulation and the Role of the Built Environment

Political economy draws on Marxist analysis, which takes the works of Karl Marx as its core. Marx's approach centred on the division of society into classes, of which the working class and the owners of capital (capitalists) are the most important categories. This is because the economic system, upon which capitalist societies are based, works by capitalists exploiting the working class. Exploitation results from the need of members of the working class to sell their labour in order to have the means to survive; they have no capital (financial or in the form of land or manufacturing equipment) to rely on. This analysis was developed in nineteenth-century Europe, which was characterised by two features. First, manufacturing was shifted from artisans who worked with their own equipment in their homes to factories where people came to work for a wage in exchange for their labour power. Second, this was linked to a shift of the population from rural areas, where people may have had some access to land to provide an element of subsistence, to the urban areas where the factories were located. Hence this was a period when the working class was created as a class without any assets but their ability to work by selling their labour power.

The classical Marxist analysis of capitalism sees value as deriving purely from labour value, that is the work of the working class. Capitalists can seek to increase the rate of exploitation by investing in fixed capital, that is machinery. The idea was that the worker equipped with such machinery would be able to produce more and be the source of a higher rate of profit-making. However, there is a limit on the ability to increase profits and the rate of exploitation of labour by these means, a kind of law of diminishing returns. This is considered one of the key causes of recurrent crises within capitalism, crises which were evident in nineteenth-century industrial Europe.

Such political economy is clearly a theory of how the economy works rather than of planning processes per se. But during the later twentieth century a number of theorists looked to classical Marxism to inspire a new view of how the state worked. These theorists—sometimes termed neo-marxists—in turn inspired urban theorists, and from here, new accounts of urban planning emerged (Broadbent 2007; Dunleavy 1980; Harvey 1988). These have varied as political economists have sought to understand the changing economic context of the twentieth and twenty-first centuries. It is in the nature of the Marxist approach that each historical period has its own analysis and explanation of the key trends.

In the 1970s and 1980s, the main insight of political economy was that during the twentieth century the growing public sector had increasingly been playing a role in the social reproduction of the labour force. In effect, this meant that the state was undertaking a variety of functions that made the working class more effective from the point of view of capitalist production. Some of this was about making the working class healthy enough to be productive. Early state investment in housing, for example, was linked to the medical examinations during the call-up of soldiers to the First World War, which revealed more widely the appalling standard of health of the working class, and also to the evidence of poor housing standards in rapidly urbanised areas recorded in the late nineteenth century by Marx's collaborator, Frederick Engels, and by Booth and Chadwick.

The political economy accounts from the 1970s onwards have tended to move away from seeing urban planning as supporting capitalism through provision for the working class via the welfare state, to seeing such planning as being constrained and limited to enabling urban development and enhancing the profits therefrom.

An excellent example of how the circulation of capital within the economic system can be linked to change in the built environment and the associated oppression of a social group is found in Pasternak and Dafnos' work on infrastructure development in Canada and how the land rights of indigenous peoples are implicated in this (Pasternak and Dafnos 2017). The argument is that the logistics sector has an increasingly important role within capitalism and is, indeed, restructuring it along leaner, faster lines of accumulation. Ensuring the availability of infrastructure to support distribution activities in line with logistics is essential, and the state, through infrastructure planning, becomes involved in this. The assertion by indigenous people of their rights over land can be seen as a threat to this new mode of accumulation, and thus the ways in which the state responds to this are worthy of analysis.

Pasternak and Dafnos analyse this situation in terms of the uncertainty that indigenous rights pose for capital accumulation and identify two responses, two forms of risk mitigation that have resulted. The first is configuration of indigenous jurisdiction as a 'legal risk' by central government and the imposition of a socio-economic agenda to integrate indigenous communities into the market economy through political and financial investments. This enables the state and private sector to access land, resources and transport networks within indigenous jurisdictions. Capital can literally flow through these areas which had otherwise been potentially barred to it. The second is the configuration of indigenous jurisdiction as a potential 'emergency' in the context of infrastructure for national needs, permitting action against indigenous land rights. In these ways, capital within a logistics-dominated economy can flow readily, and infrastructure planning facilitates this.

Planning as Responding to Crisis

The oil prices crisis of 1973–1974 created a depression more severe than any since the interwar period. Much of the industrialised world seemed to be affected again by a crisis of imbalance between the quantum of goods and services being produced and the global ability to pay for these, that is a crisis of overproduction (or, as O'Connor chose to term it, under-consumption; O'Connor 1973). At the core of such crises is the inherent inability of capitalism to provide sufficient income through paid wages to fund such purchases. Imports and exports can be used to try and separate out the geographical location of the underpaid workforce from that of the market-place with the financial ability to purchase. Social differentiation between the working class and a middle-class with this all-important ability to pay can also play a role. But there is an intrinsic instability at the core of capitalism that renders recurrent crisis inevitable, according to political economy.

This gives the state a new role to play, looking at how capital is deployed within capitalism. Key possibilities include trying to speed up the rate at which capital circulates and switching capital between different investment opportunities. This can involve devaluing capital which has already been invested in fixed forms, such as machinery and buildings. In effect, this neo-Marxist analysis provides an explanation of urban decline, suggesting a systemic reason why land and buildings become abandoned and ripe for redevelopment. The decline of value on abandonment represents the devaluation of capital, so that new investment in these areas will (eventually) reap higher rates of return. Urban planning will be directly implicated in these processes of devaluation of urban assets and their revaluation through urban regeneration.

David Harvey has provided an important account of the specific role that urban planning can play in response to such crises (Harvey 1982, 1985, 1988, 2010). He points to the way that a crisis can require capital to be devalued so that it can support a new round of capital accumulation from a lower base. He also sees this as a form of switching between different types of capital and argues that the built environment, as a form of fixed capital sunk in buildings and land, has a particular role to play here. When there is a crisis of profitability in capitalism, then there is a need to devalue capital, and resources will switch from the built environment to other forms of investment, engineering a massive devaluation of properties in the built environment.

Harvey identifies inter-related circuits of capital which flow between: the processes of the production of values and surplus value; the consumption of commodities and the reproduction of labour power; state functions; and the capital market including financial and state intermediaries. In addition to the primary exchange of payment for labour power (wages) for consumption goods, there are circuits concerned with: fixed capital; the consumption fund; social expenditures (on education, health, welfare, policy, etc.); and technology, science and administration. Crises arising in the system can potentially be resolved by switching capital between circuits, devaluing capital in one circuit and building it up in another. The built environment features both as fixed capital and as part of the consumption fund, and thus periodic devaluations of parts of the built environment and reinvestment in other parts of the built environment can be seen as a tactic of addressing crises of profitability and return within capitalism. This provides a distinctive interpretation of why some property markets suffer rapid decline, and why, with the assistance of planning policies and actions such as local government land transfers, investment funds flow into new areas to create profitable urban development opportunities.

During the early 1970s a debt-fuelled commercial property boom in London was brought to an abrupt halt by the increase in interest rates following the Arab-Israeli war and the associated restrictions on the supply of oil set by the cartel of oil-producing Arab countries. The result was an economic recession with wider spatial consequences, leading to inflation and unemployment. Interest rates rose rapidly, and this rendered many developments that had been debt-financed unviable, reinforcing the effect of declining demand for new buildings from potential occupants (Ambrose and Colenutt 1975).

In 2008, again, the trigger point for a broader economic crisis was the excessive use of debt to fuel property markets. But here the particular problem was lending for the domestic market in the USA and elsewhere. Not only was mortgage lending leading to very high debt-to-income and debt-to-equity ratios, but these debts were being parcelled up into portfolios and then securitised, that is divided up into new paper debt-backed assets for onward sale. This securitisation was even happening repeatedly. These debt-backed assets were selling for far in excess of the value of the underlying debt; in addition, the link between the securitised assets and the original mortgages was often obscured by the securitisation process. When the over-valuation of assets became obvious, however, the links led back to the property market and asset values resulting in falling property values. Banks that had lent extensively into these mortgage markets also found themselves under-capitalised and in danger of collapse.

In each of these cases the response was devaluation of the landed property assets as predicted by the political economy framework. In the 1970s, commercial and industrial property lay empty and unlettable until its value fell, the economy restructured and planning led a new wave of property-led regeneration. Planning, as a public sector activity, both came under direct attack and was required to operate in a context whether the private sector rather than the public sector guided much urban change. Major public sector housebuilding and other development programmes—as in the New Towns of the 1960s and 1970s—were replaced with the urban regeneration of the Urban Development Corporations, led by the private sector and fuelled by the transfer of land and other subsidies to private developers.

After 2008, the exemplar of a depreciated property market was Detroit in Michigan. Here the major employer of General Motors went into liquidation. Vast swathes of the city were abandoned as households literally walked away from their houses and the associated mortgages (a possibility that exists in the USA). The local economy collapsed as a resulted and population out-migration ensued. The idea of down-sizing the city started to drive urban planning as plots and whole neighbourhoods were bull-dozed. Community activity started to take up some of the financially worthless land with urban agriculture and related activities (see also Chap. 10), and more recently (at least until the 2020 pandemic), signs of gentrification and associated urban development were emerging.

Global Trends and the Impact on Planning

Marxists have also been able to point to the way that many national states have responded to this crisis as clearly operating in the interests of certain sections of capital, notably finance capital. The banking institutions—the key representatives of finance capital—have been given vast financial support to 'recapitalise', and this has clearly been at the expense of lower-income groups. Austerity policies have been adopted by or imposed on countries affected to reduce the public sector debt by radical retrenchment of public spending. Massive reductions in public services have followed with planning services within the public sector again affected. The political economy account here largely supports a view of the planning system as being reduced, stripped back and limited in order to avoid any substantial constraint on private sector interests.

Thus, planning gets situated within accounts of the state and the economy that emphasise a number of different processes. There is the tendency towards privatisation of state assets so that they become part of the private circulation of capital. There is the shift towards austerity politics with cuts in public budgets and the activities of the state, including the local state and its planning functions. These fit within a broader adoption of neo-liberalism as the prevailing ideology that argues for the primacy of market processes and the need to alter the role of the state (Tulumello 2015). Rolling back the state has been identified as one neo-liberal strategy, but this has been supplemented with suggestions of other ways of restructuring the state to fit new economic circumstances. In such a context—of the primacy of the market and a reduced role for the state—localities and particularly cities saw their future in terms of attracting private capital and engaging in competition with each other for mobile capitalist resources.

Alongside this has gone an analysis that the dominant economic interests are to be found in the finance fraction of capital. Back in the 1980s, Massey and Catalano argued that the industrial capital that had dominated nineteenth-century capitalism was increasingly becoming subservient to finance capital, notably banking capital but also other investment channels such as commercial land ownership (Massey and Catalano 1978). Thus the role of planning was not so much to facilitate the profitable activities of industrial capital any more but to aid the speculative profit-taking of finance capital, principally through easing urban development and the construction of speculative commercial property. By the twenty-first century, commentators were adding the refinement that capitalism was increasingly being reshaped by processes of financialisation, in which a variety of assets including the built environment were being turned in the equivalent of a paper financial claims that could be circulated, in ways similar to equities (which had transformed industrial capitalism). Since such financial assets circulated on a global scale, this was transforming built environments (or parts of them) into ways of capturing and holding financial assets rather than places designed for living in (O'Neill 2017).

The dynamics by which financialisation of land drives urban planning, rather than planning efforts leading to urban change, can be seen in a study of peri-urbanisation in Asia by Shatkin (2016). Here the rapidly increasing price of land is driving new strategies of land management, seeking to release that value either to enhance public finances or to distribute resources to powerful private corporate backers of the state. Building a historical account, Shatkin argues that this lies behind the reform agendas of governments, "liberalization of the financial sector, reforms to urban land use planning frameworks, fiscal decentralization, and other— that are quite explicitly intended to empower local governments and prod them towards a more commercial orientation in their land management" (p. 142). Using Smith's rent gap theory (Smith 1996), he argues that a number of factors have contributed to a growing disparity between current use values of land in Asian peri-urban areas and the potential value of those sites after development; among these he lists large-scale landownership of some tracts, restrictions on land uses and the politics of informality in these locations that has seen the spread of extra-legal occupations of land. The size of the rent gap has then created pressures for the monetisation of peri-urban land and private sector development.

Research Themes in Practice

The papers reviewed here look at three aspects of a political economy perspective on planning: the commodification of the environment, how capital accumulation is related to the dispossession of already disadvantaged communities (a relationship that strongly connects to studies of gentrification), and the recent trends towards financialisation and how this supports the idea of the entrepreneurial state.

Commodification

The processes by which a range of public or common goods are turned into private assets for capital accumulation have been widely examined; this is particularly pertinent where environmental goods and services are incorporated into a capitalist economy. An example of this is provided by Speake (2017) looking at the commodification of views in Malta. She looked at the regeneration of Tigné Point, a location with views across to the old town of Valletta with its distinctive architecture and sea setting. She showed how the commodification of a panoramic view became part of urban transformation and regeneration in line with the neo-liberal agenda. In doing this she connected a political economy approach with cultural geography and its use of the concept of 'the gaze'; she also connected with Lefebvre's work with his trio of 'perceived', 'conceived' and 'lived' space, a framework which works across cultural dimensions and the political economy of a situation (Lefebvre 2008). She explored how, under neo-liberalism, "panoramic views are a commodity to be bought, sold and become the property [of] the affluent élite" (p. 2921).

The methodological framework used a qualitative bricolage approach based on field observation, public and private sector documentation and interviews. This involved recording of visual observations, coding and thematic analysis of the textual material and collecting data and information about how the local property market worked from interviews with estate agents. Documents studied included property market promotional material and official planning documentation. The research question centred on how the panoramic view across Marsamxett Harbour was reflected in design and valuation activities, and this led to the manual coding of the material for analysis.

The research focussed on the details of how a panorama becomes an object for economic and political transactions and how this then can accelerate capital accumulation and contribute to further spatial inequalities. In the analysis there was parallel attention to cultural aspects such as gazing, signalling and representations, alongside the economics of property development and the role that local planning plays in this: "Interlinkages occur between panorama, gazing and the creation of city form and these are revealed during the neoliberal commodification of the aesthetics of a panoramic view into cultural and financial 'value'" (p. 2922).

Through the empirical work, Speake showed how the development of Tigné Point followed a 'classic' capitalist logic, which benefited the developers of the site, able to sell properties at a premium due to the view, and also those able to pay for the new properties and enjoy exclusive access to this view. She pointed to how "the commodification of the gaze is operationalised and the viewing subject takes ownership of the commodified gaze, in scripted, tangible, material form such as an apartment" (p. 2929), and further tracked the market value that is associated with this commodified gaze. She noted the limited possibilities for public consultation in this process; as a result local planning facilitated rather than shaped these processes in the community interest.

This research has a very detailed focus on how a view became a commodified asset for exchange, but it still fits within the broader political economy argument of how urban planning is relatively powerless to deliver in the public interest due to such commodification and the limited scope for resistance from local publics.

Balaban (2011) looked at the relationship between squatting and commodification of urban space in Turkish cities. The context for this was the rapid post-war urbanisation of Turkey and the role that illegal working dwellings called 'gecekondus' played during the 1960s and early 1980s. These gecekondus were single-storey shacks built on land previously owned by the official and semi-official religious organisations of the Ottoman Empire and non-Muslim minorities who left in the early twentieth century. The research proceeded through a chronologically organised history of the transformation of the gecekondus during the later twentieth century and early twenty-first century; this form of historical narrative is often adopted within the political economy framing. The methods were largely document based although there is also reference to interviews with some 17 local mayors, and a case study of the Bağcilar area in Istanbul was also included. Again political economy accounts often collate material—including quantitative and archive material—from a variety of sources and do not always emphasise methodology in their account of the research.

In the period up to the 1980s, gecekondus were synonymous with squatting, given the lack of a legal right to the land occupied. The social movements formed around them were concerned with giving a right to residence to low-income working-class communities, and there was pressure to regularise their land rights. The context changed in the 1980s when there was a major construction boom and a shift towards multi-storey apartment buildings for housing the working class, rather than these single-storey buildings. At the same time, there was a shift from occupation to renting. Squatters began to rent out space within their homes, and multi-storey buildings were typically occupied by renters. This began a process of commodifying the squatter settlements. The rights that squatters were given to secure their occupation were now used to support landlord-tenant relationships. Furthermore, gecekondu owners sought to build more and more multi-storey apartment blocks.

Balaban thus argues "when early squatters obtained legal status for their homes, their initially progressive-looking social movement for self-help became a major mechanism of commodification of urban space" (p. 2163). On the back of this, a conservative government put in place institutional arrangements to complete the enclosure and commodification of urban land. State violence was also used to prevent further illegal land occupations of urban spaces. The losers were the working class who were now reliant on rented accommodation and enmeshed in land-tenant relationships. The author puts the argument that this contributed to the proletarianisation of the working class and supported the neo-liberal economic policies aimed at expanding exports.

Here the process of commodifying former squatted land is linked to a number of broader structural trends including the growth of a formal rented sector, the enforced decline in informal housing, the removal of non-wage resources from the working class, and neo-liberalism influencing the state's policies. Again the specific is connected to the broader structural level.

Accumulation by Dispossession

Globally, the political economy framework has had particular purchase in studying the way that market-led development takes over areas of the city that had been settled by lower-income groups, often in so-called informal settlements. Such informally settled land has a low market value, enabling urban development in these locations to be more profitable than in more central urban locations. The emphasis here is not just on the dispossession of lower-income groups but how this connects to processes of capital accumulation. This phenomenon has been researched by

Mbiba (2017) in Zimbabwe using Harvey's concept of accumulation by dispossession to understand land-grabbing.

The concept of accumulation by dispossession is developed from the Marxist idea of primary accumulation. The emphasis though is on the means by which capitalist processes can be expanded and speeded up. Mbiba cited Springer as describing accumulation by dispossessions as "ways in which neoliberalization has transformed the matrix of city spaces, entailing intensified differentiation, displacement of the poor and a significant degree of conflict contestation" (Springer, 2017: 445). He then went on to make the point that in contexts such as Zimbabwe national and local actors can be as, or even more, important as global actors. Neo-liberalism became "home-grown" (p. 216). But in line with the political economy approach, the emphasis was on the role of the state, the mechanisms that state actors deployed and the extent to which this benefited specific capitalist groupings. The use of financial mechanisms were particularly important, including differential pricing for different groups (with poor groups getting less), differential credit and debt arrangements (again with the poor paying more on worse terms) and direct resource transfer from the poor to private capitalist interests.

Mbiba used archival data, relating to land-use change and ownership, available from public offices. This was supplemented with elite interviews with senior public officials and site visits. Archival records for specific sites were also sought "to explain the history of and arguments relating to change of use or reservation [planning designation] for each site and to identify and describe the role of different actors in each development" (p. 216). Mbiba noted the sensitive nature of some of the data he sought to access, recording the necessity to present his research in terms of "urban history and land use change" and to confirm that he was a planner and not a journalist.

The analysis from this research showed how, in a context set by a World Bank/IMF-driven structural adjustment programme oriented towards neo-liberalism and growth in exports, there had been a transfer in public land to elites and corporate entities, often through fraudulent land sales and at a significantly lower price per unit of land compared to similar land sales to poorer people. "Citizens' assets were thus transferred to private entities at below-market prices, depriving the Harare City Council of resources to provide citizens with sorely needed services" (p. 220). This was not analysed as a result of the behaviour of a few corrupt officials, but rather "a comprehensive, systematic state-led attempt at economic restructuring to build and protect indigenous capitalist agents" (p. 221).

Mbiba then followed this argument through two case studies. The first case concerned a People's Market in Harare, an area of public open space that had long served as a location for the sale of crafts and vegetables. This land was in community use but could have fetched a considerable sum if sold for commercial purposes; however, it was bartered away for a batch of new vehicles by the council in a deal with the Commercial Bank of Zimbabwe (CBZ). The area was fenced off, and traders were displaced to peri-urban locations. The second case concerned a nature reserve in Harare, involved in a contested barter with CBZ for vehicles and cash, where a key question was whether the state had followed due process in permitting the change of planning designation that would have been required to transfer the site to commercial use.

Mbiba saw both these cases and the supporting historical analysis as identifying how an indigenous capitalist system was being built through *inter alia* the transfer of public land in ways that disadvantaged poorer sectors of the population and the ability of the local state to provide public services. Here there was conflict between capitalist interests: international versus local, state-aligned versus non-state capitalists, various forms of capitalist (vigilante, briefcase and settler) versus indigenous capitalists. But this was in the context of the tendency of capitalism as a system to respond to periodic crises by switching capital between investment options. Mbiba concluded that in 1990s Zimbabwe, "capital switched from manufacturing to speculative financial deals and real estate investments" (p. 229). As the crisis deepened, fraudulent alliances were forged between local elites and capitalist interests, on the one hand, and local governments, on the other, to enable transfers of land for longer-term security and gain.

This research identifies how land is turned into a marketable asset but it spends more analytic effort in linking this to a broader analysis of shifts in capital accumulation in Zimbabwe, using a mixture of historical and case study data to build the narrative.

Research by De Weerdt and Garcia (2015) into the response to the mortgage crisis in Spain following the 2008 financial crisis tackled the situation of those facing dispossession as a result. The Platform of Mortgage Victims (PAH) was founded in Barcelona in 2009 to support those facing eviction—without discharge of their mortgage debt—when they were not able to service that debt. The researchers examined this as a form of collective social action, looking at the institutional responses and how the movement against evictions impacted on governance arrangements. The context for this was the huge expansion in home ownership in Spain, supported by state policies, to the point where it constituted almost 85% of households before the housing bubble burst. After the crisis erupted more than 400,000 mortgages were foreclosed for non-payment and faced possible eviction. Under the Spanish legal code, the debtor had to use present and future assets to pay a mortgage debt, so that eviction did not end the claim by the financial institutions. Furthermore, until 2012, debtors were not permitted to defend themselves in court during the eviction process.

The data for the analysis of PAH was based on statistics from a variety of sources, as well as participant observation of the social movement, attendance at PAH meetings, and examination of online documentation held for PAH, and protocols and data on eviction cases. In addition, there were ten semi-structured interviews with stakeholders and public officials, and a database was collected to monitor media coverage of PAH and related issues. Finally, a workshop was held of local stakeholders.

The PAH was founded in Barcelona, but the model spread to other cities in Spain so that there were 10 local platforms by mid-2011, 144 in 2013 and 205 in 2014. The Catalan platforms held regular assemblies and hosted webpages or Facebook groups. They managed to capture media attention and transform the framing of mortgages from an individual to a collective problem. The social movement was effective in that it got to the position of having the support of over 80% of Spaniards. In addition, they prepared tools to support individual households in their struggles, including ready-to-use documentation. The researchers also emphasised the importance of the links that PAH groups built out to other organisations, both locally and across scales, and how they mobilised specialist knowledge.

The PAH aimed to achieve a temporary suspension in evictions through a legal amendment and to promulgate collective renegotiation of mortgage debt for groups of households. They set up a People's Legislative Initiative, collected a petition to propose new legislation and staged protests outside the homes of politicians. They also acted at the European scale to get a ruling in the European Court of Justice, which supported legal amendments and action by justices to somewhat redress the imbalance between the financial institutions and mortgagors.

Firmly situated within a period of economic crisis, this research uses the political economy framework to investigate the roots of the crisis as it affected the housing market and those dispossessed by mortgage foreclosures. But what this detailed case study also shows is the variety of actions and activities that go into a successful social movement able to produce structural change in support of disadvantaged groups, as well as the importance of a broad social base and wider public support.

Financialisation and the Entrepreneurial State

Three examples of research framed by political economy and the concern with current trends of financialisation are discussed next.

First, Savini and Aalbers (2016) provided a study of Milan, Italy, situated in an understanding of global investment dynamics and how local government often responded by trying to anchor mobile capital through urban development policies, enabling the extraction of value from urban sites. Urban projects thus became a key site of negotiation between capital and cities. In such negotiations, Savini and Aalbers were sceptical about the ability of city government to reap benefits. They pointed to a booming real estate sector based on the availability of cheap finance, regulation that favoured larger developments, guarantees on long-term investments and greater flexibility in planning, notably land-use regulations. Land became an asset for global capital, rendered liquid (capable of being converted into money) and de-contextualised from its location. "A specific plot of land can be part of a large portfolio, owned by locally, nationally or even globally active firms. Indeed, the financialisation of land facilitates the globalisation of land" (p. 882). Thus there had been a shift in the kind of developers active in cities, away from local firms with local knowledge towards national and global players, combining capital from multiple sources and largely delinked from the localities where they operated. At the same time, land was increasingly used to leverage capital within the banking system; this was the growing trend towards land as fictitious capital envisaged by Harvey (1982: 369) whereby land was used as the security for growing amounts of debt, financing increasing amounts of urban development. Special Purpose Vehicles (SPV) were increasingly used to promote urban development, involving a variety of actors and often turning local governments into entrepreneurial partners.

Using historical data over two decades, Savini and Aalbers studied a specific project in Sesto San Giovanni, Milan—the Falck project—and related it to these trends. This was a site which had been sold four times, whose value had steadily increased and yet where the realisation of the project remained uncertain. The 150 hectares site was central, well connected to rail and metro infrastructure and the outer ring road, and yet in a highly polluted area due to its industrial past. Distinct periods could be discerned. In the immediate aftermath of the industrial use of the site, development was managed locally through local development agencies and investors, but plans faltered on the tension between the booming residential market and the desire of local government to maintain employment-generating land uses. The second phase saw an SPV created to promote residential and commercial development of the area and controlled by a single entity with strong links to local politics. Negotiations proceeded between the SPV owner and the Deputy Mayor, but a plan was never approved. The SPV was then, in the third period, sold on to a new owner, an investment company with land holdings across several countries; this was a pattern that was occurring on other sites across the city. Competition between these sites drove the master-planning which now involved several 'flagships', almost doubled the density of development and increased the proportion of high-value housing. "A more ambitious real estate programme reflected the need to reach higher gains for both investors and the municipality" (p. 887). Higher financial returns (partly to service the increased debt) were required when the municipality asked for more public facilities.

However, and into the fourth period, the crash of 2008 sent the originator company of the SPV (Risanamento SpA) towards bankruptcy. The planning negotiations now lost all leverage and became entirely dependent on the decisions being made by financial markets and actors. Risanamento Spa recapitalised and, as a condition of this, sold the Falck site to a new company, who also formed an SPV with a highly complex ownership structure including investors from across a variety of economic sectors. The requirements of these investors necessitated the realisation of a modified project for the site: "the Falck land was repackaged and subdivided among numerous investors, and this process took place under the expectations that the municipality would complete the project" (p. 888).

The local government had to pick up the risk but did so in conditions where the project became increasingly complex (driven by investor requirements) and the collapsing housing market undermined the financial model for development. The municipality approved a master plan with more retail and office space, with less high-end housing and manufacturing and with sites earmarked for health care and medical research under a cash injection from the regional government. In this case the role of urban land in financial markets was made clear, along with the complexity that this produced for urban projects. The implications for local planning were restrictive, given that the municipalities became increasing dependent on realising financial returns from the scheme and had to adjust their policies accordingly.

The political economy framing supported research that clearly demonstrated Harvey's argument (Harvey 1982) that land is increasingly becoming fictitious capital, not only flowing into and through land via physical development but being used as financial collateral to leverage debt for further investment. Land and sites become decontextualised from their locality as they form part of complex trans-spatial financial arrangements, and urban planning authorities lose much control as they are increasingly tied to the priority of capturing value from land to enable any development to proceed.

MacDonald (2019) provided an account of the entrepreneurial state or rather the entrepreneurial city in Sydney. Her research addressed key question of: how does the local entrepreneurial state respond to the contradictory pressures of providing the public benefits they have promised and also maintaining profitability when faced with large-scale urban development? And how does this impact the planning system and its practices? These questions were answered through a case study of waterfront redevelopment in Barangaroo, the last vacant central city waterfront site in Sydney. She framed this in terms of a new phase of financialisation, "one in which the state acts as an entrepreneur in its own right" (p. 2). Drawing on prior research on financialisation, she postulated that investors are relying on developers, planners and related agencies to 'anchor capital' by jointly producing a high-yielding built environment in financial terms. Where local authorities could bring their own land to the development project, this encouraged them to view that land largely as a financial asset.

The methodology for the case study was not detailed, unfortunately, but can be reconstructed from the reported research. There was an emphasis on building a chronology of the project and detailed reference to a range of documentation associated with the development and its passage through the planning system. There was no quotation material from interviewees, but there was considerable attention to the context for the case, including the institutional arrangements of government in the region, the changing legislation, policy and procedures for planning in the area. The various nuances of the planning process and how challenges could be mounted were covered. In this way, the details of the specific case were situated within a broader understanding of the structural arrangements for planning and urban development, and this supported the political economy analysis of these details.

MacDonald found, from her empirical research, that the state—acting as an entrepreneurial state—faced a conflict of interest between enhancing the profitability of their asset and delivering the expected public benefits from the development, and in that situation, they renegotiated the public benefits in favour of enhancing the value of the public asset. This outcome was partly due to the concentration of planning powers at the New South Wales 'state' scale and the granting of considerable discretion to the Ministerial level. This limited the public consultation that occurred and led to a drawing back from the promises on such consultation that previous administrations had made. This Ministerial discretion was seen as involving "a disproportionate degree of power to approve concept plan modifications that significantly increase the project's impact and dilute the promised benefits" and further that this was "used to maximise State revenue through regulatory concession that increase development intensity" (p. 6).

The story of the case study was constructed from the empirical evidence as an account where the state prioritised the amelioration of risk and the increase of development returns. This impacted the nature of the development including visual intrusion, a more limited contribution to the provision of affordable housing and the small scale of public space provided. It was argued that claimed public benefits such as more sustainable construction and access to transportation infrastructure could equally be seen as enhancing property values and thus constituted private benefits. Furthermore, it seemed that in pursuit of a profitable development, the state had taken on certain costs that should have been borne by the developer as part of their entrepreneurial role, rather than assumed by the state. The conclusion was that "Barangaroo has been a highly 'financialized' project, in two senses: it has served to 'anchor capital' ... by remaking the built environment to the benefit of investors and developers, but it has also used public land speculatively, to generate substantial financial returns for the State government" (p. 10). This strategy of the entrepreneurial state was not without problems though, as MacDonald claimed it had further eroded trust in the planning system and intensified questions about its legitimacy.

Here the concept of the entrepreneurial state or city enabled the researcher to consider how the risks and returns of urban development were spread between public and private interests. This led to the conclusion that the public sector was disproportionately carrying risks while the returns accrued to the private sector.

A more optimistic study (at least initially) was provided by Vogelpohl and Buchholz (2017), who looked at three policy experiments in Hamburg, Germany, which have challenged the city's prevailing entrepreneurial approach. They were interested in the counter-example of a city where, since 2009, there has been an attempted break with neo-liberalism, supported by "unparalleled German urban movements fighting for the right to the city" and "the rediscovery of a political will for regulating the housing market" (p. 266). This shift was promulgated by the election of a Social Democratic Party (SDP) Mayor and, after his re-election, an SPD-Green coalition. So this case raised the question of the circumstances under which political officials were able to pursue such innovative policies and whether they were sufficient to overcome the prevailing neo-liberal direction. This research thus picked up on the social movements literature that was reviewed in Chap. 6 but was less concerned with examining the internal dynamics of such movements; rather it considered how their activism related to the apparently structural shifts towards neo-liberalism, financialisation and the entrepreneurial state.

The research narrative built a historical account of the three chosen policy initiatives. First, there was a study of the International Building Exhibition (IBA) for the Elbe islands, a low-income area across the river from the high-value HafenCity development; such IBAs were a commonly used tool in German planning to build visions for new (re)development areas. Second there was the use of regulation for rent control under the Social Preservation Statute (SPS). The third case was the creation by the Hamburg government of an Alliance for Housing in Hamburg, to create affordable housing with an accelerated housebuilding rate. The methods of data collection in each case were slightly different: for the IBA, data was collected through participant observation of public IBA events, interviews with local activists and IBA project managers, and analysis of IBA documentation; for the SPS, the authors reviewed SPS papers and interviewed the officers responsible for implementation in two boroughs; and for the Alliance, the focus was on key policy papers and local media reports.

The analysis suggested that the IBA introduced greater respect for lower-income residents and prevented direct displacement through guaranteeing the right for existing residents to remain and providing periods of low rent; but it was not able to prevent longer-term displacement due to increasing property prices, and it lacked significant public engagement, retaining an expert-led approach. The identification of the Elbe islands as a site for an Olympic Games bid suggested that elements of the entrepreneurial city approach remained in place. Turning to the SPS, the enhanced regulation prevented certain types of building modifications as a way to prevent rent increases and displacement of existing tenants. However, these covered only very specific changes to buildings which were bound to be limited in their effect. Ways around the regulations were all too easy to imagine. Thus the authors concluded that regulation that challenged the neo-liberal paradigm would need "to change the very framework by hitting the core of neoliberalization, such as property rights, maximum rents, legal bases of speculation" (p. 276). Finally, on the Alliance, this promoted a new policy called 'concept bidding' to replace the requirement that public land policy should aim at the highest possible price from land sales and hence income from land transfer tax. Central to this was the requirement that a third of new housing should be subsidised or affordable housing. While the authors detailed how this requirement was not always reached, their main comment was that, given the paucity of investment opportunities in Hamburg, much more progressive changes in housing policy could have been attempted: "The Alliance thus represented only a softly mitigated paradox of urban neoliberalism" (p. 278).

Thus they conclude that while the experiments attempted by the Hamburg state sought to break with neo-liberalism, each can be considered ambiguous in its implementation and showed the continued influence of the entrepreneurial agenda within the state's practices. Here the research used the frame of local state entrepreneurialism to consider three positive challenges to neo-liberalism but found in each case some limitations on their ability to push back against the structural trends.

Conclusions

Political economy is centred on understanding how capital is accumulated and profits are generated within a capitalist society and then, further, the role that the state and by implication state planning can play. Such state activity could be a response to struggles by the working class against their exploitation and/or an attempt to support the profitability of capitalist enterprise by improving the workforce in some relevant way. However, analysis can also be based on the analysis of capitalism as a

crisis-prone system. There are two rather different views of what planning does arising from a political economy perspective, although they are related. From the analysis of capitalism and how its structures largely determine outcomes at the local
scale, planning systems become seen as part of a capitalist state and implicated in
maintaining the profitability of capital and avoiding or responding to economic crises. From here come a long tradition of planning research that shows how planning
fails to prioritise the needs of disadvantaged social groups or operate in the public
interest as it claims, but rather is constrained to facilitate capitalist dynamics.

But there is another view of planning that sees the potential within the planning
system to support the activism of social groups in their struggles with capitalist
interests. Rather than seeing such state provision as being purely functional for
capitalist interests, this perspective sees the working class as responding to their
exploitation by engaging in struggles against capitalists not only through traditional
workplace-related means such as the withdrawal of labour, but through campaigning
for the state to provide benefits. Here the housing, more sanitary urban areas and
better living environments provided through public sector action are a triumph for
the working class. It is largely a matter of chosen emphasis whether one sees the
public sector planning as more involved in supporting the functionality of capitalism
or responding to political struggles by the working class.

Key Theoretical Readings

Campbell and Fainstein (2003) Ch. 5.
Hillier and Metzger (2015) Ch. 6.
Gunder et al. (2018) Chs 14 and 22.

Key Research Readings

Balaban, U. 2011. The Enclosure of Urban Space and Consolidation of the Capitalist
    Land Regime in Turkish Cities. *Urban Studies* 48 (10): 2162–2179.
De Weerdt, J., and M Garcia. 2016. Housing Crisis: The Platform of Mortgage
    Victims (PAH) Movement in Barcelona and Innovations in Governance. *Journal
    of Housing and the Built Environment* 31: 471–493.
MacDonald, H. 2019. Planning for the Public Benefits in the Entrepreneurial City:
    Public Land Speculation and Financialised Regulation. *Journal of Planning
    Education and Research.*
Mbiba, B. 2017. Idioms of Accumulation: Corporate Accumulation by Dispossession
    in Urban Zimbabwe. *International Journal of Urban and Regional Research.*
Savini, F., and M.B. Aalbers. 2016. The De-Contextualisation of Land Use Planning
    Through Financialisation: Urban Redevelopment in Milan. *European Urban and
    Regional Studies* 23 (4): 878–894.

Speake, J. 2017. Urban Development and Visual Culture: Commodifying the Gaze in the Regeneration of Tigné Point, Malta. *Urban Studies* 54 (13): 2919–2934.

Vogelpohl, A., and T. Buchholz (2019). Breaking with Neoliberalization by Restricting the Housing Market: Novel Urban Policies and the Case of Hamburg. *International Journal of Urban and Regional Research.*

Bibliography

Ambrose, Peter J., and Bob Colenutt. 1975. *The Property Machine*. Harmondsworth: Penguin.

Balaban, Utku. 2011. The Enclosure of Urban Space and Consolidation of the Capitalist Land Regime in Turkish Cities. *Urban Studies* 48 (10): 2162–2179.

Broadbent, Thomas Andrew. 2007. *Planning and Profit in the Urban Economy*. London: Routledge.

Campbell, Scott, and Susan Fainstein, eds. 2003. *Readings in Planning Theory*. 2nd ed. Oxford: Blackwell.

Dunleavy, Patrick. 1980. *Urban Political Analysis*. London: Macmillan.

Giddens, Anthony. 1986. *The Constitution of Society: Outline of the Theory of Structuration*. Cambridge: Polity Press.

Gunder, Michael, Ali Madanipour, and Vanessa Watson, eds. 2018. *The Routledge Handbook of Planning Theory*. London: Routledge.

Harvey, David. 1982. *The Limits to Capital*. Oxford: Basil Blackwell.

———. 1985. *The Urbanization of Capital*. Oxford: Blackwell.

———. 1988. *Social Justice and the City*. Oxford: Basil Blackwell.

———. 2010. *The Enigma of Capital and the Crises of Capitalism*. London: Profile.

Hillier, Jean, and Jonathan Metzger, eds. 2015. *Connections: Exploring Contemporary Planning Theory and Practice with Patsy Healey*. Farnham: Ashgate.

Lefebvre, Henri. 2008. *Critique of Everyday Life*. Trans. John Moore. London: Verso.

MacDonald, Heather. 2019. Planning for the Public Benefit in the Entrepreneurial City: Public Land Speculation and Financialized Regulation. *Journal of Planning Education and Research*. https://doi.org/10.1177/0739456X19847519.

Massey, Doreen, and Alejandrina Catalano. 1978. *Capital and Land: Landownership by Capital in Great Britain*. London: Edward Arnold.

Mbiba, Beacon. 2017. Idioms of Accumulation: Corporate Accumulation by Dispossession in Urban Zimbabwe: Idioms of Accumulation. *International Journal of Urban and Regional Research* 41 (2): 213–234.

O'Connor, James. 1973. *The Fiscal Crisis of the State*. New York & London: St. Martin's Press and St. James Press.

O'Neill, Phillip. 2017. Managing the Private Financing of Urban Infrastructure. *Urban Policy and Research* 35 (1): 32–43.

Pasternak, Shiri, and Tia Dafnos. 2017. How Does a Settler State Secure the Circuitry of Capital? *Environment and Planning D: Society & Space* 36 (4): 739–757.

Robbins, Paul. 2012. *Political Ecology: A Critical Introduction*. 2nd ed. Chichester: Wiley-Blackwell.

Savini, F., and M.B. Aalbers. 2016. The De-Contextualisation of Land Use Planning Through Financialisation: Urban Redevelopment in Milan. *European Urban and Regional Studies* 23 (4): 878–894.

Shatkin, Gavin. 2016. The Real Estate Turn in Policy and Planning: Land Monetization and the Political Economy of Peri-Urbanization in Asia. *Cities* 53: 141–149.

Smith, Neil. 1996. *The New Urban Frontier: Gentrification and the Revanchist City*. London: Routledge.

Speake, Janet. 2017. Urban Development and Visual Culture: Commodifying the Gaze in the Regeneration of Tigné Point, Malta. *Urban Studies* 54 (13): 2919–2934.

Tulumello, Simone. 2015. Reconsidering Neoliberal Urban Planning in Times of Crisis: Urban Regeneration Policy in a 'Dense' Space in Lisbon. *Urban Geography* 37 (1): 117–140.

Vogelpohl, Anne, and Tino Buchholz. 2017. Breaking With Neoliberalization by Restricting The Housing Market: Novel Urban Policies and the Case of Hamburg. *International Journal of Urban and Regional Research* 41 (2): 266–281.

De Weerdt, Julie, and Marisol Garcia. 2015. Housing Crisis: The Platform of Mortgage Victims (PAH) Movement in Barcelona and Innovations in Governance. *Journal of Housing and the Built Environment* 31 (3): 471–493.

Chapter 8
Discourse, Knowledge and Governmentality: The Influence of Foucault

Framing the Research

This chapter looks a collection of theoretical approaches which unsettle our taken-for-granted view of the world. Their benefit is that they take an aspect of current planning and make one see it in quite a new and different light. In particular they focus on how actors perceive the governing of the world through planning and support a re-interpretation of such governing. By looking at the way that planning is framed, these concepts enable a new understanding of what planning is. In Chap. 4 the concept of discourse was introduced as a way of understanding how cultural dimensions shape planning practice. There the operation of discourse was linked to the views of individuals and the prevailing culture of organisations. Here a much broader understanding of how society is culturally shaped is adopted with a more critical perspective on the role of actors' perceptions.

This approach largely derives from the work of Michel Foucault, a twentieth-century French intellectual. Foucault's work is wide ranging and ambitious, with a historical sweep that few planning researchers will be able to emulate or feel the need to in the face of contemporary planning problematics. But it has proved an inspiring oeuvre to planning researchers, highlighting aspects of planning practice that have hitherto remained opaque or overlooked. For Foucault the way that discourses shaped society was the key issue of interest. Through historical studies of madness and sexuality, he explored what it meant to be categorised in certain ways and the discursive processes involved. He further showed how institutional arrangements were involved, at societal level, in creating and maintaining these discourses. This means close attention to the way that language is involved in shaping dominant societal understandings. The communications in the mass media, within organisations and even in interpersonal discussion, are both enabled and constrained by language. This is the effect not just of the words that are available but of how they

Y. Rydin, *Theory in Planning Research*, Planning, Environment, Cities, https://doi.org/10.1007/978-981-33-6568-1_8

are understood at a particular time and in a particular context. Thus, work in this paradigm begins from the insight that the way that we perceive, talk about and communicate on issues matters.

If discourses matter, how does this affect the framing of research into planning processes? A starting point is to map out the prevailing patterns revealed by studying language, images and other modes of communication with planning. This can focus on documents of various kinds as texts to be read and analysed, but it can also extend to instances of planning practice, looking at how communication occurs between actors within planning arenas. This picks up from the emphasis on social construction processes in Chap. 4 and communicative action discussed in Chap. 5. However, the Foucauldian approach focusses in more depth on the way that communication can be understood across multiple instances of interaction, looking for the broader patterns rather than studying individual engagements between actors. The idea of discourse is that there are societal patterns that can be understood and are revealing, that shape, enable and constrain the opportunities available to actors and hence their agency. It also goes beyond the worldviews that may prevail in an organisational setting.

This can lead researchers to think of planning processes in terms of the inter-relationships between societal or institution-wide discourses and planning practices. This follows the emphasis that Foucault increasingly placed on practices as opposed to words during the lifetime of his research. The way that the micro-practices of planning are influenced by and in turn influence the prevailing discursive patterns sheds a new light on how planning works and why it often does not work in the way that might be expected from policy pronouncements. Such research can get at the hidden processes involved in planning without assuming in advance particular structural tendencies towards, say, promoting capital accumulation. In this way, Foucauldian research provides a new entry point into debates on structure and agency. It is less actor-centred than the research into planning suggested by the approaches in Chaps. 2, 3, 4, 5 and 6 and yet less structuralist than much work with the political economy tradition of Chap. 7. It is the interface between institutionalised discourses of planning systems and the micro-practices within those planning systems that is revealed by this perspective on planning research.

This provides a new way of looking at power and planning. Planning studies was particularly influenced by the work of Bent Flyvbjerg (1998), who drew on Foucault's ideas for this study of transport and urban planning in Denmark to provide an analysis in which discourse was used to rationalise certain decisions, strategies and lines of action in a way that benefited certain groups within the locality, effectively amplifying their powerful positions. Mapping the discourses of planning and understanding how they shape our perceptions and have agency can indicate what Lukes called the third dimension of power (2005). To reiterate, the first and second dimensions of power are overt and covert power, within an actor-centred viewpoint. The third dimension considers how the way that we look to the world is shaped by such discourses and then has implications for outcomes and the impacts on different groups in society. It means that individuals and groups do not always take action that is in their interests because of the influence of institutionalised discourses present within the world.

This means that planning policies that would appear to have one set of goals may be shown to be serving quite different goals. Planning presents itself as operating in the public interest, but this self-presentation cannot be assumed to be the case. There will be institutionally embedded reasons why particular forms of the public interest dominate within a planning system, and this can be shown empirically. The key argument is that the discursive patterns surrounding planning processes and associated practices have implications for how power operates within society and how governing is, therefore, achieved through planning. Thus, research within this approach tends to raise questions about how planning relates to broader modes of governing and the implications for the operation of power of the complex ways that discourses, practices and institutions are interconnected.

One way in which this analysis has been developed is through seeing planning as a form of governmentality, in which actors come to see their interests aligned with those of the state, through the influence of societal and policy discourses and through the operation of 'governmental technologies'. These include processes of categorisation, classification and statistical representation; this is discussed further later. This perspective does not assess this as 'tricking' people as part of a strategy on the part of governmental actors; rather this is about understanding how the processes of representation circulating within society at a general level impact on the relationships between the state and civil society and, in this case, on the operation of planning systems.

The notion that these societal dynamics lead to changes in how self-interest is understood and actors' practices are shaped is close to the insights from using the aligned concept of performativity. Coming from modes of analysis that play close attention to language use, the idea of performativity is that the act of using discourses through specific practices can give rise to entities that otherwise are presented as pre-existing those discursive acts and practices (Rydin et al. 2018b). Thus, many of the categories and elements of planning practice that seem self-evidently to exist—such as community say—only come into effect through those acts and practices. This has been used within the new cultural economy (Callon 2010) to discuss how markets are generated and operate, but it is also relevant to how planning systems work. The key question is not what elements planning practices engage with— communities, evidence, places, sectors, categories of behaviour—but rather how these are created through the discursive dimensions and micro-practices of planning systems.

Dynamics of Analysis: Key Concepts

The following discussion begins by unpacking the nature of circulating discourses more fully, before considering the nature of knowledge as power (and vice versa) and then concluding with an account of the governmentality framework.

Circulating Discourses

One of the first insights to be taken from a Foucauldian perspective is the importance of societal discourses and how they frame issues and solutions. It leads to a body of work mapping the nature of discourses circulating within planning practice, particularly within planning documentation. Such work is typically based upon a form of discourse analysis of such documentation, although the precise nature of this can vary. For example, Tozer's analysis of the discourse of local climate change planning in Canada showed the work done by language and the discourses of sustainability and climate change circulating within Canadian local government (Tozer 2018). By looking at sustainability plans, a discourse analysis identified different aspects of sustainability (social, environmental, economy) as well as topics related to culture and cross-cutting themes. This kind of analysis can also be used to support arguments for hegemonic positions within policy processes (Sager 2015).

But the dynamic issue is how these circulating discourses have an impact. One way is through the imposition of categories that are then taken for granted. Thus, in one of Foucault's classic analysis, what counts as madness is shown to be contingent on particular discourses and institutions of a certain time. Categories are not self-evident or pre-existing or 'out there' but rather created by these discursive practices. The discursive analysis questions everything: how ways of presenting the world arose and what the implications are. Planning practice is full of categories: land allocations categorised on a map, designations for a variety of conservation and regeneration reasons, development that does and does not need explicit consent, and so on. A discursive approach queries these rather than taking them on their own, explicit terms.

Pollution is a good example here. This has been famously defined by Mary Douglas as 'matter out of place' (Douglas 1966). So describing something as a pollutant puts it on one side of the appropriate elements to be found in air or water or the ground. Some pollutants may be considered obvious—as with visible smoke. Others are invisible but detected by chemical analysis and move to the 'wrong' side of the pollution boundary due to evidence of harm, usually to health but also to environmental systems. Changes in scientific understanding of the impacts of polluting elements and changes in the ability to detect smaller amounts of existing pollutants or new pollutants all alter the way that pollution is defined. It took a campaign to turn lead in the air into a pollutant and then into something to be measured and regulated. The decision by the US Environment Agency to consider carbon a pollution reframed the climate change caused by carbon emissions into a pollution issue and thus put it under the remit of pollution control measures. These categories are linked through to issues of knowledge discussed later.

In addition to categorisation, a variety of other concepts are often used within the analysis to try and pinpoint how discourses have agency. A paper discussed here uses the idea of 'ruts'; another deploys that of 'fantasmic' logics. Calculations are often a key part of emphasising the authority of a discourse alongside other markers of evidence, expertise and knowledge (Rydin et al. 2018a). Or there can be recourse to a variety of cultural tropes that carry weight such as pathos, the use of the jeremiad, invoking significant images that act as metonymy such as national signifiers. Techniques from rhetorical analysis can be introduced here to assist the research, and this has proved particularly useful in the environmental planning field (Myerson and Rydin 1996).

Hajer has provided a further way of understanding the impact of circulating discourses through his concept of the 'discourse coalition' (Hajer 1995). This derives from an engagement between Foucauldian thought and Habermasian accounts (discussed in Chap. 5), where the bringing-together of actors to deliberate together is emphasised. The discourse coalition concept draws attention to the way that effects arise from groups of actors—coalitions—working in concert. However, while conventional coalitions comprise actors who meet with each other and communicate directly, the discourse coalition concept suggests that the effects arise from a group of actors using a specific discourse. This discourse ties the group together even though they may never meet or even be aware of each other. The impact arises from the repeated use of this discourse by different actors in different contexts. This repetition embeds the key tropes of the discourse in everyday communication and thus affects the way that actors interact and the resultant outcomes.

This detailed focus on discourses and how they are operationalised through the details of micro-practices can throw new emphasis on the artefacts of planning. Here Foucauldian-inspired approaches can come close to the material turn discussed further in Chap. 9. The point is that documents, plans, models and other forms of artefacts can play an active role in generating, maintaining and circulating discourses. The concept of the boundary object, taken from museum studies originally (Leigh Star 2010), has proved useful in accounting for how certain artefacts can transmit specific discourses and governmental technologies across organisational boundaries. This will be shown in some of the research reviewed later.

Knowledge as Power

One aspect that carries considerable importance within a Foucauldian approach is what counts as knowledge (and what does not). Foucault put a particular emphasis on the construction of knowledge within society and how this constitutes the operation of power within society. He saw knowledge-power or *savoir-pouvoir* as an indivisible duality, two sides of the same coin. Thus, a study of how knowledge and power are intertwined becomes a key way of understanding society and of the role of planning within that society. Power here is not a resource held by a social actor. The influence of Foucault goes alongside a rise in a relational perspective (see also Chap. 9) in which power is seen as diffused throughout society, rather than concentrated in certain social groupings. It is a capillary action not a stock, the flow of blood through the vessels of the body social and politic rather than the store of bags in the blood bank.

The idea of knowledge as power is a potent one for planning studies. After all John Friedmann famously defined planning as knowledge in action (Friedmann 1987). Much planning work is about synthesising across different forms of knowledge—social, economic and environmental, for example—and there are multiple examples of assessment systems that constitute knowledge claims. Sharp and Richardson's work uses a Foucauldian framework to good effect to understand Environmental Impact Assessment (Sharp and Richardson 2001). More broadly one could point to the use of statistics as part of the survey-analysis-plan framework for planning (see Chap. 2). Data, statistics and information are all seen as essential prerequisites to planning activity, whether plan-making or regulation. The importance of such sources and the categorisations that they use was analysed by Foucault in his studies of bio-politics, which saw the politics of population change as shaped by the data used to define that population change. What is involved here is the enactment of the population categories contained in the statistical data through politics. Again, the categories emerge through the circulation of discourses, here discourses of quantitative statistics which are constituted as knowledge.

Considering the issue of pollution more fully, the focus on knowledge and particularly quantitative statistical knowledge raises the importance of considering how pollution is measured. What counts as the level of pollution of a given pollutant? This involves a range of assumptions and decisions. How much of the pollutant—defined as a chemical element or compound—is found in a given quantity of the relevant media—air, water or land? How much of the media is 'captured' to work out this quantity? When in the day or night? Where is the measuring equipment located? How often is the pollutant recorded? Or is there real-time monitoring? Once the details of how the pollutant is measured are decided, then what is the benchmark against which this is measured? Not all presence of the pollutant will count as a pollution episode or sign of contamination. Thus, guidelines have to be drawn up by key organisations, such as the World Health Organisation or the European Union or the US Environment Agency.

One issue that has been very prone to calculative practices is sustainable development. The association of this issue with ambiguity and multiple definitions is widely noted. As sustainable development is defined either in rather generic terms (as with the elegant, fascinating but quite frustrating definition in the Brundtland report, WCED 1987) or through the combination of economic, social, environmental and (sometimes) institutional aspects, then such ambiguity and proliferation should perhaps not be unexpected. But this does mean that in specific contexts, whether particular cities, countries, industrial sectors or companies, there is a perceived need to provide a more specific definition. There has been considerable growth in sustainability indicator sets as a means of providing definition in place of ambiguity and offering an opportunity for calculating progress on this issue. How sustainability is so defined not only provides more detail on calculative processes but also suggests implications for policy and practice. A different definition in Mexico as opposed to France, in New York as opposed to Texas, in housebuilding as opposed to shopping centre development and in this development company as opposed to that—all these have implications for how planning practices may take place.

The Foucauldian approach highlights the importance of what counts as knowledge within society, and this can be brought down into the planning arena to understand planning practice more fully. There is a close link here with the field of science and technology studies or the sociology of scientific knowledge. These provide detailed understanding of how particular knowledge claims arise, how contestation over these claims occurs and how this is resolved so that particular claims become warranted or accepted as legitimate. In environmental policy contexts, the work of Sheila Jasanoff has been particularly influential with her idea of 'serviceable truths' suggesting the kind of knowledge that is found within planning contexts (Jasanoff 2015). There is a fine line here between identifying the kinds of knowledge that can be shown to be sufficient to guide planning practice, policy and decision-making and developing a critique of that knowledge, including highlighting what is excluded by constructing knowledge in this way. Some research has also drawn on the insights of Actor-Network Theory, with its roots in understanding scientific practices; this will be covered in Chap. 9 as it has a distinctive concern with materiality within assemblages that fits with the relational approaches discussed there.

Governmentality

Interesting as the study of societal discourses may be in itself, Foucault provided in a late set of lectures at the Collège de France a suggestion of how they may be implicated in projects of the state, and thus potentially in urban policy and planning (Foucault 2010). These lectures were suggestive rather than a fully fledged theory, and much of their influence has been filtered through the work of Miller and Rose (2006), who have provided an account of the relevance of the concepts outlined for the contemporary period of neo-liberalism.

The key concept here is that of governmentality. The idea of governmentality responds to the apparent lack of direct capacity that urban governance theorists also identified but suggests that there has been a rather different kind of response. Governmentality describes a set of institutional arrangements and prevailing discourses in which governmental projects are not delivered by explicit public sector action but rather by other actors delivering on the state's behalf. Thus, the state does not govern directly (as assumed in Chap. 2 and elsewhere) or even in collaboration with others (as in governance approaches discussed in Chap. 5) but rather governs from a distance. Governing is not about direct action but about the conduct of conduct, shaping how other actors behave (see, e.g. Bresnihan 2019).

A key aspect of this is shaping actors' perceptions of how they should and even want to behave. This is called self-responsibilisation whereby other non-state actors feel it incumbent upon them to take actions which will deliver a government project (Raco 2003; Raco and Imrie 2016). A key aspect of this is the reshaping of actors' identities so that they see it as in their interests or in line with their values to undertake these actions. This is where the power of discursive formations is again felt, in the way that words can shape understandings, categories and perceptions. In particular, it has been suggested that these forms of discourse, emphasising steering and self-responsibilisation are consistent with the trend towards neo-liberalism discussed in Chap. 7 and with the growth of post-politics (Etherington and Jones 2018).

A variety of governmental technologies are implicated in such governing from a distance, and particular emphasis has been put on the way that knowledge and associated calculation (as discussed earlier) are involved. For example, the governmentality approach can provide a new reading of new public management (NPM), the shift in the way governing has occurred since the late twentieth century. NPM refers to the way that direct public provision has increasingly been replaced by contractual arrangements that require public services to be provided in line with targets, with performance measured by a range of indicators; the aim is to align the indicators and the targets. In the case of some services, incentives and sanctions are invoked when performance indicators fall short of desired targets. While NPM has often been justified from a rational choice perspective (see Chap. 3) as a way of aligning the incentives of individual actors to drive decision-making in line with public sector goals, it can also be seen as a more societal trend in which discourses circulate at the institutional or societal level so as to enable larger-scale shifts, say towards neo-liberalism. From a Foucauldian perspective the strength of NPM is the way that prevailing discourses result in service providers changing how they operated regardless of the incentives and sanctions they faced. They internalise the targets, and this changes their behaviour, rather than rational calculation based on likely performance and costs/benefits. The discourses of NPM are as important as the institutional arrangements and are intrinsic to the apparatus of contracts, indicators and targets, which collectively could be considered governmental technologies.

An example is provided by De Wilde and Franssen (2016), who looked at how deprivation is measured within the neighbourhood policy for Amsterdam, thereby showing how such deprivation is constructed and becomes a social fact from the use of particular metrical devices within planning texts. The process of quantification is seen as a practice that constitutes policy itself, not a technical or neutral activity. The research focusses on the quantified object of the Normal Amsterdam Level (NAP), which is used to in the Amsterdam Neighbourhood Policy programme and the analysis traced the life-span of the NAP from birth to it afterlife (after the policy programme ended, the NAP was still referred to by politicians). It looked at how it acted as a generative devise that helped to assemble and organise the world. This involved a variety of techniques labelled as semiotic, statistical and visual techniques. Through these, 'hard' facts about deprived neighbourhood were produced to justify distinguishing these areas in terms of policy and specific interventions. The planning approach was legitimised through such quantification which judges the targeted neighbourhood against the idea of a city-wide average. The dynamics involved here included: simplification of a complex social reality to a figure (or a small set of figures), objectification in an apparently transparent way so that it seems as if the policy problem and intervention can be clearly seen, normalisation to emphasise the potential for comparison of neighbourhoods using the NAP, and the creation of evidence to justify and legitimise policy interventions.

Research Themes

The research papers reviewed here concern the mapping of discourses in planning, the role of knowledge and resistance to the governmentality mode of governing.

The Discursive Nature of Planning

It has been suggested above that the identification of the importance of discourses in shaping the 'taken for granted' within planning processes can lead to a strand of research that seeks to specify and define these discourses into distinct narratives or storylines. However, there is also the possibility for richer and more complex forms of planning research looking at how discourses emerge, evolve, interconnect with each other and are shaped by their context. Three examples are discussed here.

Daly's research (2016) underpinned an account of the impact of the neo-liberal agenda on spatial planning and urban development in Ireland during the so-called Celtic Tiger period of 2002–2007. He explored "the genealogy of governance land-scapes, institutional rationalities and the analogous restructuring of planning, together with the intertwined dynamics between them, through which planning policy decisions were taken and legitimated" (p. 1644). Methodologically, Daly used a discourse analytic approach to key public policy documents, including the National Spatial Strategy but also material in national archives from different periods of Irish planning. He also employed two case studies of housing development in the Upper Shannon region and large-scale commercial development in County Meath; here he relied also on local authority records including planning officer reports, planning statistics and meeting minutes. This was supplemented by a database drawn from online local authority planning records for 2002–2007 and detailed records of unfinished housing developments from the National Housing Survey.

The initial focus of the research was on the publication of the National Spatial Strategy in 2002 and how it acted as a key discursive resource for the national state to facilitate capital switching (see Chap. 7) into property development and thereby contribute to growth of GDP. This was set against the backdrop of a "remarkably stable compact among society at large" (p. 1648), which saw supply-side macro-economic policies as necessary for economic and social reasons and which functioned at ideological levels and shaped institutions. The modern Irish planning system emerged in this context and the National Spatial Strategy reflected this discourse, although Daly also acknowledged the influence of the European intellectual reformulation of planning as spatial planning with an emphasis on designating growth nodes and improving means of connectivity of all kinds (people, goods, communications). Daly, thus, showed how neo-liberal thinking became enmeshed in the restructuring of Irish spatial planning through key policy documentation; he further argued that this implicated Irish planning in the speculative property boom associated with the Celtic Tiger period and its eventual collapse.

The consequences of this could be seen in the two case studies. In Upper Shannon a massive oversupply of new housing resulted, with sufficient land zoned for residential development to accommodate a 75% increase in the population, much of it in unsustainable locations outside urban areas (p. 1652). Here he noted, from archival research, "the typically perfunctory and compliant level of assessment by planning in cases of planning applications for major new development proposals" (p. 1652). In County Meath, he found a series of planning applications for major commercial development on remote, un-zoned and un-serviced sites being granted permission without (after one initial case) any opposition.

Daly did not 'blame' Irish planners for the property bubble but rather pointed to "a distinct narrowing of intellectual horizons" (p. 1655) and a lack of critical introspection, which meant the planning profession had been unwilling to address the emergent boom-and-bust cycle but rather fuelled the rate of urban development. This 'narrowing of … horizons' is exactly the kind of dynamic that attention to discourses can pinpoint; and, as Daly suggests, critical introspection is necessary to challenge taken-for-granted viewpoints and ways of seeing, talking and writing within planning.

Fuller and West (2017) similarly used a discourse analytic approach to consider how 'urban austerity' was constructed in the local authority of Birmingham, beginning from the premise that this was an under-explored aspect of accounts of the urban crisis; they saw "neoliberalism as partly an incomplete discursive formation" (p. 2088) and set out to explore this. They positioned themselves as operating with a post-structuralist theory of discourse and hegemony but then amplified this with the 'logics' approach identifying three logics—social, political and fantasmatic—although the analysis concentrated on the last two. Political logics relate to the ways of thwarting antagonism and preventing new demands being articulated so as to disrupt the status quo. Fantasmatic logics involve "both foretelling of disaster and guaranteeing future harmony" (p. 2092) so as to smooth over difficulties; they are involved in securing the identification of subjects and embedding these in the social imaginary. Fuller and West were particularly interested in how such fantasmatic logics were involved in 'crisis talk' within austerity urbanism (see later). They also acknowledged that these discursive formations are imbricated with socio-spatial relations.

Birmingham City Council was chosen as the municipality had a long-term profile in urban regeneration and economic development, as well as being subject to considerable austerity measures (i.e. budget cuts and their consequences). The methods deployed included analysis of relevant policy documents, political speeches and public debates in the media; this was conducted at both national and local levels, and a total of 70 documents were analysed together with a database of 32 media reports from 2010 to 2015. In addition, interviews were undertaken with 15 senior managers and officers in departments within the City Council dealing with economic development, regeneration and planning policy. The focus of the interviews was on the role of political rhetoric and the affective in the context of the prevailing austerity measures: budget and service reductions, restructuring of services and efficiency drives. All the material was coded and examined using NVivo software.

The analysis began from the insight that 'austerity urbanism' had been character-ised in terms of processes of 'destructive creativity', followed by 'deficit politics' and 'devolved risk' down to the local level; across this, 'crisis talk' was likely to be a critical element. However Fuller and West raised the question of "why substantial, collective resistance to austerity is lacking" (p. 2090), why passivity appeared to be the norm. They argued that many accounts of austerity urbanism fail to comprehend that the hegemonic and institutionalised aspects of neo-liberalism need to be con-tinually performed in order to become 'business as usual', to be normalised in this way. A discourse-based approach is well placed to examine these normalisation processes.

The analysis identified a number of ways that the two dimensions of fantasmatic logics were expressed discursively. For example, the Council blamed an external 'other' for austerity, fatalistically pointing up the futility of resistance; at the same time, they posited a 'beatific fantasy' in which "austerity is presented as the harbin-ger of Birmingham's economic recovery" (p. 2096), often drawing on the industrial heritage of the city and past economic survival. This discursive combination meant that austerity, poverty and welfare dependency could justifiably co-exist with local economic growth and job creation. Indeed, austerity could even be recast as a virtue, leading to future economic development. Within this, the decline of local govern-ment capacity and the need to rely on market-based business models were accepted; local government, therefore, repositioned themselves as a civic entrepreneur.

Thus, the analysis provided a picture wherein "these logics and their interactions with the everyday is complex, with actors reconciling multiple logics and socio-spatial relations in a mixture of resistance and acquiescence" (p. 2097). It detailed the prevailing discourses but further identified how they were maintained and ren-dered difficult to challenge or even look beyond.

A similarly rich and many-sided analysis was provided by Lucas and Warman (2018) in their study of discourse coalitions and storylines around forestry and cli-mate change planning in Tasmania, Australia. They sought to disrupt the polarisa-tion around environmental issues that was notable in Tasmania and combined a focus on entrenched discourse coalitions and storylines with the concept of 'ruts', which perpetuate such entrenchment over time. There also made a connection to Beck's idea of sub-politics that he developed within his *Risk Society* (Beck 1992). Within such sub-politics, negotiations moved outside the realm of formal politics or corporatist relations with major economic interests and, in decentralised encoun-ters, opened up expert systems to contestation by lay groups.

Their research sought to understand how "polarized attitudes formed through disputes over the use of natural resources can affect the social organization and public understanding of subsequent environmental conflicts" (p. 988). The method-ology adopted was a mixed one. They drew on the Hobart Values Survey of 522 local participants that looked at how attitudes to climate change intersected with other values and issues. A sample of nine respondents were then asked to engage in a series of repeated interviews to discuss this in more depth. These interview tran-scripts were analysed for narrative structures. In relation to the forestry activities, the researchers looked at public records of negotiations, particularly around the

Select Committee hearing of the Tasmanian Parliament into the Tasmanian Forests Agreement Bill 2012; 12 days of hearings were analysed alongside over 130 submissions, together with various other relevant public documents. The discourse analysis of the entire body of data was guided by the questions: what were the significant conditions that made the process possible, and how did the process impact or disrupt polarised discourse coalitions?

Their analysis showed how the 'ruts' were formed out of certain discourse coalitions and associated storylines, and how these emphasised certain values and defined risk in certain ways. They identified these as a resource development discourse coalition and a reactive conservation discourse coalition, each associated with a number of storylines such as promoting 'balanced' use of resources and avoiding natural resources being 'locked away', on the one hand, and protecting the local environment which was seen as 'wilderness', on the other. These ruts were shown to be persistent over time, from conflicts over the construction of hydroelectric dams through to later disputes over forestry activities. The divide between environmental arguments for protection and economic arguments for local prosperity that had formed around the dam project persisted into the forestry debates.

The researchers showed how these ruts were also present within climate change debates, even though local forestry interests arguably had common cause with environmentalist here. Statistical analysis of the Hobart Values Survey here supplemented the discourse analysis. This enabled them to identify the shared factors associated with the membership of the two discourse coalitions. For the 'pro-forest development' plus 'unconcerned about climate change' coalition, these were concern for security and social order, prioritising tradition and maintaining the status quo. For the opposing coalition, the factors were mainly care for nature. There were also different framings of risk, seeing it variously as a threat to the degradation of nature, a threat to traditional hierarchies or a threat from regulation to individual freedoms. There are resonances with the use of cultural theory discussed in Chap. 4; however, the researchers here went on to look in detail at the discursive practices of the interviewees to show how these different tropes were combined together to underpin the two discourse coalitions in terms of a discourse of nature-as-wilderness or of human-authority-over-nature.

Looking at the case study of negotiations around forestry, they detailed an attempt within the realm of sub-politics to disrupt these ruts and develop a more collaborative process. In this case they found evidence of the reflexive modernisation that Beck has suggested is a more positive mode of policy and politics. They identified enabling conditions for the emergence of negotiations: the emergence of new storylines associated with the sub-political activities of environmental NGOs and the growth of corporate social responsibility in the forest sector, shifts in the market conditions for the timber industry and a change in government to a Green-Labour ruling coalition. This resulted in a storyline that emphasised the costs of conflict and the need for 'peace' emerging alongside existing storylines; this supported negotiations in sub-political spaces, sidestepping traditional negotiating arenas. The result was an agreement that largely survived later changes in government.

This study, like Fuller and West's, showed some of the complexities of the ways that discourses operate within planning processes, and the potential for challenge to established and institutionalised patterns. They suggested three conclusions. First, sub-political negotiating spaces may be better suited to disrupting entrenched polarisations. Second, for risk negotiations between polarised discourse coalitions to be effective, there needs to be a mutual understanding of the socially constructed nature of risk. Third, disruptive moments in the political or economic environment can allow new storylines to emerge and new discourse coalitions to become established. Thus, in addition to mapping the discourses and specifying the discourse dynamics, this research used these concepts to suggest new means of changing established discursive and institutional patterns.

Knowledge Within Planning

The work inspired by Foucault on the role of knowledge within planning studies starts from the centrality of discourses in shaping what counts as knowledge. For example, Tafon et al. (2019) put a concern with discourse centre stage in their study of offshore wind energy in Estonia, where they focussed on the proposed wind farm at Hiiumaa and the associated roll-out of Estonia's first marine spatial plan. The research had two elements. The first related to strategies of political mobilisation that were deployed including the rival discourses of expertise and sustainability. The second looked at how discursive and legalistic strategies were used to displace key areas of contestation, depoliticise the issues and legitimate the offshore wind energy plan. This analysis was situated within a view of marine spatial planning as employing a modernist discourse of rational technocratic planning and thereby contributing to depoliticisation, marginalisation of opponents and the promotion of neo-liberal forms of governmentality.

A sixfold conceptualisation of discourse was adopted as a relational social practice, radically contingent in its interpretation, articulated in moments which yield certain orders of meaning, involving nodal points and empty signifiers, related to a particular space and positioning subjects within the discourse. This helped guide the detailed analysis of the data that was collected. Their methodology centred around ways that different social actors symbolised and responded to the events involved in the Hiiumaa wind farm and the marine spatial plan more generally, and they traced this over five years from 2012 to 2017. Of particular interest was the emergence of a resistant subjectivity among residents in the vicinity of the Hiiumaa infrastructure.

The methodology comprised 17 open-ended interviews with local resident objectors (13), the Estonian Wind Power Association (1) and central government (3) of 2–3 hours in length. Interviews were recorded, transcribed and coded through an inductive process focussing on discourses, interests, priorities and power dynamics, and based on the above sixfold characterisation of the role that discourses played. In addition, there were four open-ended email questionnaires with county planning representatives. These, therefore, covered the three groups of opponents to the wind farm proposal: local residents, local state actors and central state actors. Finally, there was an analysis of documentation and also site visits.

The researchers found that rival discourses of expertise and sustainability had been integral to the process by which residents and municipal actors contested the offshore wind project. Contestation centred around the role of local knowledge held by residents about the local geology of karst limestone rock and the incidence of sinkholes in Hiiumaa, particularly one near a certain village, Pihla. The question was whether construction for the wind farm would destabilise the water table and cause further sinkholes. Residents asked for independent scientific studies, to be corroborated in an Environmental Impact Assessment (EIA). However, such studies were postponed, and there was a shift to the use of a Strategic Environmental Assessment (SEA) in place of an EIA; an SEA, which focussed on the marine spatial planning process rather than individual project approval, and had reduced requirements for scientific evidence in the form of formal studies and less detailed analysis.

They followed through the decision-making on the marine spatial plan and the way that discourses were involved in the alignment of interests around it. They saw the 'we-don't-want-wind-farms' discourse acting as a nodal point or empty signifier for a coalition of interests: "Empty signifiers are thus able to bind differences together, while conferring a more overdetermined identity. But in so doing, they may also conceal the differences they connect" (p.12). The ability by certain actors to construct a common opposition was at the expense of assumed homogeneity among the opposing interests. The researchers then examined how discourses were used—alongside legal resources—by developers, planners and a legal court to displace contested issues and depoliticise them. On the one hand, 'othering' was a key discursive resource used to put key actors into different and divergent camps in opposition to each other hand; on the other, 'dis-othering' was used to emphasise common interests, such as evoking the climate change agenda. These tactics disrupted the opposition to the scheme.

Thus, by following the discursive tactics—including the construction of relevant knowledge—within the planning processes around offshore wind power, the researchers highlighted the interplay of means of consolidating and disrupting the opposition to the project. The tactics of local residents were able to return "a seemingly necessary and unproblematic OWE [offshore wind energy farm] to the realm of politics", while the tactics of proponents of the scheme sought "to provide ideological cover for, and stabilize the precarious OWE scheme" (p. 16). This led the authors to suggest that the pre-planning moment—before the formal processes get under way—is the most conducive for local residents to voice their concerns in an effective way. Central to such research is the framing of knowledge as a discourse with a range of discursive interactions and links to shifting coalitions of interests.

In their study of climate change planning in Denmark, Berthou and Ebbesen (2016) began from a classic form of discourse analysis but then situated this within a broader governmentality perspective and looked at the role of knowledge including calculative practices. They looked at ten climate change plans prepared at the municipal level in Denmark and examined the discourses in play to identify a number of themes and patterns that were clearly dominant across the documents. They then used 'abductive' reasoning to explore the processes giving rise to these themes and patterns. In doing so they drew on fieldwork in two municipalities, comprising participant observation of meetings and seminars, informal and semi-structured interviews with public sector policy actors and (in one location) interviews plus focus group discussion with local citizens. However, it is interesting to note that while they relied on the fieldwork research to build a narrative explaining the results and exploring the implications of the discourse analysis, they did not use the interview and conversational material for further discourse analysis. Indeed, they noted that there was sometimes a conflict or tension between the oral and the textual material, and they chose to focus just on the policy documentation, arguing that "we are mainly interested in the reality the documents produce" (p. 502).

They identified a distinctive discursive pattern across these plans: three justifications in terms of the need for action on climate change; the responsibility on behalf of local authorities to act and the potential win-win outcomes; the identification of target areas for action based on carbon budgets; targets defined in reduction percentages and some other variation in objectives; and methods linked primarily to public services and emphasising collaboration between municipalities, business and citizens. This then led to an exploration of how governmentality processes may be implicated in climate change policy at the local level. They did this by using a structure of headings: fields of visibility, forms of knowledge, formation of identities and technical aspects. Using the term 'fields of visibility' to consider which issues were made explicit and which were not, they pointed to how municipalities were defining climate governance as a matter of governing 'systems'. Furthermore, this was presented "as evidence and legitimate sites of interventions, as outcomes can be tangibly measured and since they are sites of interest that the municipalities have a right and duty to govern" (p. 506). This was contrasted with the private realm of the everyday lives of citizens, even though the one clearly had implications for the other. Thus citizen-oriented activities were "pooled into another area" (p. 507) and denoted as awareness raising, behaviour change campaigns and information distribution.

Turning to the kinds of knowledge that were invoked in climate change governing, they noted the emphasis on demonstrating numerically that carbon reductions are compatible with economic goals and then suggested that the identification of win-win options can tip over into a form of neo-liberalism and deference to the market. This was linked closely with technical aspects and the importance of calculative practices in climate management, since carbon reductions cannot be seen but had to be calculated to be rendered visible. They again turned to the implications for citizens, arguing that such calculative practices had the consequence of rendering the citizen passive. Finally, looking at the formation of identities, Berthou and Ebbesen interpreted the discourse analysis and the individual documents as showing a distinction between the municipality as "the responsible, authoritative, problem-defining, and problem-solving actor" and the citizen, again, as passive (p. 512). This passive citizen was supposed—through enhanced awareness of climate change, more information and knowledge of how-to-change behaviour—to

make "good choices" and self-regulate their behaviour in the name of climate protection. This fitted with the Foucauldian emphasis on self-responsibilisation but
Berthou and Ebbesen's discourse analytic research interestingly connected this with
passivity on the part of the citizen in the political realm.

Thus a discourse analysis was linked to the role that knowledge plays, particularly through calculative practices, and how this distinguishes expertise from passive citizens while also requiring self-regulation from the citizenry.

Resistance Within Governmentality

The governmentality framework emphasises the way that actors outside the state
'self-responsibilise' to deliver the state's project, enabling governing by steering
from a distance. However, much planning research within this framework has come
to explore the ways that actors resist these dynamics. The final two examples of
research discussed in this chapter are of this kind.

Rosol (2014) provided a study of a planning conflict in Vancouver, Canada, from
a governmentality perspective, arguing that this provided a more nuanced response
to the identification of post-political times by Swyngedouw (2009, 2011) among
others. While accepting that the governmentality idea of governing through steering
the conduct of others accorded well with the idea of depoliticisation of contentious
issues, Rosol argued that this could be too one-sided an account of how these issues
are handled in practice. Therefore, he highlighted the importance of resistance and
seeing such resistance as ongoing and not a single moment of rebellion. Resistance
was not external to power; it was intrinsic to the relations of power. Rosol used the
concept of counter-conduct to capture this framing of resistance within his research.

The research took the form of a case study of an application for rezoning an
industrial area on the southern fringe of Vancouver City for a 'big-box' store, a form
of highway-oriented retail development. The application was approved after a three-
day public hearing in November 2007. The methodology was not discussed in any
detail but appears to have involved closely following this case, through documents
and observation, as well as an unspecified number of interviews. In particular, Rosol
focussed on "practices and strategies used in this struggle' by members of an organisation known as CVIC (Community Vision Implementation Committee), which
had been charged by the City Council "to watch over the implementation of the
results of a participatory neighbourhood planning process" (p. 71), that is the
CityPlan Community Visions. This participatory process operated at the city level
but also more locally; thus, the big-box application was considered by local residents to be in conflict with the Sunset Community Vision for the adjoining area.

Using this material, Rosol identified a key aspect of governmentality that operated by side-lining the CVIC, "disqualifying the expression of opposition by members of the CVIC as inappropriate" and requiring it to "define itself as a neutral,
information-sharing forum, which did not see it as their role to 'take sides on
issues'" (p. 77). However, Rosol also found three modes of resistance as

counter-conduct to this positioning of the community organisation. First, the CVIC struggled to get acknowledged as a legitimate actor with a position vis-à-vis this controversy, so they spoke out in opposition in the name of the CVIC. Second, the CVIC expounded the argument that they were basing their opposition on the defence of a formal city policy, that is the Sunset Community Vision. Third, they sought to influence the conduct of others by using knowledge of the rezoning and the City Visions processes to get city councillors and committee members to reconsider the appropriateness of what they were doing. In addition, local actors—including members of the CVIC—created other forums for expressing their views; this was a challenge to depoliticisation. Rosol characterised this as "attempting to 'not be governed like that'" (p. 80). The governmentality framework allowed for identification of strategies of resistance in a case that could otherwise be positioned within post-politics, that is a process of neutralisation of conflict.

Certomà and Notteboom (2017) provided another example of research that showed the ways in which governing at a distance both works and is resisted. Their research looked at community gardens, a topic of increasing interest within planning studies. They noted that research on such community-based activism tends to position it as part of the emergence of an urban counterculture, aligned with the 'right to the city' tradition. It is thus oppositional politics, in line with the approaches discussed in Chap. 6. However, Certomà and Notteboom argued that "this perspective, while offering an important interpretative key, does not allow an in-depth appreciation of the phenomenon" (p. 52). They therefore turned to the governmentality framework and asked: "what kind of governmentality does it [community gardening] build upon?" They considered that this provided a new lens onto the kinds of informal urbanism represented by such collective gardening, one which saw urban gardening as not just a spontaneous, grassroots phenomenon but rather one that was also mediated by local authorities and private landowners. Urban gardening was not necessarily local authority led (as with council allotments) or generated from within civil society.

Their case study was of Ghent in Belgium, a city that had consciously adopted a self-image of the 'pocket size metropolis', not cosmopolitan but rather open and creative. It had attracted young and highly educated people, interested in sustainable lifestyles and contact with nature. The city government had been based around a coalition of parties, lately including green politicians. Two urban gardening platforms existed to bring together community interests and link them with policy makers and the municipal administration. Thus the urban gardening movement could be seen as integral to the self-presentation of Ghent and how it was governed to produce the green, dense, creative, sustainable city at a small scale, one that was also assumed to be the most economically productive.

Within Ghent, the researchers looked at three projects with common characteristics: including some vegetable plots, common areas and facilities; involving participatory processes; located on the periphery and former industrial land with the goal of ecological restoration; and engaging with local people, particularly cultural minorities and disadvantaged groups. The methodology involved six months of desk-based research and fieldwork including analysis of the urban context and both scientific and grey literature. Founding members, group leaders and key sector representatives for the urban gardening projects were interviewed, including at least one person who had been involved from the beginning. Seven semi-structured interviews amounting to 20 hours of material were supplemented with transect walks, during which multimedia data was collected (presumably photos, sound recordings and/or videos).

The three projects provided examples of the different ways that the urban gardening communities engaged with the dominant rationality of governing in Ghent. The De Boerse Poort project was located at the intersection of two working-class areas and a nature reserve. Its planning rationality was seen as "a product of the *bobos'* [bourgeois-bohemian] image of Ghent as a modern, inclusive, progressist (sic), grassroot and environmentally friendly city" (p. 65) and thus fits with the prevailing mode of governmentality. However, the De Site project involved an organisation (Samenlevensopbouw) which used community gardening as a form of welfare provision for marginalised, deprived and ethnic groups; the provision of self-cultivated food was a significant addition to household budgets. And the 't Landhuis project had roots in "the extreme left-anarchist urban counterculture for an autonomous reappropriation of city space" (p. 66) with the aim of operating separately from the municipality.

Certomà and Notteboom concluded that these projects sometimes involved a form of resistance that was entangled with the formal system rather than either simply complying with dominant modes of governing or simply challenging them. They saw potential for actors activating connections with the institutions of governmentality to their mutual benefit and, thereby, challenging neo-liberalism itself: "the new transactive governmentality (which in Ghent has been defined as 'green-socialist-liberal') generated by such a dynamic, fluid and temporary purpose-oriented network [for urban gardening] is able to generate a variety of informal modes of planning" (p. 66). Here governmentality is shown to be a more fluid framework, not just identifying the necessary implications of neo-liberalism for civil society but capable of encompassing resistance at the same time.

Conclusions

The Foucauldian approach is centred around the mobilisation of the concept of discourse but in a broader sense than in Chap. 4; here the focus is on societal patterns and links to broader institutional patterns, and there is also a particular emphasis on knowledge and governmental technologies. But the research effort will be focussed around understanding the pattern of discourses using discourse analysis (e.g. see Fairclough and Fairclough 2012) but also approaches borrowed from the humanities such as narrative analysis or dramaturgy, looking for characterisation, storylines or plot-lines and dramatic developments. Hajer made the identification of storylines a key focus of his analysis of environmental planning, as a way to understand the development of acid rain politics and policies (Hajer 1995). There is also the possibility to go back to classical antecedents and look for modes of argumentation, perhaps using rhetorical analysis to identify how such argumentation works. Such rhetorical analysis can involve identifying key tropes of debate, the use of devices such as synecdoche and metonymy, the ethos that is invoked and the way that debates are closed down (Myerson and Rydin 1996). In addition, the role of graphic images of all kinds—pictures, photos, cartoons and so on—in creating discourses can be analysed.

Increasingly, with large collections of discursive material, formal coding using specialist software such as Atlas-ti or NVivo is being adopted. These packages are generally easy to use and flexible, allowing the analyst to set the codes for the analysis and even adjust these during the analysis. Such discourse analysis, however useful the software proves, does not take away from the core task of reading or examining the texts and images closely. With words, such close reading has been the central activity of humanities research for centuries. Texts and images are intended for a reader, a spectator, and so the response of that person is key. The researcher is standing in for that audience and trying to consider possible responses. The coding and use of software is just a way to record that response for later comparison across a large database. Code runs allow a large quantum of material to be sifted so that a reasonable amount for closing reading and viewing is selected. It remains down to the analyst to deduce the key themes that distinguish discourses and consider how they have effects, looking particularly at the micro-practices that they are linked to.

Key Theoretical Readings

Campbell and Fainstein (2003), Ch. 17.
Mandelbaum et al. (1996), Chs. 14, 16 and 17.
Hillier and Healey (2008), Ch. 8.

Key Research Readings

Berthou, S.K.G., and B.V. Ebbesen. 2016. Local Governing of Climate Change in Denmark: Recasting Citizens as Consumers. *Journal of Environmental Planning and Management* 59(3): 501–517.

Certomà, C., and B. Notteboom. 2017. Informal Planning in a Transactive Governmentality. Re-reading Planning Practices through Ghent's Community Gardens. *Planning Theory* 16(1): 51–73.

Daly, G. 2016. The Neo-liberalization of Strategic Spatial Planning and the Overproduction of Development in Celtic Tiger Ireland. *European Urban Studies* 24(9): 1643–1661.

Fuller, C., and K. West. 2017. The Possibilities and Limits of Political Contestation in Times of "urban austerity". *Urban Studies* 54(9): 2087–2106.

Lucas, C., and R. Warman. 2018. Disrupting Polarized Discourses: Can We Get Out of the Ruts of Environmental Discourses? *Environment and Planning C: Politics and Space* 36(6): 987–1005.

Rosol, M. 2014. On Resistance in the Post-political City: Conduct and Counter-conduct in Vancouver. *Space and Polity* 18(1): 70–84.

Tafon, R., D. Howarth, and S. Griggs. 2018. The Politics of Estonia's Offshore Wind Energy Programme: Discourse, Power and Marine Spatial Planning. *Environment and Planning C: Politics and Space* 37(1): 157–76

Bibliography

Beck, Ulrich. 1992. *Risk Society: Towards a New Modernity; translated by Mark Ritter*. London: Sage Publications.

Berthou, Sara Kristine Gløjmar, and Betina Vind Ebbesen. 2016. Local Governing of Climate Change in Denmark: Recasting Citizens as Consumers. *Journal of Environmental Planning and Management* 59 (3): 501–517.

Bresnihan, Patrick. 2019. Revisiting Neoliberalism in the Oceans: Governmentality and the Biopolitics of 'Improvement' in the Irish and European Fisheries. *Environment and Planning A: Economy and Space* 51 (1): 156–177.

Callon, Michel. 2010. Performativity, Misfires and Politics. *Journal of Cultural Economy* 3 (2): 163–169.

Campbell, Scott, and Susan Fainstein, eds. 2003. *Readings in Planning Theory*. 2nd ed. Oxford: Blackwell.

Certomà, Chiara, and Bruno Notteboom. 2017. Informal Planning in a Transactive Governmentality. Re-Reading Planning Practices through Ghent's Community Gardens. *Planning Theory* 16 (1): 51–73.

Daly, Gavin. 2016. The Neo-Liberalization of Strategic Spatial Planning and the Overproduction of Development in Celtic Tiger Ireland. *European Planning Studies* 24 (9): 1643–1661.

Douglas, Mary. 1966. *Purity and Danger: An Analysis of Concepts of Pollution and Taboo*. London: Routledge and Kegan Paul.

Etherington, David, and Martin Jones. 2018. Re-Stating the Post-Political: Depoliticization, Social Inequalities, and City-Region Growth. *Environment and Planning A: Economy and Space* 50 (1): 51–72.

Fairclough, Norman, and Isabela Fairclough. 2012. *Political Discourse Analysis*. London: Routledge.

Flyvbjerg, Bent. 1998. *Rationality and Power: Democracy in Practice*. Trans. Steven Sampson. Chicago; London: University of Chicago Press.

Foucault, Michel. 2010. *The Government of Self and Others: Lectures at the Collège de France, 1982–1983*. Ed. Frédéric Gros and Trans. Graham Burchell. Basingstoke: Palgrave Macmillan.

Friedmann, John. 1987. *Planning in the Public Domain: From Knowledge to Action*. Princeton: Princeton University Press.

Fuller, Crispian, and Karen West. 2017. The Possibilities and Limits of Political Contestation in Times of 'Urban Austerity'. *Urban Studies* 54 (9): 2087–2106.

Hajer, Maarten A. 1995. *The Politics of Environmental Discourse: Ecological Modernization and the Policy Process*. Oxford: Clarendon Press.

Hillier, Jean, and Patsy Healey, eds. 2008. *Contemporary Movements in Planning Theory*. Aldershot: Ashgate.

Jasanoff, Sheila. 2015. Serviceable Truths: Science for Action in Law and Policy. *Texas Law Review* 93 (7): 1723.

Leigh Star, Susan. 2010. This Is Not a Boundary Object: Reflections on the Origin of a Concept. *Science, Technology, & Human Values* 35 (5): 601–617.

Lucas, Chloe, and Russell Warman. 2018. Disrupting Polarized Discourses: Can We Get out of the Ruts of Environmental Conflicts? *Environment and Planning C: Politics and Space* 36 (6): 987–1005.

Lukes, Steven. 2005. *Power: A Radical View*. 2nd ed. Basingstoke: Palgrave Macmillan.

Mandelbaum, Seymour, Luigi Mazza, and Richard Burchell, eds. 1996. *Explorations in Planning Theory*. Rutgers, NJ: The State University of New Jersey.

Miller, Peter, and Nikolas Rose. 2006. Governing Economic Life. *Economy and Society* 19 (1): 1–31.

Myerson, George, and Yvonne Rydin. 1996. *The Language of Environment: A New Rhetoric*. Vancouver: UBC Press.

Raco, Mike. 2003. Governmentality, Subject-Building, and the Discourses and Practices of Devolution in the UK. *Transactions of the Institute of British Geographers* 28 (1): 75–95.

Raco, Mike, and Rob Imrie. 2016. Governmentality and Rights and Responsibilities in Urban Policy. *Environment and Planning A* 32 (12): 2187–2204.

Rosol, Marit. 2014. On Resistance in the Post-Political City: Conduct and Counter-Conduct in Vancouver. *Space & Polity* 18 (1): 70–84.

Rydin, Yvonne, Lucy Natarajan, Maria Lee, and Simon Lock. 2018a. Black-Boxing the Evidence: Planning Regulation and Major Renewable Energy Infrastructure Projects in England and Wales. *Planning Theory & Practice* 19 (2): 218–234.

———. 2018b. Local Voices on Renewable Energy Projects: The Performative Role of the Regulatory Process for Major Offshore Infrastructure in England and Wales. *Local Environment* 23 (5): 565–581.

Sager, Tore. 2015. Ideological Traces in Plans for Compact Cities: Is Neo-Liberalism Hegemonic? *Planning Theory* 14 (3): 268–295.

Sharp, Liz, and Tim Richardson. 2001. Reflections on Foucauldian Discourse Analysis in Planning and Environmental Policy Research. *Journal of Environmental Policy & Planning* 3 (3): 193–209.

Swyngedouw, Erik. 2009. The Antinomies of the Postpolitical City: In Search of a Democratic Politics of Environmental Production. *International Journal of Urban and Regional Research* 33 (3): 601–620.

———. 2011. *Designing the Post-Political City and the Insurgent Polis*. London: Bedford Press.

Tafon, Ralph, David Howarth, and Steven Griggs. 2019. The Politics of Estonia's Offshore Wind Energy Programme: Discourse, Power and Marine Spatial Planning. *Environment and Planning C: Politics and Space* 37 (1): 157–176.

Tozer, Laura. 2018. Urban Climate Change and Sustainability Planning: An Analysis of Sustainability and Climate Change Discourses in Local Government Plans in Canada. *Journal of Environmental Planning and Management* 61 (1): 176–194.

De Wilde, Mandy, and Thomas Franssen. 2016. The Material Practices of Quantification: Measuring 'Deprivation' in the Amsterdam Neighbourhood Policy. *Critical Social Policy* 36 (4): 489–510.

World Commission on Environment and Development. 1987. *Our Common Future*. Oxford: Oxford University Press.

Chapter 9
Relational Approaches: Assemblages, Materiality and Power

Framing the Research

The early twenty-first century saw a growth in planning research that represented a radical shift from earlier work which tended to look for specific patterns or causes of change and worked by focussing in on particular theoretically informed aspects of planning processes. The search was for a causal relationship that shed more light on the dynamics of planning. However, philosophical explorations such as that conducted by Deleuze and Guattari (1988) were representatives of a shift away from trying to find such limited causal connections and towards a recognition that change tended to occur because many different elements came into combination in a particular place at a particular time. What was important was to understand the relationships between these different elements *in toto*. The relationships were considered to be key to understanding change, agency and power.

A further distinctive aspect of this approach was that many theorists and researchers increasingly emphasised the importance of non-human actors (Rydin 2014). All the approaches discussed so far in this book have considered how actors, individually and collectively, shape planning processes. These actors may be people, groups, organisations but they are social actors in a social world. They may respond to or be shaped by economic, political, social or cultural considerations, but there has been little consideration of the materiality of both the actors and the world that they inhabit. Hence the 'material turn' urges researchers to consider both these aspects of materiality, and given that everyone is both a social and physical entity and that we live in a world that is both social and physical, this call has led to some fruitful research responses.

But while these may be the theoretical shifts that were shaping academic debates on planning, the context of policy and practice was also shifting, with a strong sense of the diminution of the power of the planner as an actor and the shift of interest to planning practices that were operating outside of formal state structures. The

Y. Rydin, *Theory in Planning Research*, Planning, Environment, Cities, https://doi.org/10.1007/978-981-33-6568-1_9

governance trend noted in Chap. 5 had, as has been discussed, led to more actors being drawn into planning practices. But now it seemed that some of the interesting and innovative planning actions were happening within civil society or through informal mechanisms. This was associated with a realisation that planning systems in the 'North' or higher-income countries had a lot to learn from those in the 'South' or in countries where informal and bottom-up actions often took the lead in reshaping cities or resisting the negative consequences of market-led development.

Whereas planning studies in the early-mid twentieth century was characterised by enthusiasm and optimism about what state-led planning could achieve, the experiences of and empirical research into the reality of urban planning have led to repeated demonstration of the inability of planning systems to deliver on their promises and of the challenges that are placed in the way of planners by internal and external factors. Many of the conceptual approaches explored in this volume (certainly from Chap. 4 onwards) suggest ways of understanding and empirically investigating the limitations of planning practice. Relational planning is another way of exploring this by seeing planning as just one part of a bigger puzzle.

This has led away from seeing planning solutions in terms of state-led policies, projects and initiatives, even if in conjunction with other actors. Rather planning is involved in small, tactical work on the part of the state or even happens outside the state altogether. This relational perspective has gone alongside a growing interest in informal urban change, in experimental urbanism and in the idea of the city as self-organising. These all challenge the ideal of planning that has informed many of the other chapters in this book. Rather than looking at planning as an intervention intended to achieve a certain effect, planning becomes reconsidered in terms of how it can play a part within emergent self-organisation, support small-scale initiatives and provide just the right intervention to promote desirable outcomes in urban and environmental systems.

But perhaps more significant than this shift in the focus of planning research is the shift in the characterisation of planning implied by a relational perspective. Relational approaches have a common ontology across all the different entities and processes involving those entities that are considered; they look for how different elements come together into a collectivity, often termed an assemblage. These are not the tight networks of Social Network Analysis (SNA; see Chap. 5) or the rigid systems of governmental approaches (see Chap. 2). Rather these networks are defined by the fluid set of elements they bring together. These are not nodes and links but something much more open to alternative interpretations and the collectivities that result have been described in a number of ways, including assemblage and network but also rhizome and even goo.

The key insight is that elements come into connection with each other and that this connection has effects (see for diverse examples: Merriman 2019; Richmond 2018). Outcomes are a result of such connections being made (or not), and agency is thus seen as a distributed effect of the connections rather than residing in any individual actor or alliance of actors and their associated resources. Change, agency and indeed power are thus emergent rather than the effect of a specific link or resource that is exercised. And the actors themselves are not fixed entities either.

They are co-defined by the assemblage, the collectivity shaping the individual elements and the individual elements, taken together, shaping the assemblage. In some accounts, individual actors themselves can be disaggregated into a network, an assemblage, a set of associations, in a fractal form of reasoning.

This can be quite a slippery mode of theorising and analysis because the level of generality in the concepts and the mode of argumentation is quite high. However, it is used to understand planning processes and the outcomes that result, by considering the contingent way that elements come together, and this means that the empirical research tends, paradoxically, to be rather specific, as the examples discussed later in this chapter show. Broad notions of assemblage, contingent agency and relational power are used to explain the naming of an urban regeneration project, a local referendum on a development proposal or the use of data in aquaculture; often these are examples of things that are overlooked in other modes of planning studies. In all cases, planning systems, processes and actors are not the key focus of study but rather are one element within a collective that drives change (or prevents it). The broader urban or environmental or socio-ecological system is the frame for research, and the research questions concern how planning operates within that frame in one or more specific instances.

The difficulty of tying down the role of planning systems, processes and planners relates to the view of planning as mired in complexity. Complex systems are discussed further below, but they are distinguished from simpler forms of systems that identify causal linkages amenable to interventions by planning organisations through a variety of tools and means. Appreciating complexity means a more modest idea of what planning can achieve and a much more indirect way of achieving that. This also relates to the search for resilience within urban, environmental and socio-ecological systems and the attempt to use planning to enhance such resilience. Again, this is expanded later.

Key Dynamics and Concepts

Three key aspects of relational thinking will be discussed: the importance of complexity thinking, the nature of the assemblages and networks involved in planning, and the import of the material turn.

Planning Under Complexity

At some level, planning is about trying to exert a degree of control over the built and natural environment and to manage associated change. The strongest statement of this is represented by the public administration framework discussed in Chap. 2. But as discussion in that chapter and subsequent chapters has shown, there are many limitations on the abilities of the planner and planning organisations to achieve such control and to manage change. One way of understanding this is to begin from a critique of the simple systems approach that was outlined in Chap. 2 on public administration, that is a linear set of cause-effect relationships able to be affected by specific interventions oriented towards desired ends. The theory of complexity has rewritten this view of systems. It has emphasised the existence of a number of features about how elements are inter-related in systems that disrupt this more simple cause-effect model. These include the following.

First, relationships within systems are often non-linear in nature so that a change of a certain quantum in one part of the system may produce a change of many times greater or, conversely, many times smaller magnitude. And the relationship between the size of the initial change and the resultant change may alter as more of the initial stimulus is provided. So, a certain initial change—say a subsidy for brownfield development—may have a big impact to begin with but then that impact may become less as the subsidy is increased.

Second, some non-linear relations may also demonstrate threshold effects whereby the link between cause and effects becomes radically different once a threshold for the stimulus has been exceeded. A change may cause, say, a consequence of double magnitude in quite a predictable way until the threshold is reached, after which the impact of that same change is radically variable. This can happen when considering habitats for flora and fauna and how they are impacted by anthropogenic change.

Third, systems may have many feedback loops that complicate the cause-effect relationship. The initial stimulus may have an effect but that may then produce a feedback loop, creating a new stimulus which then has a further effect, and so on. The feedback loops may amplify the consequences of the original stimulus, even leading to a runaway effect, or it may dampen down the implication of the original stimulus. Either is a possibility, indicating that if one recognises feedback loops, it is no longer easy to work out the likely effect arising from a specific stimulus. An added complication is the recognition of feed-forward loops as well. These are loops from the consequences of an initial stimulus that do not feedback to the site of that stimulus but rather have an impact elsewhere in the system. They may affect changes to several links in the chain from the original stimulus. The complexity of urban systems means that such multiple feedback/feed-forward loops are usually evident.

Fourth, there is the possibility of cocktail effects. These occur when the effect of two or more stimuli occurring at the same time is different from the sum of the effects of each stimulus happening on its own. Such cocktail effects are very prevalent in environmental systems subject to pollutants. Thus, multiple additions to the atmosphere may interact with each other to create a quite distinct and often magnified consequence in terms of air pollution.

The implications of the complexity of these types of inter-relationship within a system are that prediction of the outcomes resulting from a specific stimulus becomes very difficult. This hits at the very foundation of planning as it no longer becomes possible to say with even a degree of confidence what the effect of a certain planning policy or decision will be. At worst the system may demonstrate aspects of chaotic behaviour as a result of a stimulus, careering between different states in an unpredictable way. It calls for a rethinking of what constitutes effective planning (Chettiparamb 2019; McGreevy 2018; Skrimizea et al. 2018).

The discovery of the nature of complex systems raised significant questions for how planning could be expected to operate and, rather than enhancing the status of planning organisations, led to a call for greater resilience. If a complex system could not be planned or managed, then perhaps, at least, the system could be made more resilient to change. In effect, the aim was to help shape the system so that it could manage itself in terms of achieving more desirable outcomes and, particularly important, avoiding the less desirable ones.

So, the question becomes how to understand resilience and the conditions creating resilience. The term resilience itself has undergone a shift over recent years. Originally it was focussed on the so-called engineering definition whereby a system was resilient if it returned to its original state after a shock. However, it was increasingly recognised that this might not be the best option as it would lay the system open to similar shocks again. Thus, it was suggested that it would be better if the system changed so as to be more able to cope if such a shock occurred. A simple example would be the ability of a city to cope with flooding. Restoring a flooded city to exactly the pre-flood situation would not make the city more resilient. It would be better for the city to be adapted to cope with flooding through a mix of hard and soft engineering works, altered ground management practices in the catchment area and better information for local residents and businesses on how to protect their premises.

Thus, resilience is now interpreted as building into a natural or built environment system the ability to cope with shocks without excessive negative consequences (Janssen et al. 2006). These could be environmental shocks but also social or economic ones. These 'shocks' could also be considered as slow-burn changes over time as well as short-life catastrophic events. A resilient system is also seen as one that is able to self-organise and respond to these various shocks and pressures by continuous adjustment; planning then becomes just part of such adjustments. This has given rise to planning as framed by autopoiesis of urban and environmental systems. Broadening the understanding of resilience in this way has also broadened the range of actions that are suggested for building resilience. This is less about major works to restore environments to the pre-disaster scenario. Rather it is about fostering the ability of a system to meet the uncertainty of the future. Resilience theory holds that a number of features of systems enable them to be more resilient. These focus largely around being more diverse in various ways. Included in this is a shift away from the overarching plan and control being concentrated in one organisation towards more fragmentation of management and planning.

It is here that the ideas of self-organisation and informality enter. The central idea is that enabling localised self-organisation of the urban and natural environments through action inside and increasingly outside the state will render them more resilient to future changes, whether slow or sudden (Eizenberg 2019; Moroni et al. 2019; Nunbogu and Korah 2017; Portugali 2008). The key dynamics that a self-organisation perspective draws attention to concern the role of endogenous, small-scale, bottom-up and localised initiatives (Devlin 2018; Meijer and Ernste 2019; Silva and Farrall 2016; Song 2016). Community-based action comes to seem much more significant within this perspective, and the question is what planning can do to foster this.

Implications of a Relational Approach

Relational approaches do not just emphasise the way that elements happen to be brought together in specific circumstances; they also emphasise the way that for *this* outcome to occur, then *this* very specific set of elements had to be arranged in *this* very specific way. It looks to the contingency of outcomes, how they arise from certain circumstances at certain times. A variety of analytic terminology have been developed to try and give some conceptual structure to this idea, which otherwise can seem rather loose and all-encompassing. For example, De Landa has used language from computer science to suggest the relevance of certain elements being able to be removed from one assemblage and inserted—with new consequences—in an alternative assemblage (De Landa 2006). He uses the terms of alterity and interiority to describe this. He also emphasises the importance of identifying stabilising and destabilising factors with regard to an assemblage. McFarlane, coming from geography, has used the relational approach to discuss places as relational, multi-scalar, temporally situated and politically powerful networks of meaning; places are dense and highly unstable arrangements where boundaries act as a powerful mediating force with impacts upon place-identity (McFarlane 2018).

Latour and Callon's Actor-Network Theory (ANT) is firmly based within a relational approach and seeks to understand what has happened in particular instances by tracing threads of connections back and back (Rydin and Tate 2016). Agency, understood in terms of making change occur, results from the way that different elements are associated with each other, and thus a first task of planning research inspired by this approach is to identify the networks, assemblages and so on that gave rise to the change. But it also has a toolkit of concepts available for describing how these associations occur which can prove useful.

Translation describes the way that two elements are brought together, and this may involve a variety of work. It involves translation in the mathematical sense of moving and changing shape so that the connection is made; it also involves the linguistic sense of translation in that different language, and other communicative forms may be needed for that connection. The word 'translation' is perhaps a rather awkward one to use here as it has these specific meanings. But within ANT the focus is on the variety of ways in which the connections are forged, and the varieties of work that need to be done before that connection is firmly made.

Another key term is enrolment, and this focusses on the way that the connections between elements all together form a network (or assemblage or rhizome). It is important here to see the difference between the networks of ANT and those of Social Network Analysis (SNA) as discussed in Chap. 5. There the network was a set of nodes connected by links. Here the network is a metaphor for the sets of associations between elements, nothing more. It is not a fixed thing that can be measured, and Latour has regretted the connotations of stability that the word 'network' can imply.

Finally, the idea of ANT's flat ontology should be outlined. The networks of ANT go wherever they need to in order to explain processes of association and outcomes. There is no sense of levels or hierarchy. Links may be made across scales without any sense that the higher level somehow shapes the lower level. Rather the outcomes are the result of these cross-scalar links just as they are the result of links that happen to be within a scale. This is a more radical sense of working across scales that the multi-level governance discussed in Chap. 5.

These terms seek to describe processes that occur within planning, but more than this, they describe the work that has to happen. For networks in the ANT sense are always unstable and they require work to make them even temporarily stable. Thus, Latour says that society is the thing that needs to be explained, that is, the way that things appear to behave in predictable ways, although this is always an illusion (Latour 2005). A key part of the analysis within ANT is to understand the way that certain connections are making the network more stable or, on the contrary, are contributing to its destabilisation. It may be that adding further elements to the network will be important in creating stability or instability. Thus enrolment, in the sense of bringing other elements into the network, can play an important role in embedding the network within social ways of being.

This can be a key way that planners can contribute to stabilising networks potentially generating desired outcomes. But it is very subtle work. It involves understanding the network sufficiently to see what needs to be added (or taken away) to generate the desired agency and outcomes. Planners do not have power as such, since power is seen as distributed through the network (akin to Foucault's capillary power), but they can have an impact through this kind of enrolment activity. They may act directly as mediators or intermediaries in promoting such enrolment and connecting new elements to the network. But they may also use mediators or intermediaries, such as planning artefacts, to help create these connections. Planning work does involve a wide variety of such artefacts—plans, maps, photos, models, environmental assessments, noise modelling, statistical presentations and so on. These can all act as mediators or intermediaries in creating new network connections and changing the stability and effect of the overall network.

The Agency of Materiality

As indicated above, the early twenty-first century has seen some researchers within planning studies embracing the 'material turn' and seeking to place material elements more centrally within their theorising. This was quite distinct from earlier (nineteenth and early twentieth centuries) engagements with the material which generally took the form of environmental determinism; here planners sought to shape social behaviour and economic decisions by intervening in the physical environment, both built and natural. The material was seen to have a key role in determining socio-economic dynamics but as a context or container for those dynamics.

The current material turn is quite different and has been influenced by the work of Bruno Latour and his colleagues Michel Callon and John Law (see Law and Hassard 1999). Initially they looked at the processes by which scientific knowledge was generated, and this had strong connections with the Foucauldian approach discussed in Chap. 8, where power and knowledge were seen as two sides of the same coin. The resulting Actor-Network Theory (ANT), however, developed a quite distinct trajectory of its own, with some of the specific analytic tools discussed above.

Arguably the most contentious aspect of ANT was its radical symmetry in which it sought to treat social and material elements alike, coining the term 'actant' instead of 'actor' to describe this. This meant that aspects of materiality could enter into associations and thereby contribute to agency. There are many aspects of planning that exhibit materiality and thus can be said to contribute to the agency of planning processes. There is the physical environment—natural and built or usually a combination—that planning is directed at; that is, sites and their context. There is the materiality of the many impacts of urban development and change such as pollution to various media to traffic congestion along specific roads. There is the materiality of the developments that are at the heart of planning visions and decision-making.

But there is also the materiality of the planning process itself (Rydin and Natarajan 2016). Planning takes place in specific loci and arenas such as offices, public halls for public inquiries and community halls for public participation. It involves site visits and traverse across development locations and urban areas. As mentioned above, it also involves a range of material artefacts that are central to debates, deliberations and decision-making: maps, plans, reports, modelling exercises, 3D models and so on. Many of these embody key knowledge claims and act as conduits for knowledge to enter into planning processes.

Such artefacts can sometimes act as a black box (Rydin et al. 2018a). This useful ANT concept suggests that some parts of a network may be clustered and hidden within a black box, so that the work involved in creating those associations becomes forgotten or not visible. Indeed many of the artefacts that planners may use to try and shape the network will themselves be black boxes. A statistical report, an evaluation of a landscape or an analysis of retail shifts or of a particular habitat will all be the result of a particular network. This gets lost in the emphasis on outcomes within the planning process.

Finally, the social actors—planners, developers, communities—are themselves physical, material entities, and their embodied nature could be considered to be a relevant part of planning. Not only do the site visits mentioned above involve the materiality of the site but they also encompass the embodied experience of the social actors involved in these activities. Indeed, raising the materiality of social actors emphasises that all these actants can be thought of as socio-material; humans are embodied and materially situated, while no material element escapes the social construction processes that define and present it in the world.

Research Themes in Practice

The papers selected for providing examples of relations approaches focus on three themes: the mapping of assemblages, the search for new forms of power and the role of experimentation and self-organisation.

Tracing Assemblages

Researching assemblages is quite elusive and involves choices about where to draw the boundaries. How far to go in tracing connections and linkages?

Wideman and Masuda (2018) took a novel approach to assemblage theory approaching it through the lens of critical toponymy (the investigation of the historical and political implications of place naming). This made a link between the concern with discourse discussed in Chap. 8 and the assemblage approach. Within toponymy, naming is seen as a socially constructed process of discursive power, but the process can be analysed through the assemblage lens. So the researchers investigated a local planning process in Downtown Eastside, Vancouver, Canada, as a toponymic assemblage in which the relational activity of naming was a source of power and agency. This planning process took place over 2011–2014, and despite stated intentions to be participatory, local area planning generated "derision from stakeholders for its potential to generate dramatic capital-led transformations" (2018: 1). The toponymic assemblage analysis sought to understand why this was the case.

The methodology was based on participatory action research working with a variety of organisations including those representing low-income households, the Japanese-Canadian community, and mental health and housing sectors. Interviews ($n = 14$) were conducted with city planners and members of the relevant planning committee, in order to trace toponymic patterns. Similarly some 194 planning documents were analysed. The analysis throughout was organised around themes of discourses, aesthetics and materialities as they emerged through the local area planning process. This was conceptualised as a "generative, fluid and relational process that reworked the toponymic assemblage" of the Downtown Eastside (2018: 6). The researchers were interested in how the local plan-making process "acted as a participatory yet exclusionary assemblage-making arena" (p. 6). They asked how toponymies worked to depoliticise certain community activist claims and encourage market-led development, thus providing another window onto depoliticisation processes.

The key focus of analysis was in the naming that occurred and the use of maps to define and name space. These material artefacts were seen as highly significant in establishing the accepted nature of the area of Downside Eastside, in bounding and containing certain communities (notable lower-income communities) and in prescribing the aesthetics of the proposed 'Japantown' in highly racialised ways. They noted how the nomenclature for the area moved from 'Downtown Eastside'—a political assemblage coalescing around labour activism and focussed on housing, human rights, social services and social justice but also used to denigrate the area as one subject to drug use, poverty, homelessness and violence—to being termed 'Downtown Eastside Communities, 'Community Based Development Area' and in particular 'Japantown'.

Boundaries were a particular focus of the analysis, looking at how they were transformed by place naming and how this impacted on place identities, with consequent effects. "In particular, planning maps acted to rescale and reconfigure the boundaries of the neighbourhood, and they gave legitimacy to depoliticized techno-rational depictions of the area" (p. 15). Maps were thus seen as material, as essential elements in assemblages and also as governmental technologies (again nodding to a Foucauldian approach) in that they impacted identities: "Maps are highly contested technologies of government (operating at multiple scales and deployed by multiple actors), and they help to reinforce the boundary-making assemblage work of toponymy, even as boundaries themselves remain fluid and open to revision" (p. 5).

Their findings were fourfold. First, they found that the local area planning process generated new territorial conflicts. Second, it worked to depoliticise community activism in a low-income community of marginalised residents. Third, it co-opted racialised and class-based histories of displacement and dispossession through its use of the trope 'Japantown' to stimulate urban change. A final and unanticipated impact was the generationn of anti-gentrification politics including activism and new alliances being formed. They thus found naming was used to frame place in oppressive and marginalising ways but also resulting in liberating effects. This latter impact was related to the role of place naming in generating political solidarity, place attachment and social cohesion as well as stigma, dispossession and conflict.

The focus on naming helped to shape the description of the assemblage and identified certain key dynamics which produced agency through the relations between the elements of the assemblage. That agency, in this case, was seen to support racialisation and displacement of a community but also—paradoxically—activism and resistance by that community.

Another way in which the assemblage framework has been nuanced is through the idea of policy mobilities. This has looked at the way that ideas about ideal forms of urban development and city change circulate internationally and thus have global impact. Examples of this are flagship buildings as anchoring urban regeneration efforts, increasingly standardised designs for urban public spaces, the use of waterfronts to shape urban projects and the idea of a sustainable city or urban development project. These normative discourses of what cities should look like and how they should change have an impact on planning practice across the world and can be linked to assemblages involving specific images and tropes, the micro-practices of international consultancy or architectural firms and the interaction of global economic interests with national and local governments. Fairbanks (2019) used this concept to study the US offshore aquaculture governance with a specific interest in how policy models and ideas moved across geographies, time and institutional scales. He picked up the interest in how policy ideas are not simply transferred but translated and how stability in any related policy assemblage is often temporary.

The methods for the research, which extended over three years, were shaped by the intention to 'study up' through state structures and processes and also 'study out' across time, space and scale. Relevant policy documents for the period 1970–2015 were studied, looking across public and private sector reports, proposed and passed legislation, historical and internal government documents, hearings, minutes and public comments. Sixty-five in-depth, semi-structured interviews with government, industry and other actors were undertaken. These interview transcripts were coded for "common themes, ideas and discourses, as well as for descriptive information about policy developments and mobility" (p. 851). In addition to a national-scale focus, two developments were considered as case studies: California's Sustainable Oceans Act 2006 and the Fisheries Management Plan for Regulating Offshore Marine Aquaculture in the Gulf of Mexico 2009.

Fairbanks identified three emergent strands of proposed reform within the offshore aquaculture policy assemblage: federal legislation, which while not successfully passed proposed an enabling framework for commercial offshore development; regional management, which adopted a rationalisation approach and also aligned itself with a neo-liberal perspective, but offered scope for community involvement and consideration of social issues; and administrative cooperation, which was built into the baseline policy framework and promised a form of multi-level governance. These three strands were fluid, inter-related and neither linear nor exclusive, resulting in "iterative and relational policy processes where activities in different times, places and scales shape each other" (p. 856). He emphasised that the assemblage moved its centre of focus from policy idea to policy idea, transforming them along the way.

The analysis also emphasised the socio-materiality of policy and that "policy and governance are emerging in different localized, territorialized, and assembled forms dependent on the actors, spaces, and environments involved". It concluded that the mobilities led to a precautionary approach at the national scale, a critical re-interpretation of their policy authority by the National Oceanic and Atmospheric Administration and greater interest in shellfish aquaculture and cooperation between administrations across scales. While the policy assemblage remained provisional, the analysis suggested a new trajectory for planning and regulation.

This might be considered an analytic, but less critical use of the assemblage concept with the researchers applying the framework to identify how different elements—including policy ideas—are brought together in different ways at different scales. This offers scope for suggestions on how the policy process might be improved through altering the assemblage at the margin.

New Forms of Power

As with the Foucauldian approach discussed in Chap. 8, relational perspectives offer a new analysis of power, seeing it as emergent from the relationships and links between actors and between actors and things (and things and things). Agency is the combined result of these relationships, and thus power is diffused and not the result of an actor and her resources. There are a number of research papers that seek to take advantage of this new insight.

In another aquaculture example, Ascui et al. (2018) looked at the role of Big Data within environmental governance, considering the case of salmon aquaculture management in Macquarie Harbour, Australia. They used the classic paper by Callon et al. on the management of scallop fishing as a backdrop to their research (Callon 2017) and built on this to develop an analysis of how Big Data has emerged to become a significant actant in environmental governance. This arises from the use of sensors on the fish themselves, providing real-time data and increasing the spatial and temporal resolution of the information involved in environmental management. They argued that Big Data now takes 'centre stage', and the consequences are the fracturing of historic alliances, resulting in greater uncertainty and shaping the ongoing legitimacy of the industry.

The data for the analysis was collected over 20 months using a variety of documents (academic literature on the case, government and industry reports, and online, TV and print media) as well as nine interviews with fisheries scientists (3), fisheries managers (3), sustainability certifiers (2) and an environmental NGO (1). This was set in the context of a wider set of 17 interviews with environmental Big Data experts and a two-day workshop attended by 30 invited experts. This material was analysed using the framework of the classic Callon paper: problematisation in which the actors are defined together with the obligatory passage point; interessement, a process in which actors are locked into place; enrolment involving negotiation and the allocation of roles; and mobilisation in which representatives are created. This enabled the researchers to trace and thereby identify the agency of Big Data, rather than it being a passive input or influence.

They began by identifying the key actors (the salmon farmers, the salmon, the 'local community', the regulator and the scientific community) and the obligatory passage point (the regulation of the expansion of fishing activity). At this point the theoretical construct of 'sustainable carrying capacity' was pinpointed for its importance in building alliances around development. They then looked at how the actors were brought into alliances and the role that the ECO Lab model for assessing 'sustainable carrying capacity' played in aligning actors. The next stage involved detailing the negotiations that occurred and how this resulted in new roles being assigned to different actors, in particular farm operators were charged with an environmental regulatory role through monitoring. Through monitoring activity, as influenced by the prevailing environmental model, three parameters came to represent 'water quality' in a necessarily partial way: nitrates, dissolved oxygen and ammonia.

The monitoring model appeared to act as a black box with regard to water quality, that is resolving inputs into simplified outputs through a hidden complex process. However, this 'mobilisation' was only temporary as data emerged that did not conform to the model—'uncooperative data'—and this led to protests and contestation. A counter-narrative emerged that was critical of the use of public waterways for public gain, and this was aired at a Senate inquiry. Although the inquiry sided with the fish farm developers, this led to later political moves calling for independent real-time monitoring of all salmon leases. The relational approach allowed the researchers to identify power or agency as emergent from the assemblage brought together through Callon's categories of work. This further then led them to the identification of the agency of specific data, with clearly apparent political implications.

Still staying with water as a context but moving to Africa, Wissing (2019) provided an account in which the materiality of power took centre stage, looking at the contested relationships around the Volta River in Ghana and the construction of the Akosombo Dam. This dam was a central feature of Nkrumah's attempt to reshape Ghanaian society in this southern area through control of water. This area was the traditional homeland of the Akwamu people; Wissing stressed that they had different views of how water could be controlled and by whom. They saw deities as centrally authoritative in any human engagement with water. Thus, there was a clash between the Akwamu understanding of hydro-sociality and the vision of Nkrumah which was linked to the concept of a hydraulic society. This was a historical piece of research, looking at developments in the 1960s. Methods were not detailed, but the account relied on a retelling of the insights from previous studies and accounts of the period; the paper also referred occasionally to unnamed 'informants'. In this retelling the different aspects of the story were counterposed and related to each other in an original way. Thus, historical and anthropological accounts informed each other in ways that allowed relationships, particularly with the materiality of water, to be traced; this suggested the agency and power of the water itself.

Wissing began with an autobiographical account of an encounter with the materiality of water during a rain downpour on her daily commute in Ghana; this sets the tone of the analysis. She then established the Nkrumah vision for modernising Ghana through hydro-electric power, picking out the connections that were nevertheless made to African tradition, for example, in the ceremony for opening the dam. Wissing then focussed on the Akwamu purification ritual performed within the Odwira festival. The full-scale Odwira festival, which served to recognise traditional leaders of the past and to first subvert and then restore social cohesion in the present, had not been performed for many years, but elements were still practised, including the use of water from certain rivers for purification and blessing. The ritual fitted within a complex set of cultural and material relationships between the Akwamu and water, particularly the Volta River. Wissing argued that "the exclusive relationships that the Akwamu assert with water and their gods may be utilised to resist national notions of control over water and humans" (p. 8).

Bringing the story up to date, Wissing related how the purification ritual was used during a drought (and subsequent power outages) in 2015. These outages of electricity were due to low rainfall for the Akosombo Dam—the "uncooperative nature of water" (p. 3). She saw this as disrupting the model of hydraulic control implied by the construction and management of the dam and reasserting the material agency of water: "we may see in the fluid, unruly nature of water creative opportunities for local resistance, rather than reinforcement, of national or global claims to power over water and work within such frameworks to counter effects such as climate change" (2018: 15). The material agency of water was harnessed to a political challenge to state control of both water and people, firmly set in the context of a long-standing and ongoing cultural, spiritual and religious engagement between local people and water. The planning implications of this were that it opened up "the possibility … for water management solutions to incorporate notions of divine protectors in relationships with human responsibility to the environment, thus strengthening human intervention with a perceived to be greater (hydro-)power" (p. 15).

This is a retelling of water planning which enables a re-interpretation of a rational modernist planning effort and the suggestion of alternative modes of planning based on appreciating the material agency of water.

Metzger et al. (2017) began from a view of power as the outcome of social processes rather than a causal variable behind them, in line with the relational view of ANT. They studied a referendum that was held concerning a major urban development in the Swedish municipality of Upplands Väsby north of Stockholm. The proposal was for a new urban area by Lake Mälaren, named Väsby Sjöstad. The Green Party amongst others opposed the development, and in 2010 a referendum was proposed by opposition campaigners. This was taken up and held in September 2014, alongside the general election vote. The results went against the development, and the urban development plans were shelved. Hence the way that power was implicated in this resistance to an urban proposal was the research question they addressed.

The research into this event was based on 17 semi-structured interviews held soon after in October–November 2014. The questions sought to elicit general information but also focussed on the detail of the process including which competences were brought in from outside the locality, arguments that were deployed for and against the development, motivations for the development and the referendum, and the conduct of the plebiscite. The aim was to uncover the micro-politics of power, rejecting the assumption of a dominant economic power or pre-existing coalitions of actors. All interviews were recorded and transcribed for analysis.

In this analysis the researchers uncovered how "the 'winners' succeeded by drawing upon unexpected resources, making unforeseen connections, displacements and translations" (2017: 211). These led to new sets of relations being made and remade in a way that can explain the referendum outcome. For example, the No-side (the eventual winners, just to be clear) organised a boycott against a local food store as the owner was involved in the development plans; this boycott led to the owner stepping back and taking a more passive role as well as disincentivising other local businesses getting involved in the Yes-side. Again, the No-side deployed the local media feeding stories that portrayed the proposed development as an 'elite project' for wealthy people or as a 'concrete project' in a natural area, and distinguishing it from the famous Hammarby Sjöstad, often held up as a sustainability model.

The researchers also uncovered other examples of the No-side acting contingently to shift the public position on the development including aligning different interests in a coalition, forcing a clear choice between Yes/No on the development which precluded negotiations for a compromise, renegotiating local geographical boundaries and associated values, and delegitimising local community participation efforts. The analysis, thus, uncovered the way the agenda was formed and the alliances that were mobilised in detail, showing how one activity or decision followed on others.

However, following the relational perspective, they emphasise that "(n)one of the resources deployed were 'power tools' lying around waiting to be deployed or 'power reservoirs' waiting to be tapped" (p. 211). Rather they stressed the inventiveness of actors and the ability to go beyond the expectations of a local development referendum. They suggest that while this occurred in the context of asymmetries between actors, "creative and innovative practice may function to undermine and subvert existing power relationships" (2017: 216). The focus on power and agency in assemblages allowed for new contingent forms to emerge.

Self-Organisation and Experimentation

The final set of research papers to be discussed look at instances of urban self-organisation and experimentation. Here the fluidity and creativity of a relational perspective is used to discuss novel forms of planning without any preceding assumptions about how these would operate and what would contribute to their success. This is a very open form of researching suitable for experimental cases.

In a study of sustainable transport experimentation in Greater Manchester Hodson et al. (2018) explored the interface between place-based priorities and national interests. Their research argued that the national conditioning of localised, place-based priorities shaped urban experimentation. They limited the possibilities of experimentation through the setting of priorities, stipulations and funding. The mode of experimentation and particularly the associated political priorities were then embedded materially in the city. The established processes of governing and constituting capacity were instrumental in this. This was a key argument that the researchers made to develop thinking on experimentation and take work within this frame away from the purely localised project. They then further argued that the feedback loop back to the national level occurred only weakly so that learning through experimentation was limited.

The empirical research questions they posed were twofold:

1. How have multi-scalar urban governance configurations shaped place-based sustainable transport priorities?

2. What kinds of spaces of sustainable transport experiments are opening up, which social interests are involved and with what effects? (And—they added—leading to what lessons?)

The methodology deployed was based on document analysis (particularly looking at the national and city-regional levels) and interviews with transport authority officials, local authority officers, NGOs, transport activists and 'others'. Greater Manchester was chosen as a 'critical' case study, "exemplifying place-based priorities and experimentation in a context of state-spatial and governance restructuring" (p. 8); presumably this also built on local contacts and ongoing observation of developments in the researchers' university city. The specific experiments that they concentrated on were associated with cycling infrastructure: a city centre Cycle Hub providing parking but also cyclist facilities such as showers and lockers; and a segregated cycle lane along Wilmslow Road including 'floating' bus stops between the cycle lane and the road.

The analysis emphasised five themes which amounted to five elements for conditioning experimentation. The first was the importance of fusing together instrumented, measured forms of experimentation with more flexible, trial-and-error assessments within the materially embedded infrastructure. Second, there was the need to constrain local discretion to experiment to favour the nationally promoted (and funded) initiatives. Third, the meaning of sustainability was narrowed through the experiments to highlight the economic benefits. Fourth, while there was a strategic vision, the episodic funding associated with conditions mean that a somewhat fragmented infrastructure resulted; and, fifth, experiments had on occasion to be truncated to sustain the status quo.

In all these ways, the influence of national interests and priorities on experimentations with sustainable urban transport options in Greater Manchester was apparent, and, thus, experimentation could not be relied on to "effectively and strategically restructure existing urban governance" (p. 15). While there were a variety of conditions that shaped experimentation, the processes involved in such experimentation had only a very limited impact on broader conditions. The researchers concluded that experiments were involved in governance dynamics whereby responsibility but not funding was devolved to the local level, encouraging cities into "a hyper-competitive game whereby they must produce a narrative of innovation to get money" (p. 16). The result was an "unbalanced" form of experimentation promoting "the constant production of novelty over the process of learning" (p. 16).

Cugurullo (2018) used the term 'Frankenstein urbanism' to describe the impact of the experimentation on urban change, looking at Hong Kong and Masdar City, Abu Dhabi. In particular he looked at how the ideas of the eco-city and the smart city have been used as typologies of experimental urbanism globally. The framing for the research was based on understanding the fragmentation that characterises smart and eco-city projects both as part of a broader historical trend seeing city development as 'fragmented artefacts' shaped by a variety of forces, and also as a result of the specificity of individual case studies.

The methodology for the case studies was based on 14 months of fieldwork including 24 semi-structured and 18 structured interviews with the key actors involved in the projects: public sector policy makers, developers, local council spatial planners, architects, investment companies and clean-tech multinationals. This was supported by document review including master plans, development agendas and environmental reports. The projects were regarded as rather controversial so that the interview quotes had to be anonymised. Rather modestly, Cugurullo saw this as contributing "a 'midlevel formulation' whose explanatory power remains open and revisable" (p. 75).

He began by noting the tension between the presentation of these smart and eco-city projects as homogeneous entities, developed in a systematic way following a master plan, and the fragmentation, heterogeneity and chaos that is found at the root of urban experimentation. Thus, the case studies were explored in relation to this conceptualisation of urban experiments to reveal their nature as a "plethora of sub-projects" (2018: 75). This resulted in a distinct narrative of analysis for the two cases.

In Masdar City it was clear that the construction of the so-called eco-city had not been led by a coherent and precise master plan. Cugurullo described a "patchwork made of incongruence parts developed by different actors with different interests" (2018: 82). The result had limited its sustainability potential despite the claims made for this new city development. For example, the public rapid transport system worked well as did the electric car project, but the one seemed to undermine the other. In Hong Kong, there was a similar fragmentation into "a number of smart buildings, infrastructures and technologies which are not integrated in a broader system, and function independently as separate entities" (2018: 84). This resulted in a divorce from the ecological dimensions of the smart city concept; in addition, there was an exclusive focus on office buildings and the use of real-time smart monitoring that was unrelated to the broader urban context.

The failure of such projects related to the inability to embrace their organic nature, so that urban unsustainability and inequality often resulted. In particular, the attempt in both cities to fit together different elements—spaces, infrastructures, technologies—to create a new type of urban settlement resulted in individual elements working well, but existing in tension with each other so as to destabilise the overall experiment. The term 'Frankenstein urbanism' that he used to characterise his research implied that urban experiments were differentiated by scale and degree, that they were not complemented by experimentation at the macro scale (the city and the region) and that they created fragmentation and disconnection. Thus, he concluded that these types of urban experimentation were "reproposing traditional, chaotic urban models which have been around for millennia" (2018: 87) rather than achieving sustainability goals.

Finally, Zhang and de Roo (2016) used evidence from Nanluoguxiang, a residential area within the inner city of Beijing in China to look at the interdependency of self-organisation and planning. The case study was chosen because it had experienced transformations which appeared to have self-organising properties. It was deteriorating in terms of its physical qualities and liveability, but it was considered a successful example of organic regeneration by balancing development and preservation while incorporating resident participation. Of particular note was the preservation of the historic spatial pattern of a main street crossed by small lanes and residential dwellings organised around an internal courtyard.

The case study method was used to reconstruct the phases of development of the area since the 1950s using desk research and site visits. A questionnaire supplemented with detailed interviews was used to inquire about people's interpretations of space, their quality of life and their attitudes towards the renewal plan; the aim was to understand the motives behind their responses to the situation. The questionnaire was used in two rounds, before and after the 2006 revitalisation of the area. The 2006 round concentrated on local residents' perceptions of their living conditions and their attitudes towards potential changes; 98 validated responses were received. The second round in 2011 covered local residents ($n = 169$) but also tourists ($n = 81$) and shopkeepers ($n = 79$). This focussed on the interpretation and appreciation of the local environment, their knowledge and opinions about conservation and the plans for development, and their views on future developments.

The analysis was framed by an understanding of self-organisation as non-linear transformation that involved several steps. First there was a break in symmetry; this built up tension until criticality was reached; this meant adjustments in behaviour, each responding to but autonomous from each other; out of this new patterns emerged, the consequences of which could not be anticipated. The densification of the development of the quadrangle residential courtyards in Nanluoguxiang was seen as an illustration of this process, as the open courtyards had been filled with buildings creating "warrens" of "a chaotic mix of extensions of existing houses and stand-alone buildings" (2016: 259). This was associated with two phases in shifts of ownership. Before 1949 most courtyards were privately owned and in single occupancy. State socialisation transferred ownership in the 1950s to the state, and this meant that the properties were subdivided into small rooms and rented out to low-income tenants. More recently, the housing pressures led to self-building that densified the courtyards into warrens, at first quite tentatively and then on a more substantial scale. The population growth and housing stresses were seen as the symmetry break; the halt to the socialisation policy was the criticality; this triggered people to change their behaviour, and self-build led to spontaneous new patterns of urban form.

This occurred in the context of spatial planning which influenced certain aspects of the urban development but was eventually overwhelmed by that spontaneous change. The linear thinking of traditional spatial planning could not cope with the nature of such self-organisation. The undesirable unintended consequences of this form of urban change also could not, therefore, be managed by such planning. Thus, the research traced the dynamics and consequences of self-organisation but concluded that the side-effects required an engagement with an alternative form of planning to promote the public interest.

Conclusions

Within relational approaches, the focus is on understanding the complex contingency of situations, which rather suggests that it will not be straight-forward to identify the role that planning systems and planners can play in achieving specific desired outcomes. This is not a world in which a plan can be readily implemented. The plan becomes reduced to an artefact circulating within multiple associations between actors, between actants. When the complexity of current situations is acknowledged, then it becomes much more difficult to see a single intervention as necessarily connected to specific outcomes across multiple linkages. So the planner cannot readily be said to 'cause' or 'create' certain pathways for the city or the environment. In this framing, planning becomes reinterpreted as 'small work', as many specific interventions within networks, trying to create associations, linkages and connections which may be implicated in chains leading to a certain outcome. This is not the world of big claims for planning or planners. But this does not mean that planning has no role to play. Rather it emphasises the importance of planners understanding the way that the world they are trying to influence arises from complex network relations. On the back of this understanding, then planners can seek to create new associations, enrol key actors into networks and create artefacts that will play a role in stabilising networks. Where a network seems to be creating beneficial effects, then the role of the planner will be to stabilise that network by bringing in new actants that strengthen associations.

Particularly important is the way that planners deploy artefacts. As emphasised above, there are many different artefacts that are used within planning. Many of these are in forms—plans, reports, visualisations—that black box the work that went into creating them. The processes of collaborative discussion, of detailed environment or economic assessment, of the choice and creation of key images are all forgotten as the artefact circulates and becomes the means of connection. The use of artefacts in this way is key planning work. But this may be problematic work as it hides power relations. Planners need to be aware of such hidden power. They have to be aware of the possible consequences of deploying such artefacts and it may be that they should seek to create other associations to challenge it. This puts the emphasis on the researcher beginning somewhere and then being very responsive to the developments in the fieldwork and where it takes her. The researcher has to be open to following different lines of inquiry, seeing where an association with an actor or actant goes.

Key Theoretical Readings

Hillier and Healey (2008) Chs 14, 21, 22, and 23.
De Roo et al. (2012) Chs 1-3, 5-11, 12, 13 and 16.
Hillier and Metzger (2015) Ch. 5.
Gunder et al. (2018) Chs 15, 18, 25, 26 and 27.

Key Research Readings

Ascui, F., M. Haward, and H. Lovell. 2018. Salmon, Sensors and Translations: The Agency of Big Data in Environmental Governance. *Environment and Planning D: Society and Space* 36 (5): 905–925.

Cugurullo, F. 2018. Exposing Smart Cities and Eco-Cities: Frankenstein Urbanism and the Sustainability Challenge of the Experimental City. *Environment and Planning A: Economy and Space* 50 (1): 73–92.

Fairbanks, L. 2019. Policy Mobilities and the Sociomateriality of U.S. Offshore Aquaculture Governance. *Environment and Planning C: Politics and Space* 37 (5): 849–867.

Hodson, M., J. Evans, and G. Schliwa. 2018. Conditioning Experimentation: The Struggle for Place-Based Discretion in Shaping Urban Infrastructures. *Environment and Planning C: Politics and Space.*

Metzger, J., L. Soneryd, and K.T. Hallström. 2017. "Power" Is That Which Remains to Be Explained: Dispelling the Ominous Dark Matter of Critical Planning Studies. *Planning Theory* 16 (2): 203–222.

Wideman, T., and J. Masuda. 2018. Toponymic Assemblages, Resistance and the Politics of Planning in Vancouver, Canada. *Environment and Planning C: Politics and Space.*

Zhang, S., and G. de Roo. 2016. Interdependency of Self-Organisation and Planning: Evidence from Nanluoguxiang, Beijing. *Town Planning Review* 87 (3).

Bibliography

Ascui, Francisco, Marcus Haward, and Heather Lovell. 2018. Salmon, Sensors, and Translation: The Agency of Big Data in Environmental Governance. *Environment and Planning: Society & Space* 36 (5): 905–925.

Callon, Michel. 2017. Some Elements of a Sociology of Translation: Domestication of the Scallops and the Fishermen of Saint-Brieuc Bay. *Logos* 27 (2): 49–90.

Chettiparamb, Angelique. 2019. Responding to a Complex World: Explorations in Spatial Planning. *Planning Theory* 18 (4): 429–447.

Cugurullo, Federico. 2018. Exposing Smart Cities and Eco-Cities: Frankenstein Urbanism and the Sustainability Challenges of the Experimental City. *Environment and Planning A: Economy and Space* 50 (1): 73–92.

Deleuze, Gilles, and Félix Guattari. 1988. *A Thousand Plateaus: Capitalism and Schizophrenia.* London: Athlone Press.

Devlin, Ryan Thomas. 2018. Asking 'Third World Questions' of First World Informality: Using Southern Theory to Parse Needs from Desires in an Analysis of Informal Urbanism of the Global North. *Planning Theory* 17 (4): 568–587.

Eizenberg, Efrat. 2019. Patterns of Self-Organization in the Context of Urban Planning: Reconsidering Venues of Participation. *Planning Theory* 18 (1): 40–57.

Fairbanks, Luke. 2019. Policy Mobilities and the Sociomateriality of U.S. Offshore Aquaculture Governance. *Environment and Planning C: Politics and Space* 37 (5): 849–867.

Gunder, Michael, Ali Madanipour, and Vanessa Watson, eds. 2018. *The Routledge Handbook of Planning Theory.* London: Routledge.

Hillier, Jean, and Patsy Healey, eds. 2008. *Contemporary Movements in Planning Theory*. Aldershot: Ashgate.

Hillier, Jean, and Jonathan Metzger, eds. 2015. *Connections: Exploring Contemporary Planning Theory and Practice with Patsy Healey*. Farnham: Ashgate.

Hodson, Mike, James Evans, and Gabriele Schliwa. 2018. Conditioning Experimentation: The Struggle for Place-Based Discretion in Shaping Urban Infrastructures. *Environment and Planning C: Politics and Space* 36 (8): 1480–1498.

Janssen, Marco A., et al. 2006. Toward a Network Perspective of the Study of Resilience in Social-Ecological Systems. *Ecology and Society* 11 (1): 15.

De Landa, Manuel. 2006. *A New Philosophy of Society: Assemblage Theory and Social Complexity*. London: Continuum.

Latour, Bruno. 2005. *Reassembling the Social: An Introduction to Actor-Network-Theory*. Oxford: Oxford University Press.

Law, John, and John Hassard. 1999. *Actor Network Theory and After*. Oxford: Blackwell.

McFarlane, Colin. 2018. Fragment Urbanism: Politics at the Margins of the City. *Environment and Planning:, Society & Space* 36 (6): 1007–1025.

McGreevy, Michael Patrick. 2018. Complexity as the Telos of Postmodern Planning and Design: Designing Better Cities from the Bottom-Up. *Planning Theory* 17 (3): 355–374.

Meijer, Marlies, and Huib Ernste. 2019. Broadening the Scope of Spatial Planning: Making a Case for Informality in the Netherlands. *Journal of Planning Education and Research*. https://doi.org/10.1177/0739456X19826211.

Merriman, Peter. 2019. Relational Governance, Distributed Agency and the Unfolding of Movements, Habits and Environments: Parking Practices and Regulations in England. *Environment and Planning C: Politics and Space* 37 (8): 1400–1417.

Metzger, Jonathan, Linda Soneryd, and Kristina Tamm Hallström. 2017. 'Power' Is That Which Remains to Be Explained: Dispelling the Ominous Dark Matter of Critical Planning Studies. *Planning Theory* 16 (2): 203–222.

Moroni, Stefano, Ward Rauws, and Stefano Cozzolino. 2019. Forms of Self-Organization: Urban Complexity and Planning Implications. *Environment and Planning: Urban Analytics and City Science* 47 (2): 220–234.

Nunbogu, Abraham Marshall, and Prosper Issahaku Korah. 2017. Self-Organisation in Urban Spatial Planning: Evidence from the Greater Accra Metropolitan Area, Ghana. *Urban Research & Practice* 10 (4): 423–441.

Portugali, Juval. 2008. Learning from Paradoxes About Prediction and Planning in Self-organizing Cities. *Planning Theory* 7 (3): 248–262.

Richmond, Matthew Aaron. 2018. Rio de Janeiro's Favela Assemblage: Accounting for the Durability of an Unstable Object. *Environment and Planning D: Society and Space* 36 (6): 1045–1062.

De Roo, G., J. Hillier, and J. van Wezemael, eds. 2012. *Complexity and Planning: Systems, Assemblages and Simulations*. Farnham: Ashgate.

Rydin, Yvonne. 2014. The Challenges of the 'Material Turn' for Planning Studies. *Planning Theory & Practice* 15 (4): 590–595.

Rydin, Yvonne, and Lucy Natarajan. 2016. The Materiality of Public Participation: The Case of Community Consultation on Spatial Planning for North Northamptonshire, England. *Local Environment* 21 (10): 1243–1251.

Rydin, Yvonne, Lucy Natarajan, Maria Lee, and Simon Lock. 2018a. Black-Boxing the Evidence: Planning Regulation and Major Renewable Energy Infrastructure Projects in England and Wales. *Planning Theory & Practice* 19 (2): 218–234.

Rydin, Yvonne, and Laura Tate, eds. 2016. *Actor Networks of Planning: Exploring the Influence of ANT*. New York: Routledge.

Silva, Paulo, and Helena Farrall. 2016. Lessons from Informal Settlements: A 'Peripheral' Problem with Self-Organising Solutions. *Town Planning Review* 87 (3): 297–319.

Skrimizea, Eirini, Helene Haniotou, and Constanza Parra. 2018. On the 'Complexity Turn' in Planning: An Adaptive Rationale to Navigate Spaces and Times of Uncertainty. *Planning Theory* 18 (1): 122–142.

Song, Lily K. 2016. Planning with Urban Informality: A Case for Inclusion, Co-Production and Reiteration. *International Development Planning Review* 38 (4): 359–381.

Wideman, Trevor J., and Jeffrey R. Masuda. 2018. Toponymic Assemblages, Resistance, and the Politics of Planning in Vancouver, Canada. *Environment and Planning C: Politics and Space* 36 (3): 383–402.

Wissing, Kirsty. 2019. Assistance and Resistance of (Hydro-)Power: Contested Relationships of Control over the Volta River, Ghana. *Environment and Planning C: Politics and Space* 37 (7): 1161–1178.

Zhang, Shuhai, and Gert de Roo. 2016. Interdependency of Self-Organisation and Planning: Evidence from Nanluoguxiang, Beijing. *Town Planning Review* 87 (3): 253–274.

Chapter 10
Conclusion: On Doing Planning Research

Introduction

This book has sought to introduce a variety of theoretical and conceptual frameworks, perspectives and approaches. Each of these has a distinctive way of discussing planning processes and framing planning activities as an object of study, as summarised in Table 10.1. Where one starts with a research project has an influence on the nature of findings that result, although a good researcher should always be alert to findings that do not fit with their preconceived ideas, including those shaped by their theoretical readings. But, nevertheless, it matters where one starts. Reading down the list in Table 10.1, you may have an instinctive preference for one or the other way of looking at the planning system. Or you may have assumed that planning was, say, an orderly set of procedures but are intrigued by an alternative perspective.

I first considered doing a PhD when I was working as a chartered surveyor, mainly supporting residential developers, superstore operators, mineral extractors and building societies in getting development consent, often on appeal to central government. I spent many days in public inquiries listening to various professionals read out their 'proofs of evidence' and be questioned about them, usually in a form of cross-examination by lawyers. The great revelation for me from my undergraduate degree had been that developers hold much of the power within planning processes. While the appeal system and the operation of public inquiries seemed also to demonstrate this (we usually won planning consent against the local authority), I had a feeling that something else was going on. Why was this power being cloaked behind so much procedure and such detailed discussion of evidence? In the event, I did my PhD at a time when political economy approaches were in the ascendance, and my thesis sat rather uneasily between this and emerging governance approaches. But I soon began to explore the role of discourses in planning and how they shaped processes, finding many institutionalist approaches convincing alongside

© The Author(s), under exclusive license to Springer Nature Singapore Pte Ltd. 2021
Y. Rydin, *Theory in Planning Research*, Planning, Environment, Cities,
https://doi.org/10.1007/978-981-33-6568-1_10

Table 10.1 Different framings of planning

Theoretical Approach	Planning should be understood as ...
Governmental Model	An orderly set of procedures deploying the resources of the state
Rational Choice	A structured set of interactions between rational self-interested actors
New Institutionalism	A culturally appropriate set of behaviours
Governance Theory	Collaboration within networks of actors across different sectors
Urban Politics	An intervention in urban conflicts
Political Economy	An attempt to maintain the profitability of capitalism
Foucauldian Approach	Arena for the construction of knowledges and self-interests
Relational Approaches	An attempt to stabilise certain networks by enrolling key actors/actants

governance theories, before finding my way into the fascinating (to me) literature using Foucault's ideas and concepts and discussing Actor-Network Theory. But the value of adopting these different theoretical literatures was ultimately about understanding the planning system I was observing, starting from my intellectual instincts about what was important to consider in more detail.

The purpose of this book is, therefore, to demonstrate how the adoption of a theoretical framework or conceptual approach can support empirical research within planning studies and make such research a more interesting and revealing activity. The emphasis has been on showing the value of each approach rather than developing a critique; as indicated in Chap. 1, such a critique is implicit in the discussion across chapters. In the final chapter, the focus turns to more practical matters of research, pulling together some key ideas on research design, considering the questions that a researcher might ask themselves about which theoretical or conceptual framing might be most appropriate and ending with a look at how change has to be accommodated within the research process for a variety of reasons.

Towards Theory-Informed Research

The central assertion of this book is that adopting a theoretical framework is fundamental to planning research as it provides a framing for empirical work and, further, that framing enables a broader set of claims to be made following the empirical findings. Theory-informed research can contribute to a wider debate about how planning processes work, a debate that has common assumptions, priorities and analysis of key dynamics. These commonalities provide links between planning researchers that support wider dialogue. It takes research beyond the key empirical findings to answer the 'so what' question. What does it matter if the details of planning processes are like this or like that? What more general views does this research support about planning, and how it fits into society? But for this to be effective, theory-informed planning research needs to conform to the Golden Triangle, as I have termed it. This is illustrated in Fig. 10.1.

Fig. 10.1 The Golden
Triangle of theory-
informed planning research

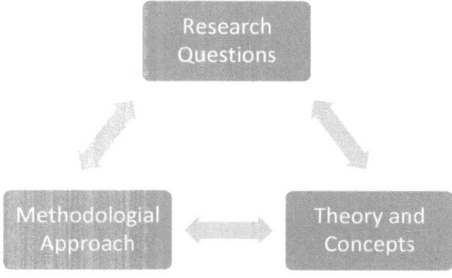

There are three links within this Golden Triangle. The first is between theory and the research questions. This is about the way that a theoretical framework and the associated concepts frame the empirical inquiry and thus set the focus of the research. This is captured in the research questions set for a project. Precise and clear research questions are the *sine qua non* of social science research. They clarify the purpose and contribution of the research and answer the first obvious question: what are you researching and why? What are your aims? What will be your contribution?

The second link is between theory and methods. One strong argument of this book is that the methods of empirical research into planning need to be carefully chosen to match the conceptual framing of that research. This covers both the methods of data collection and of data analysis. This is an important distinction, which is often lost. The techniques used to collect data allow datasets to be built; these don't have to be quantitative data and the dataset does not need to be captured in a spreadsheet. Datasets are just the totality of material that has been collected for analysis. It should not be a random selection of data; the methods should ensure that the data will support analysis that will help answer the research questions.

These datasets are then analysed using different techniques. The way that data is collected shapes the possibilities of data analysis. If you don't ask a question in interviews about organisational structure, you cannot analyse those interviews with a view to seeing if organisational structure is important and how it may shape planning processes. Thus, both data collection and data analysis techniques need to have regard to the theoretical framing. Otherwise it will not be possible to build a coherent analysis of research findings and take advantage of the scope for theory to move research beyond the detailed empirical account to broader understandings of planning.

The third link is between research questions and methods. Data collection and analysis methods need to be such as to enable the specific research questions to be answered. The theoretical framing will not specify these questions alone; they only do so when used to consider a particular problem that initial observation of planning processes has thrown up. But if there is a strong connection between the theoretical framing and the methods for data collection and analysis that have been deployed, then this should close the loop. The objective of the research is achieved in that the questions should have an answer.

In essence, what the Golden Triangle is drawing attention to is the importance of research design. This is the need to make sure that all the different elements of research are aligned before the empirical research is undertaken. This is the task of research design. It may involve more than just 'adopting' one specific framework. Research may nuance that framework—perhaps developed in a specific geographical or other context—so that it is relevant to a different context. Researchers may seek to combine frameworks to give a more complex and developed account of planning, although care always has to be taken not to combine the incompatible. Each theory has its own roots in a particular ontology—view of what the world is—as well as epistemology—view of how the world can be known; moving across ontological and epistemological boundaries can produce incoherent frameworks.

It should be clear that this is not just about applying theory in the way that one chooses to follow the recipes in a cookbook. This is about building an argument through the analysis of research findings and using a theoretical framework, with the concepts that it offers, to make that argument persuasive as it moves from empirical data to general finding and back again (and back again). The theory does not remain outside the empirical analysis but may have light shed on it by the empirical research. Such research can suggest modifications to the theoretical approach, at least for studying the particular case or issue at hand. This is one of the further excitements of undertaking theory-informed research.

Activating the Golden Triangle

So where does one start in order to generate this Golden Triangle? As suggested above, the starting point has to be something that one has seen in the world of planning practice or policy and considered interesting. Research begins from an issue, a problem or a puzzle. But as an academic activity, it also relates from early on to the existing research literature on the issue, the problem, the puzzle. Very few things have not been researched at all; perhaps the exact topic is slightly to the one side or the geographical location is different, but it is always an early task in a research project to see what has already been done. This is partly to try to understand the current state of understanding about this aspect of planning, but it is also centrally to consider where the gaps, contradictions and weaknesses are. In this way, planning research can hope to advance understanding rather than repeat findings.

Through the interaction of puzzlement about the world of planning and a thorough reading of what has already been researched, the research questions will hopefully arise. There is a temptation to use planning research to make an argument—not in terms of using data rigorously to explore possible interpretations but, rather, in terms of expanding on a viewpoint that one already holds. Of course, the choice of a research topic and theoretical framing implies, as has been repeatedly emphasised, the values and interests of the researcher. However, if research is to differ from other expository forms of writing, the researcher needs to be open to the interpretation of data leading to new and different conclusions. And this means that the research questions need to be capable of being answered in potentially different ways; they are not there to be demonstrated or proven.

Often (one might say, always) the research questions require refinement over some period of time. This may be due to new information that emerges about the topic of research: it might be an attempt to make the research more original and avoid replicating existing findings, or it might be the identification of a more interesting angle on the research arising from wider theoretical reading. For the research literature is not just about amassing research findings. Every account of planning research has a conceptual approach explicit or implicit within it, even if it is an empiricist one. A wide-ranging literature review will bring in literature with a variety of such theoretical perspectives, and this may lead to an adjustment in the questions one wants to address.

Thus, a process of iteratively refining the research questions in engagement with the research literature will occur. Some may be more descriptive, some more analytic and some more theoretical. For example, in a project on the governance of renewable energy projects, some research questions may map the extent and nature of such projects in a locality, others may consider the governance networks and consider how different actors engage with each other, and others may consider whether collaboration works effectively through such networks or the planning process needs to be reconceptualised in terms that go beyond collaborative governance.

However, it is key moment in any research project when the research questions become fixed (at least for now) and their relationship to the theoretical framing is clarified. Once the research question and theoretical framing have been settled in this way, then it is possible to devise the relevant methodologies for both data collection and data analysis. The examples of research surveyed and discussed in this book have used a variety of methods, although case study research (often justified by reference to Yin's categories (2017) with document analysis, surveys and interviews probably dominates. These methods tend to be relevant across the different theoretical frameworks deployed. But the different frameworks also have distinctive methodologies that fit particularly well within that approach; these are summarised in Table 10.2. It is often beneficial to incorporate these distinctive methodologies within a research design to ensure the maximum leverage from adopting a specific conceptual approach.

The key point is that the theoretical approach and the concepts that it deploys should suggest the details of how these diverse methodologies will be used. For example, they could suggest proformas for interviews and coding schedules. If adopting a Foucauldian approach, say, this could identify different aspects of governmental technologies—such as the role of statistical metrics and calculative practices—and how they operate. With a political economy approach, the questions could instead specify different forms of capital and how they are invested, the prevalence of neo-liberal arguments and assumptions about the role of the state. It should be possible to identify the conceptual framing from such details of data collection and analysis, rather than having a generic reliance on qualitative or quantitative research methodologies. The devil is indeed in the detail here. Ethics approval,

Table 10.2 Distinctive methodologies associated with different theoretical approaches

Theoretical Approach	Distinctive methodologies
Governmental Model	Policy evaluation methodologies; testing existing/new procedures and tools with stakeholders
Rational Choice	Modelling planning as a game including incentives/payout matrices; experimentation or game playing
New Institutionalism	Organisational mapping supplemented with discourse analysis or interpretive policy analysis
Governance Theory	Stakeholder mapping including resource inter-dependencies; network analysis (formal or informal)
Urban Politics	Case studies of conflict pursued through action research, embedded ethnography or emic research on participants' perspectives
Political Economy	Historical research using economic data, particularly encompassing periods of boom and crisis and identifying where capital flows
Foucauldian Approach	Examining micro-practices of constructing knowledge and exercising governmental technologies, including through classification
Relational Approaches	Tracing associations involving social and material actors and 'following the actor' to identify configurations that result in agency

while often seen as a bureaucratic frustration, can actually be helpful due to the level of specificity that it typically requires.

Choosing a Theoretical Framework

The importance of the choice of which theoretical framework to adopt has been emphasised throughout this book. But how does one choose a framework? If the choice of a research topic is based on what one had noticed as interesting, puzzling or intriguing, what guides the choice of concepts and theoretical ideas that will be deployed to investigate this? Table 10.3 provides a summary of the various frameworks discussed in terms of their key focus for research and the nature of the dynamics that they theorise as characterising planning processes. This makes clear the distinctive nature of each perspective.

So, the relevant questions are about how the perspective of a specific theoretical framework aligns with more general views of the researcher on relevant aspects. Possible questions for the researcher to ask themselves are as follows:

- Are you interested in what the individual planner or planning organisation does or in the way they fit into relationships within society?
- Are you more interested in the conflicts and tensions found in the planning system or in the potential for reforming that system?
- Do you tend to emphasise the possibilities for change or focus in on the reasons that things tend to stay the same?

Table 10.3 Theories in planning research: a summary

Theoretical approach	Key focus	Nature of dynamics
Governmental Model	How planning policy is made and implemented	Striving to achieve public policy goals
Rational Choice	How actors pursue their interests within the planning system	Goal-seeking, involving competition or strategic cooperation
New Institutionalism	How organisational and the wider culture shape planners' actions	Appropriate behaviour, following norms and routines, and shaped by worldviews
Governance Theory	How capacity to act is built through networks	Recognition of mutual inter-dependence and interactions, including communicative action, potentially leading to social capital within networks
Urban Politics	How social conflicts shape planning processes and outcomes	Conflict between different social groups (based on class, ethnicity, etc.) and with the state, and associated direct action
Political Economy	How capitalism determines the activities of the planning system	Drive to accumulate capital, switching between different forms of capital and response to economic crises
Foucauldian Approach	How societal discourses create dispersed power dynamics	The social construction of discourses, particularly around knowledge, through micro-practices and the role of specific technologies
Relational Approaches	How associations between heterogeneous elements generate agency	The work needed to stabilise specific sets of associations within networks (or assemblages, etc.) and the particular agency associated with material elements

- Do you tend to focus on structural aspects or the agency of actors? Put another way, do you think that broader shifts in society and the economy explain things, or do you focus more on the actions that individuals and organisations take?
- Thinking about the interests of actors, do you think that actors take decisions on the basis of their interests?
- Do you assume that actors know what their interests are? Do you take their assertion of their interests for granted or are you interested in looking behind these assertions?
- What is your view of power? Do you tend to identify powerful actors and consider what they do, taking into account the resources at their disposal?
- Or do you think that agency is a better way of considering why things happen and see this as arising in a continent fashion from the relationships at a particular time?
- Do you wish, in your empirical analysis, to zoom in on the detail of what is happening or to zoom out and present the big picture about an issue?
- Do you wish to consider how everyday, normal or average patterns shape the planning system or focus on the unusual, the atypical and experimental?

Reflecting on the answers to such questions can help identify which conceptual framing is most likely to resonate and thus take the researcher forward to a deeper understanding of planning processes.

Finally, it can also help to consider one's own writing style and which research papers most closely approximate to this (or which one would like to emulate). After all, relating research results is a writing task. Each theoretical framing leads to a slightly different way of telling the story of an empirical research project, as the various papers discussed in this book show. Reflecting on writing style can help clarify which theoretical approach is most likely to produce a story one is comfortable and confident telling.

Allowing for Change

The book ends with a word about the need to be flexible to some extent within the research process. Research design emphasises the need to align research questions, theoretical framework and methodological approach. This needs thinking through in detail in the specific context of the empirical work being undertaken. This design will probably be captured in a research proposal, a grant application or a PhD upgrade or progression document. Once captured in this way, the research design should act as a template for the rest of the research project and can seem immutable. However, things can change, and it can be necessary to adjust the research design as one goes along. There are a number of reasons why relevant change can occur.

First, if one is studying contemporary planning processes, the world can change around one and render the research proposal less relevant. A political economy study into the way that planning systems contribute to stability in the housing market may be affected by an economic crisis with plummeting house prices and abandonment of development sites. In this case, the political economy framework may still seem entirely relevant, but the research questions need to be reframed to capture a shifting relationship between state action and capital accumulation, with an apparent rapid devaluation of capital occurring in the housing sector. Changes in current situations may not mean that the conceptual framework is rendered in appropriate; it may mean that more thinking is needed about how it could interpret these changing circumstances.

But, second, it may be that the findings from the empirical research suggest a change in direction in terms of conceptual thinking. If the governance analysis of stakeholder relationships throws up the importance of the way that knowledge was constructed within those relationships and, further, how those relationships were shaped by those knowledge claims, then there may be a need to consider how a Foucauldian perspective could add to the analysis. This can lead to refining the research design, possibly adding new research questions, suggesting new paths for empirical investigation and possibly adapting the theoretical framing. The driving question should be: is the theoretical framework helping me understand my data and research context? If not, then there is the potential for a creative approach, and nuancing that framework may be an important element of the research.

Third, it can be that practical difficulties encountered during data collection (and less commonly in data analysis) can prompt a rethink. Empirical research often faces barriers. People do not want to give interviews, survey response rates are low, permission cannot be obtained for observational studies and so on. More seriously, the fieldwork location may become out of bounds for reasons of public health emergency (such as the coronavirus prevalent as I write), political upheaval (also currently affecting research in Hong Kong) or economic crisis (wrecking the budget of a project or rendering other practice aspects of the research impractical). Sometimes the difficulties just require a rescaling of the project (as with changes in personal circumstances discussed next), but, in other cases, the extent of the challenges requires a more radical rethink. In such situations, it can be a real problem to decide how far to change a project in response; it can also be easy to lose sight of the need to keep the Golden Triangle aligned as amendments and adjustments are made. But without such alignment, the potential of producing meaningful responses to the research questions can be significantly undermined.

Finally, there will sometimes be personal circumstance that requires a change in research design. Any research project has a practical dimension to it and demands a degree of pragmatism in response to its progress (or lack of it). Here there may be a need to scale back or otherwise adjust the research design. However, this kind of change should not alter its fundamentals in terms of the alignment of research questions, theoretical approach and methodology. One case study may be undertaken instead of two, or the location of the case study may be changed to something more convenient. The ambitions may be limited, but the essence of the project will probably remain the same.

Research is a difficult process, and the challenges are significant. But the rewards are also large in terms of intellectual growth and greater understanding. Hopefully, a theory-oriented research process will help in your understanding of our complex planning systems and how they work. And with that … good luck!

Bibliography

Yin, R. (2017). *Case Study Research and Applications: design and methods*. 6th ed. London Sage Publications.

Bibliography

Agyeman, Julian. 2005. *Sustainable Communities and the Challenge of Environmental Justice.* New York: New York University Press.

Ambrose, Peter J., and Bob Colenutt. 1975. *The Property Machine.* Harmondsworth: Penguin.

Anderson, Matthew B., et al. 2018. Prior Appropriation and Water Planning Reform in Montana's Yellowstone River Basin: Path Dependency or Boundary Object? *Journal of Environmental Policy & Planning* 20 (2): 198–213.

Ascui, Francisco, Marcus Haward, and Heather Lovell. 2018. Salmon, Sensors, and Translation: The Agency of Big Data in Environmental Governance. *Environment and Planning: Society & Space* 36 (5): 905–925.

Bache, Ian, and Matthew Flinders, eds. 2004. *Multi-Level Governance.* Oxford: Oxford University Press.

Bachrach, Peter, and Morton S. Baratz. 1963. Decisions and Nondecisions: An Analytical Framework. *The American Political Science Review* 57 (3): 632–642.

———. 2012. Two Faces of Power. *The American Political Science Review* 56 (4): 947–952.

Balaban, Utku. 2011. The Enclosure of Urban Space and Consolidation of the Capitalist Land Regime in Turkish Cities. *Urban Studies* 48 (10): 2162–2179.

Barrett, Susan, and Colin Fudge, eds. 1981. *Policy and Action: Essays on the Implementation of Public Policy.* London: Methuen.

Beaumont, Justin, and Maarten Loopmans. 2008. Towards Radicalized Communicative Rationality: Resident Involvement and Urban Democracy in Rotterdam and Antwerp. *International Journal of Urban and Regional Research* 32 (1): 95–113.

Beck, Ulrich. 1992. *Risk Society: Towards a New Modernity; translated by Mark Ritter.* London: Sage Publications.

Beebeejaun, Yasminah. 2006. The Participation Trap: The Limitations of Participation for Ethnic and Racial Groups. *International Planning Studies* 11 (1): 3–18.

———. 2017. Gender, Urban Space, and the Right to Everyday Life. *Journal of Urban Affairs* 39 (3): 323–334.

Berthou, Sara Kristine Gløjmar, and Betina Vind Ebbesen. 2016. Local Governing of Climate Change in Denmark: Recasting Citizens as Consumers. *Journal of Environmental Planning and Management* 59 (3): 501–517.

Bickerstaff, Karen, and Gordon Walker. 2005. Shared Visions, Unholy Alliances: Power, Governance and Deliberative Processes in Local Transport Planning. *Urban Studies* 42 (12): 2123–2144.

© The Author(s), under exclusive license to Springer Nature Singapore Pte Ltd. 2021
Y. Rydin, *Theory in Planning Research*, Planning, Environment, Cities, https://doi.org/10.1007/978-981-33-6568-1

Bisschops, Saskia, and Raoul Beunen. 2018. A New Role for Citizens' Initiatives: The Difficulties in Co-Creating Institutional Change in Urban Planning. *Journal of Environmental Planning and Management* 62 (1): 72–87.

Blum, Elizabeth D. 2008. *Love Canal Revisited: Race, Class, and Gender in Environmental Activism*. Lawrence, KS: University Press of Kansas.

Boamah, Emmanuel Frimpong, and Clifford Amoako. 2020. Planning by (Mis)Rule of Laws: The Idiom and Dilemma of Planning within Ghana's Dual Legal Land Systems. *Environment and Planning C: Politics and Space* 38 (1): 97–115.

Booth, Philip. 2011. Culture, Planning and Path Dependence: Some Reflections on the Problems of Comparison. *Town Planning Review* 82 (1): 13–28.

Bresnihan, Patrick. 2019. Revisiting Neoliberalism in the Oceans: Governmentality and the Biopolitics of 'Improvement' in the Irish and European Fisheries. *Environment and Planning A: Economy and Space* 51 (1): 156–177.

Broadbent, Thomas Andrew. 2007. *Planning and Profit in the Urban Economy*. London: Routledge.

Brownill, Sue. 2009. The Dynamics of Participation: Modes of Governance and Increasing Participation in Planning. *Urban Policy and Research* 27 (4): 357–375.

Bulkeley, Harriet, and Michele Betsill. 2003. *Cities and Climate Change: Urban Sustainability and Global Environmental Governance*. London; New York: Routledge.

Bulkeley, Harriet, Vanesa Castán Broto, and Gareth A.S. Edwards. 2015. *An Urban Politics of Climate Change: Experimentation and the Governing of Socio-Technical Transitions*. London: Routledge.

Bunker, Raymond. 2012. Reviewing the Path Dependency in Australian Metropolitan Planning. *Urban Policy and Research* 30 (4): 443–452.

Burayidi, Michael, Adriana Allen, John Twigg, and Christine Wamsler. 2019. *The Routledge Handbook of Urban Resilience*. London: Routledge.

Butler, Chris. 2012. *Henri Lefebvre Spatial Politics, Everyday Life and the Right to the City*. New York: Routledge.

Callon, Michel. 2010. Performativity, Misfires and Politics. *Journal of Cultural Economy* 3 (2): 163–169.

———. 2017. Some Elements of a Sociology of Translation: Domestication of the Scallops and the Fishermen of Saint-Brieuc Bay. *Logos* 27 (2): 49–90.

Campbell, Scott, and Susan Fainstein, eds. 2003. *Readings in Planning Theory*. 2nd ed. Oxford: Blackwell.

Campbell, Heather, Malcolm Tait, and Craig Watkins. 2014. Is There Space for Better Planning in a Neoliberal World? Implications for Planning Practice and Theory. *Journal of Planning Education and Research* 34 (1): 45–59.

Cantzler, Julia Miller, and Megan Huynh. 2015. Native American Environmental Justice as Decolonization. *The American Behavioral Scientist* 60 (2): 203–223.

Castells, Manuel. 1977. *The Urban Question: a Marxist Approach, translated by Alan Sheridan*. London: Edward Arnold.

———. 1983. *The City and the Grassroots: a Cross-Cultural Theory of Urban Social Movements*. London: Edward Arnold.

Catney, Philip, and John Henneberry. 2012. (Not) Exercising Discretion: Environmental Planning and the Politics of Blame-Avoidance. *Planning Theory & Practice* 13 (4): 549–568.

Certomà, Chiara, and Bruno Notteboom. 2017. Informal Planning in a Transactive Governmentality. Re-Reading Planning Practices through Ghent's Community Gardens. *Planning Theory* 16 (1): 51–73.

de Chastenet, Cédissia About, et al. 2016. The French Eco-Neighbourhood Evaluation Model: Contributions to Sustainable City Making and to the Evolution of Urban Practices. *Journal of Environmental Management* 176: 69–78.

Chettiparamb, Angelique. 2019. Responding to a Complex World: Explorations in Spatial Planning. *Planning Theory* 18 (4): 429–447.

Chiu, Ching-Pin, and Shih-Kung Lai. 2009. An Experimental Comparison of Negotiation Strategies for Siting NIMBY Facilities. *Environment and Planning: Planning and Design* 36 (6): 956–967.

Clifford, Ben, and Mark Tewdwr-Jones. 2013. *The Collaborating Planner?: Practitioners in the Neoliberal Age*. Bristol: Policy Press.

Cugurullo, Federico. 2018. Exposing Smart Cities and Eco-Cities: Frankenstein Urbanism and the Sustainability Challenges of the Experimental City. *Environment and Planning A: Economy and Space* 50 (1): 73–92.

Dahl, Robert Alan. 1998. *On Democracy*. New Haven; London: Yale UP.

Daly, Gavin. 2016. The Neo-Liberalization of Strategic Spatial Planning and the Overproduction of Development in Celtic Tiger Ireland. *European Planning Studies* 24 (9): 1643–1661.

Davoudi, Simin. 2006. Evidence-Based Planning: Rhetoric and Reality. *disP - The Planning Review* 42 (165): 14–24.

Deas, Iain, Stephen Hincks, and Nicola Headlam. 2013. Explicitly Permissive? Understanding Actor Interrelationships in the Governance of Economic Development: The Experience of England's Local Enterprise Partnerships. *Local Economy* 28 (7–8): 718–737.

Deleuze, Gilles, and Félix Guattari. 1988. *A Thousand Plateaus: Capitalism and Schizophrenia*. London: Athlone Press.

Devine-Wright, Patrick. 2009. Rethinking NIMBYism: The Role of Place Attachment and Place Identity in Explaining Place-Protective Action. *Journal of Community & Applied Social Psychology* 19 (6): 426–441.

Devlin, Ryan Thomas. 2018. Asking 'Third World Questions' of First World Informality: Using Southern Theory to Parse Needs from Desires in an Analysis of Informal Urbanism of the Global North. *Planning Theory* 17 (4): 568–587.

Domptail, Stephanie, Marcos H. Easdale, and Yuerlita. 2013. Managing Socio-Ecological Systems to Achieve Sustainability: A Study of Resilience and Robustness. *Environmental Policy and Governance* 23 (1): 30–45.

Douglas, Mary. 1966. *Purity and Danger: An Analysis of Concepts of Pollution and Taboo*. London: Routledge and Kegan Paul.

Dowding, Keith, Patrick Dunleavy, Desmond King, Helen Margetts, and Yvonne Rydin. 1999. Regime Politics in London Local Government. *Urban Affairs Review* 34 (4): 515–545.

Dryzek, John S. 2000. *Deliberative Democracy and Beyond: Liberals, Critics, Contestations*. Oxford: Oxford University Press.

———. 2005. *The Politics of the Earth: Environmental Discourses*. 2nd ed. Oxford: Oxford University Press.

Dunleavy, Patrick. 1980. *Urban Political Analysis*. London: Macmillan.

———. 1991. *Democracy, Bureaucracy and Public Choice: Economic Explanations in Political Science*. London: Prentice Hall.

Eizenberg, Efrat. 2019. Patterns of Self-Organization in the Context of Urban Planning: Reconsidering Venues of Participation. *Planning Theory* 18 (1): 40–57.

Elander, Ingemar, and Eva Gustavsson. 2019. From Policy Community to Issue Networks: Implementing Social Sustainability in a Swedish Urban Development Programme. *Environment and Planning C: Politics and Space* 37 (6): 1082–1101.

Etherington, David, and Martin Jones. 2018. Re-Stating the Post-Political: Depoliticization, Social Inequalities, and City-Region Growth. *Environment and Planning A: Economy and Space* 50 (1): 51–72.

Fairbanks, Luke. 2019. Policy Mobilities and the Sociomateriality of U.S. Offshore Aquaculture Governance. *Environment and Planning C: Politics and Space* 37 (5): 849–867.

Fairbrass, J., and A. Jordan. 2004. *Multi-Level Governance*. In *Multi-Level Governance*, ed. I. Bache and M. Flinders. Oxford: Oxford University Press.

Fairclough, Norman, and Isabela Fairclough. 2012. *Political Discourse Analysis*. London: Routledge.

Faludi, Andreas. 1973. *Planning Theory*. Oxford: Pergamon.

Filion, Pierre, Michelle Lee, Neluka Leanage, and Kent Hakull. 2015. Planners' Perspectives on Obstacles to Sustainable Urban Development: Implications for Transformative Planning Strategies. *Planning Practice and Research* 30 (2): 202–221.

Fisher, Susannah, David Dodman, Marissa Van Epp, and Ben Garside. 2018. The Usability of Climate Information in Sub-National Planning in India, Kenya and Uganda: The Role of Social Learning and Intermediary Organisations. *Climatic Change* 151 (2): 219–245.

Flyvbjerg, Bent. 1998. *Rationality and Power: Democracy in Practice*. Trans. Steven Sampson. Chicago; London: University of Chicago Press.

Flyvbjerg, Bent, Todd Landman, and Sanford Schram, eds. 2012. *Real Social Science: Applied Phronesis*. Cambridge: Cambridge University Press.

Foucault, Michel. 2010. *The Government of Self and Others: Lectures at the Collège de France, 1982–1983*. Ed. Frédéric Gros and Trans. Graham Burchell. Basingstoke: Palgrave Macmillan.

Fougère, L., and S. Bond. 2018. Legitimising Activism in Democracy: A Place for Antagonism in Environmental Governance. *Planning Theory* 17 (2): 143–169.

Friedmann, John. 1987. *Planning in the Public Domain: From Knowledge to Action*. Princeton: Princeton University Press.

Fuller, Crispian, and Karen West. 2017. The Possibilities and Limits of Political Contestation in Times of 'Urban Austerity'. *Urban Studies* 54 (9): 2087–2106.

Furlong, Casey, Saman De Silva, Lachlan Guthrie, and Robert Considine. 2016. Developing a Water Infrastructure Planning Framework for the Complex Modern Planning Environment. *Utilities Policy* 38: 1–10.

Giddens, Anthony. 1986. *The Constitution of Society: Outline of the Theory of Structuration*. Cambridge: Polity Press.

Goodman, Robin, Robert Freestone, and Paul Burton. 2017. Planning Practice and Academic Research: Views from the Parallel Worlds. *Planning, Practice & Research*: 1–12.

Gosden, Chris. 2004. Grid and Group: An Interview with Mary Douglas. *Journal of Social Archaeology* 4 (3): 275–287.

Gualini, Enrico, and Irene Bianchi. 2015. Space, Politics and Conflicts: A Review of Contemporary Debates in Urban Research and Planning Theory. In *Planning and Conflict: Critical Perspectives on Contentious Urban Developments*, ed. Enrico Gualini. New York: Routledge.

Gualini, Enrico, and Carola Fricke. 2019. 'Who Governs' Berlin's Metropolitan Region? The Strategic-Relational Construction of Metropolitan Scale in Berlin–Brandenburg's Economic Development Policies. *Environment and Planning C: Politics and Space* 37 (1): 59–80.

Gunder, Michael, Ali Madanipour, and Vanessa Watson, eds. 2018. *The Routledge Handbook of Planning Theory*. London: Routledge.

Gurran, Nicole, Glen Searle, and Peter Phibbs. 2018. Urban Planning in the Age of Airbnb: Coase, Property Rights, and Spatial Regulation. *Urban Policy and Research* 36 (4): 399–416.

Hajer, Maarten A. 1995. *The Politics of Environmental Discourse: Ecological Modernization and the Policy Process*. Oxford: Clarendon Press.

Hall, Peter A., and Rosemary C.R. Taylor. 1996. Political Science and the Three New Institutionalisms. *Political Studies* 44 (5): 936–957.

Han, Heejin. 2019. Governance for Green Urbanisation: Lessons from Singapore's Green Building Certification Scheme. *Environment and Planning C: Politics and Space* 37 (1): 137–156.

Hartmann, Thomas, and Barrie Needham, eds. 2012. *Planning by Law and Property Rights Reconsidered*. Farnham: Ashgate.

Harvey, David. 1982. *The Limits to Capital*. Oxford: Basil Blackwell.

———. 1985. *The Urbanization of Capital*. Oxford: Blackwell.

———. 1988. *Social Justice and the City*. Oxford: Basil Blackwell.

———. 2010. *The Enigma of Capital and the Crises of Capitalism*. London: Profile.

Healey, Patsy. 1997. *Collaborative Planning: Shaping Places in Fragmented Societies*. Basingstoke: Macmillan.

Heinelt, H. Local Democracy and Citizenship. In *The Oxford Handbook of Urban Politics*, ed. K. Mossberger, S. Clarke, and P. John. Oxford: OUP.

Henly-Shepard, Sarah, Steven A. Gray, and Linda J. Cox. 2015. The Use of Participatory Modeling to Promote Social Learning and Facilitate Community Disaster Planning. *Environmental Science & Policy* 45: 109–122.

Hettinga, Sanne, Peter Nijkamp, and Henk Scholten. 2018. A Multi-Stakeholder Decision Support System for Local Neighbourhood Energy Planning. *Energy Policy* 116 (May): 277–288.

Hill, Michael. 1997. Implementation Theory: Yesterday's Issue? *Policy & Politics* 25 (4): 375–385.

Hillier, Jean, and Patsy Healey, eds. 2008. *Contemporary Movements in Planning Theory.* Aldershot: Ashgate.

Hillier, Jean, and Jonathan Metzger, eds. 2015. *Connections: Exploring Contemporary Planning Theory and Practice with Patsy Healey.* Farnham: Ashgate.

Hodson, Mike, James Evans, and Gabriele Schliwa. 2018. Conditioning Experimentation: The Struggle for Place-Based Discretion in Shaping Urban Infrastructures. *Environment and Planning C: Politics and Space* 36 (8): 1480–1498.

Holden, Meg. 2008. Social Learning in Planning: Seattle's Sustainable Development Codebooks. *Progress in Planning* 69 (1): 1–40.

Holman, Nancy. 2007. Following the Signs: Applying Urban Regime Analysis to a UK Case Study. *Journal of Urban Affairs* 29 (5): 435–453.

———. 2013. Effective Strategy Implementation: Why Partnership Interconnectivity Matters. *Environment and Planning C: Government and Policy* 31 (1): 82–101.

Hooghe, Liesbet, and Gary Marks. 2001. *Multi-Level Governance and European Integration.* Lanham, MD: Rowman & Littlefield Publishers.

Imran, Muhammad, and Nicholas Low. 2007. Institutional, Technical and Discursive Path Dependence in Transport Planning in Pakistan. *International Development Planning Review* 29 (3): 319–352.

Innes, Judith E., David E. Booher, and Sarah Di Vittorio. 2010. Strategies for Megaregion Governance. *Journal of the American Planning Association* 77 (1): 55–67.

Janssen, Marco A., et al. 2006. Toward a Network Perspective of the Study of Resilience in Social-Ecological Systems. *Ecology and Society* 11 (1): 15.

Jasanoff, Sheila. 2015. Serviceable Truths: Science for Action in Law and Policy. *Texas Law Review* 93 (7): 1723.

Jayne, Mark. 2003. Too Many Voices, 'Too Problematic to Be Plausible': Representing Multiple Responses to Local Economic Development Strategies? *Environment and Planning A* 35 (6): 959–981.

Kaza, Nikhil. 2019. Vain Foresight: Against the Idea of Implementation in Planning. *Planning Theory* 18 (4): 410–428.

Kingdon, John. 2003. *Agendas, Alternatives, and Public Policies.* 2nd ed. New York: Longman.

Kontokosta, Constantine E. 2018. Urban Informatics in the Science and Practice of Planning. *Journal of Planning Education and Research.* https://doi.org/10.1177/0739456X18793716.

Koontz, Tomas M. 2013. Social Learning in Collaborative Watershed Planning: The Importance of Process Control and Efficacy. *Journal of Environmental Planning and Management* 57 (10): 1572–1593.

Krueger, Rob, David Gibbs, and Constance Carr. 2018. Examining Regional Competitiveness and the Pressures of Rapid Growth: An Interpretive Institutionalist Account of Policy Responses in Three City Regions. *Environment and Planning C: Politics and Space* 36 (6): 965–986.

Kumar, Parveen, Davide Geneletti, and Harini Nagendra. 2016. Spatial Assessment of Climate Change Vulnerability at City Scale: A Study in Bangalore, India. *Land Use Policy* 58: 514–532.

Lafferty, William M., and Katarina Eckerberg. 1998. *From the Earth Summit to Local Agenda 21: Working towards Sustainable Development.* London: Earthscan.

Laffin, Martin. 2016. Planning in England: New Public Management, Network Governance or Post-Democracy? *International Review of Administrative Sciences* 82 (2): 354–372.

De Landa, Manuel. 2006. *A New Philosophy of Society: Assemblage Theory and Social Complexity.* London: Continuum.

Latour, Bruno. 1987. *Science in Action: How to Follow Scientists and Engineers through Society.* Cambridge, MA: Harvard University Press.

———. 2005. *Reassembling the Social: An Introduction to Actor-Network-Theory.* Oxford: Oxford University Press.

Lauermann, John, and Anne Vogelpohl. 2017. Fragile Growth Coalitions or Powerful Contestations? Cancelled Olympic Bids in Boston and Hamburg. *Environment and Planning A* 49 (8): 1887–1904.

Law, John, and John Hassard. 1999. *Actor Network Theory and After.* Oxford: Blackwell.

Lefebvre, Henri. 2008. *Critique of Everyday Life.* Trans. John Moore. London: Verso.

Leigh Star, Susan. 2010. This Is Not a Boundary Object: Reflections on the Origin of a Concept. *Science, Technology, & Human Values* 35 (5): 601–617.

Leontidou, Lila. 2010. Urban Social Movements in 'Weak' Civil Societies: The Right to the City and Cosmopolitan Activism in Southern Europe. *Urban Studies* 47 (6): 1179–1203.

Levy, Charmain, Anne Latendresse, and Marianne Carle-Marsan. 2017. Gendering the Urban Social Movement and Public Housing Policy in São Paulo. *Latin American Perspectives* 44 (3): 9–27.

Li, Bin, and Chaoqun Liu. 2018. Emerging Selective Regimes in a Fragmented Authoritarian Environment: The 'Three Old Redevelopment' Policy in Guangzhou, China from 2009 to 2014. *Urban Studies* 55 (7): 1400–1419.

Lichfield, Nathaniel, Peter Kettle, and Michael Whitbread. 1975. *Evaluation in the Planning Process.* Oxford: Pergamon.

Lindblom, Charles E. 2010. The Science of 'Muddling' Through. *Emergence: Complexity and Organization* 12 (1): 70.

Lord, Alex. 2012. *The Planning Game: An Information Economics Approach to Understanding Urban and Environmental Management.* London: Routledge.

Lord, Alex, and Philip O'Brien. 2017. What Price Planning? Reimagining Planning as 'Market Maker'. *Planning Theory & Practice* 18 (2): 217–232.

Lucas, Chloe, and Russell Warman. 2018. Disrupting Polarized Discourses: Can We Get out of the Ruts of Environmental Conflicts? *Environment and Planning C: Politics and Space* 36 (6): 987–1005.

Lukes, Steven. 2005. *Power: A Radical View.* 2nd ed. Basingstoke: Palgrave Macmillan.

Ma, Xin, Martin de Jong, and Harry den Hartog. 2018. Assessing the Implementation of the Chongming Eco Island Policy: What a Broad Planning Evaluation Framework Tells More than Technocratic Indicator Systems. *Journal of Cleaner Production* 172: 872–886.

MacDonald, Heather. 2019. Planning for the Public Benefit in the Entrepreneurial City: Public Land Speculation and Financialized Regulation. *Journal of Planning Education and Research.* https://doi.org/10.1177/0739456X19847519.

Mandelbaum, Seymour, Luigi Mazza, and Richard Burchell, eds. 1996. *Explorations in Planning Theory.* Rutgers, NJ: The State University of New Jersey.

March, James G., and Johan P. Olsen. 1989. *Rediscovering Institutions: The Organizational Basis of Politics.* New York; London: Free Press.

Martínez, Joyde Giacomini, Ingrid Boas, Jennifer Lenhart, and Arthur P.J. Mol. 2016. Revealing Curitiba's Flawed Sustainability: How Discourse Can Prevent Institutional Change. *Habitat International* 53: 350–359.

Massey, Doreen, and Alejandrina Catalano. 1978. *Capital and Land: Landownership by Capital in Great Britain.* London: Edward Arnold.

Mayer, Margit. 2010. The 'Right to the City' in the Context of Shifting Mottos of Urban Social Movements. *City* 13 (2–3): 362–374.

Mbiba, Beacon. 2017. Idioms of Accumulation: Corporate Accumulation by Dispossession in Urban Zimbabwe: Idioms of Accumulation. *International Journal of Urban and Regional Research* 41 (2): 213–234.

McFarlane, Colin. 2018. Fragment Urbanism: Politics at the Margins of the City. *Environment and Planning:, Society & Space* 36 (6): 1007–1025.

McGreevy, Michael Patrick. 2018. Complexity as the Telos of Postmodern Planning and Design: Designing Better Cities from the Bottom-Up. *Planning Theory* 17 (3): 355–374.

McLoughlin, J. Brian. 1969. *Urban and Regional Planning: A Systems Approach*. London: Faber.

McNiff, Jean. 2013. *Action Research Principles and Practice*. 3rd ed. Hoboken: Taylor and Francis.

Meijer, Marlies, and Huib Ernste. 2019. Broadening the Scope of Spatial Planning: Making a Case for Informality in the Netherlands. *Journal of Planning Education and Research*. https://doi.org/10.1177/0739456X19826211.

Merriman, Peter. 2019. Relational Governance, Distributed Agency and the Unfolding of Movements, Habits and Environments: Parking Practices and Regulations in England. *Environment and Planning C: Politics and Space* 37 (8): 1400–1417.

Metzger, Jonathan, Linda Soneryd, and Kristina Tamm Hallström. 2017. 'Power' Is That Which Remains to Be Explained: Dispelling the Ominous Dark Matter of Critical Planning Studies. *Planning Theory* 16 (2): 203–222.

Miller, Peter, and Nikolas Rose. 2006. Governing Economic Life. *Economy and Society* 19 (1): 1–31.

Molotch, Harvey. 1993. The Political Economy of Growth Machines *Journal of Urban Affairs* 15 (1): 29–53.

Moroni, Stefano, Ward Rauws, and Stefano Cozzolino. 2019. Forms of Self-Organization: Urban Complexity and Planning Implications. *Environment and Planning: Urban Analytics and City Science* 47 (2): 220–234.

Mossberger, Karen, and Gerry Stoker. 2016. The Evolution of Urban Regime Theory. *Urban Affairs Review* 36 (6): 810–835.

Mouffe, Chantal. 2013. *Agonistics: Thinking the World Politically*. London: Verso.

Murray, Cameron K., and Paul Frijters. 2016. Clean Money, Dirty System: Connected Landowners Capture Beneficial Land Rezoning. *Journal of Urban Economics* 93: 99–114.

Myerson, George, and Yvonne Rydin. 1996. *The Language of Environment: A New Rhetoric*. Vancouver: UBC Press.

NÆss, Petter, and Inger-Lise Saglie. 2000. Surviving Between the Trenches: Planning Research, Methodology and Theory of Science. *European Planning Studies* 8 (6): 729–750.

Nicholls, Walter J. 2008. The Urban Question Revisited: The Importance of Cities for Social Movements. *International Journal of Urban and Regional Research* 32 (4): 841–859.

Nilsson, Måns. 2005. Learning, Frames, and Environmental Policy Integration: The Case of Swedish Energy Policy. *Environment and Planning C: Government and Policy* 23 (2): 207–226.

Nobre, Silvana, Ljusk-Ola Eriksson, and Renats Trubins. 2016. The Use of Decision Support Systems in Forest Management: Analysis of FORSYS Country Reports. *Forests* 7 (12): 72.

Nunbogu, Abraham Marshall, and Prosper Issahaku Korah. 2017. Self-Organisation in Urban Spatial Planning: Evidence from the Greater Accra Metropolitan Area, Ghana. *Urban Research & Practice* 10 (4): 423–441.

O'Connor, James. 1973. *The Fiscal Crisis of the State*. New York & London: St. Martin's Press and St. James Press.

O'Neill, Phillip. 2017. Managing the Private Financing of Urban Infrastructure. *Urban Policy and Research* 35 (1): 32–43.

Oxley, Michael. 2004. *Economics, Planning and Housing*. Basingstoke: Palgrave Macmillan.

Pasternak, Shiri, and Tia Dafnos. 2017. How Does a Settler State Secure the Circuitry of Capital? *Environment and Planning D: Society & Space* 36 (4): 739–757.

Pennington, Mark. 2000a. *Planning and the Political Market: Public Choice and the Politics of Government Failure*. London: Athlone Press.

———. 2000b. Public Choice Theory and the Politics of Urban Containment: Voter-Centred Versus Special-Interest Explanations. *Environment and Planning C: Government and Policy* 18 (2): 145–162.

Pierre, Jon, ed. 1998. *Partnerships in Urban Governance: European and American Experience*. Basingstoke: Palgrave.

————. 2014. Can Urban Regimes Travel in Time and Space? Urban Regime Theory, Urban Governance Theory, and Comparative Urban Politics. *Urban Affairs Review* 50 (6): 864–889.

Pinho, Paulo. 1997. Local Planning and National Environmental Assessment Procedures: The Developer's Mitigated Role in Disjointed Negotiation Processes. *Urban Studies* 34 (12): 2037–2052.

Portugali, Juval. 2008. Learning from Paradoxes About Prediction and Planning in Self-organizing Cities. *Planning Theory* 7 (3): 248–262.

Poulton, Michael C. 1997. Externalities, Transaction Costs, Public Choice and the Appeal of Zoning: A Response to Lai Wai Chung and Sorensen. *Town Planning Review* 68 (1): 81–92.

Quick, Kathryn S. 2018. The Narrative Production of Stakeholder Engagement Processes. *Journal of Planning Education and Research*. https://doi.org/10.1177/0739456X18791716.

Raco, Mike. 2003. Governmentality, Subject-Building, and the Discourses and Practices of Devolution in the UK. *Transactions of the Institute of British Geographers* 28 (1): 75–95.

————. 2014. The Post-Politics of Sustainability Planning. In *The Post-Political and Its Discontents: Spaces of De-politicisation, Spectres of Radical Politics*, ed. Japhy Wilson and Eric Swyngedouw. Edinburgh: Edinburgh University Press.

Raco, Mike, and Rob Imrie. 2016. Governmentality and Rights and Responsibilities in Urban Policy. *Environment and Planning A* 32 (12): 2187–2204.

Ravazzi, Stefania, and Silvano Belligni. 2016. Explaining 'Power To': Incubation and Agenda Building in an Urban Regime. *Urban Affairs Review* 52 (3): 323–347.

Reeve, Andrew. 1986. *Property*. London: Macmillan.

Rhodes, Rob. 1997. *Understanding Governance: Policy Networks, Governance, Reflexivity and Accountability*. Maidenhead: Open University Press.

Richmond, Matthew Aaron. 2018. Rio de Janeiro's Favela Assemblage: Accounting for the Durability of an Unstable Object. *Environment and Planning D: Society and Space* 36 (6): 1045–1062.

Robbins, Paul. 2012. *Political Ecology: A Critical Introduction*. 2nd ed. Chichester: Wiley-Blackwell.

Rogers, Dallas. 2016. Monitory Democracy as Citizen-Driven Participatory Planning: The Urban Politics of Redwatch in Sydney. *Urban Policy and Research* 34 (3): 225–239.

De Roo, G., J. Hillier, and J. van Wezemael, eds. 2012. *Complexity and Planning: Systems, Assemblages and Simulations*. Farnham: Ashgate.

Rosol, Marit. 2014. On Resistance in the Post-Political City: Conduct and Counter-Conduct in Vancouver. *Space & Polity* 18 (1): 70–84.

Rydin, Yvonne. 2003. *Conflict, Consensus, and Rationality in Environmental Planning: An Institutional Discourse Approach*. Oxford: Oxford University Press.

————. 2013. The Issue Network of Zero-Carbon Built Environments: A Quantitative and Qualitative Analysis. *Environmental Politics* 22 (3): 496–517.

————. 2014. The Challenges of the 'Material Turn' for Planning Studies. *Planning Theory & Practice* 15 (4): 590–595.

Rydin, Yvonne, and Nancy Holman. 2004. Re-Evaluating the Contribution of Social Capital in Achieving Sustainable Development. *Local Environment* 9 (2): 117–133.

Rydin, Yvonne, and Lucy Natarajan. 2016. The Materiality of Public Participation: The Case of Community Consultation on Spatial Planning for North Northamptonshire, England. *Local Environment* 21 (10): 1243–1251.

Rydin, Yvonne, and Laura Tate, eds. 2016. *Actor Networks of Planning: Exploring the Influence of ANT*. New York: Routledge.

Rydin, Yvonne, Lucy Natarajan, Maria Lee, and Simon Lock. 2018a. Black-Boxing the Evidence: Planning Regulation and Major Renewable Energy Infrastructure Projects in England and Wales. *Planning Theory & Practice* 19 (2): 218–234.

————. 2018b. Local Voices on Renewable Energy Projects: The Performative Role of the Regulatory Process for Major Offshore Infrastructure in England and Wales. *Local Environment* 23 (5): 565–581.

Sager, Tore. 2002. *Democratic Planning and Social Choice Dilemmas: Prelude to Institutional Planning Theory*. Aldershot: Ashgate.

———. 2015. Ideological Traces in Plans for Compact Cities: Is Neo-Liberalism Hegemonic? *Planning Theory* 14 (3): 268–295.

Salet, Willem, Andy Thornley, and Anton Kruekels, eds. 2003. *Metropolitan Governance and Spatial Planning: Comparative Case Studies of European City-Regions*. London: Spon Press.

Sanderson, Ian. 2002. Evaluation, Policy Learning and Evidence-Based Policy Making. *Public Administration* 80 (1): 1–22.

Savini, F., and M.B. Aalbers. 2016. The De-Contextualisation of Land Use Planning Through Financialisation: Urban Redevelopment in Milan. *European Urban and Regional Studies* 23 (4): 878–894.

Schlosberg, David. 1999. *Environmental Justice and the New Pluralism: The Challenge of Difference for Environmentalism*. Oxford: Oxford University Press.

Schon, Donald A. 2008. *Reflective Practitioner How Professionals Think In Action*. New York: Basic Books.

Sharp, Liz, and Tim Richardson. 2001. Reflections on Foucauldian Discourse Analysis in Planning and Environmental Policy Research. *Journal of Environmental Policy & Planning* 3 (3): 193–209.

Shatkin, Gavin. 2016. The Real Estate Turn in Policy and Planning: Land Monetization and the Political Economy of Peri-Urbanization in Asia. *Cities* 53: 141–149.

Silva, Paulo, and Helena Farrall. 2016. Lessons from Informal Settlements: A 'Peripheral' Problem with Self-Organising Solutions. *Town Planning Review* 87 (3): 297–319.

Skrimizea, Eirini, Helene Haniotou, and Constanza Parra. 2018. On the 'Complexity Turn' in Planning: An Adaptive Rationale to Navigate Spaces and Times of Uncertainty. *Planning Theory* 18 (1): 122–142.

Smith, Neil. 1996. *The New Urban Frontier: Gentrification and the Revanchist City*. London: Routledge.

Smith, Mark C. 2018. Revisiting Implementation Theory: An Interdisciplinary Comparison between Urban Planning and Healthcare Implementation Research. *Environment and Planning C: Politics and Space* 36 (5): 877–896.

Song, Lily K. 2016. Planning with Urban Informality: A Case for Inclusion, Co-Production and Reiteration. *International Development Planning Review* 38 (4) 359–381.

Sorensen, Andre. 2014. Taking Path Dependence Seriously: An Historical Institutionalist Research Agenda in Planning History. *Planning Perspectives* 30 (1): 17–38.

Speake, Janet. 2017. Urban Development and Visual Culture: Commodifying the Gaze in the Regeneration of Tigné Point, Malta. *Urban Studies* 54 (13): 2919–2934.

Stoker, Gerry, ed. 2000. *The New Politics of British Local Governance*. Basingstoke: Macmillan Press.

Stone, Clarence N. 1989. *Regime Politics: Governing Atlanta, 1946–1988*. Lawrence, KS; London: University Press of Kansas.

Swyngedouw, Erik. 2009. The Antinomies of the Postpolitical City: In Search of a Democratic Politics of Environmental Production. *International Journal of Urban and Regional Research* 33 (3): 601–620.

———. 2011. *Designing the Post-Political City and the Insurgent Polis*. London: Bedford Press.

Tafon, Ralph, David Howarth, and Steven Griggs. 2019. The Politics of Estonia's Offshore Wind Energy Programme: Discourse, Power and Marine Spatial Planning. *Environment and Planning C: Politics and Space* 37 (1): 157–176.

Tajima, Ryo, and Thomas B. Fischer. 2013. Should Different Impact Assessment Instruments Be Integrated? Evidence from English Spatial Planning. *Environmental Impact Assessment Review* 41: 29–37.

Taylor, Zack. 2013. Rethinking Planning Culture: A New Institutionalist Approach. *Town Planning Review* 84 (6): 683–702.

Taylor, Elizabeth Jean. 2016. Urban Growth Boundaries and Betterment: Rent-Seeking by Landowners on Melbourne's Expanding Urban Fringe: Urban Growth Boundaries and Betterment. *Growth and Change* 47 (2): 259–275.

Tewdwr-Jones, Mark, and Phil Allmendinger. 2016. Deconstructing Communicative Rationality: A Critique of Habermasian Collaborative Planning. *Environment and Planning A* 30 (11): 1975–1989.

Tozer, Laura. 2018. Urban Climate Change and Sustainability Planning: An Analysis of Sustainability and Climate Change Discourses in Local Government Plans in Canada. *Journal of Environmental Planning and Management* 61 (1): 176–194.

Trapenberg Frick, Karen. 2018. No Permanent Friends, No Permanent Enemies: Agonistic Ethos, Tactical Coalitions, and Sustainable Infrastructure. *Journal of Planning Education and Research*. https://doi.org/10.1177/0739456X18773491.

Tulumello, Simone. 2015. Reconsidering Neoliberal Urban Planning in Times of Crisis: Urban Regeneration Policy in a 'Dense' Space in Lisbon. *Urban Geography* 37 (1): 117–140.

Uysal, Ülke Evrim. 2012. An Urban Social Movement Challenging Urban Regeneration: The Case of Sulukule, Istanbul. *Cities* 29 (1): 12–22.

Vogelpohl, Anne, and Tino Buchholz. 2017. Breaking With Neoliberalization by Restricting The Housing Market: Novel Urban Policies and the Case of Hamburg. *International Journal of Urban and Regional Research* 41 (2): 266–281.

Webster, Christopher J., and Lawrence Wai-Chung Lai. 2003. *Property Rights, Planning and Markets: Managing Spontaneous Cities*. Cheltenham: Edward Elgar.

De Weerdt, Julie, and Marisol Garcia. 2015. Housing Crisis: The Platform of Mortgage Victims (PAH) Movement in Barcelona and Innovations in Governance. *Journal of Housing and the Built Environment* 31 (3): 471–493.

Wenger, Etienne. 1998. *Communities of Practice: Learning, Meaning, and Identity*. Cambridge: Cambridge University Press.

Wideman, Trevor J., and Jeffrey R. Masuda. 2018. Toponymic Assemblages, Resistance, and the Politics of Planning in Vancouver, Canada. *Environment and Planning C: Politics and Space* 36 (3): 383–402.

De Wilde, Mandy, and Thomas Franssen. 2016. The Material Practices of Quantification: Measuring 'Deprivation' in the Amsterdam Neighbourhood Policy. *Critical Social Policy* 36 (4): 489–510.

Willems, Jannes, Tim Busscher, Margaretha van den Brink, and Eric Arts. 2018. Anticipating Water Infrastructure Renewal: A Framing Perspective on Organizational Learning in Public Agencies. *Environment and Planning C: Politics and Space* 36 (6): 1088–1108.

Wissing, Kirsty. 2019. Assistance and Resistance of (Hydro-)Power: Contested Relationships of Control over the Volta River, Ghana. *Environment and Planning C: Politics and Space* 37 (7): 1161–1178.

World Commission on Environment and Development. 1987. *Our Common Future*. Oxford: Oxford University Press.

Yamamoto, Arata D. 2017. Why Agonistic Planning? Questioning Chantal Mouffe's Thesis of the Ontological Primacy of the Political. *Planning Theory* 16 (4): 384–403.

Zhang, Shuhai, and Gert de Roo. 2016. Interdependency of Self-Organisation and Planning: Evidence from Nanluoguxiang, Beijing. *Town Planning Review* 87 (3): 253–274.

Zhou, Xiaoping, Xiao Lu, Hongpin Lian, Yuchen Chen, and Wu Yuanqing. 2017. Construction of a Spatial Planning System at City-Level: Case Study of 'Integration of Multi-Planning' in Yulin City, China. *Habitat International* 65: 32–48.

Index

A

Action research, 123, 179
Actor-Network Theory (ANT), 15, 85, 94, 155, 176, 178
Agonism, 14, 100–102, 111–112, 118–122
Analytic approach, 2, 157, 158
Aquaculture, 180
Archives, 137, 157
Artefact, 153, 177–179, 189
Assemblage materiality, 155, 171–190

B

Biodiversity, 5, 32, 35
Black box, 178, 183, 189
Bureaucracy, 42, 44, 45, 47, 62, 101

C

Calculation, 42, 152, 156
Capacity to act, 88, 108
Capital accumulation, 128–132, 135–137, 139, 150, 200
Capitalism, 110, 127–135, 139, 144, 145
Case study, 11, 28, 32, 34, 52, 53, 65, 67, 72, 74, 76, 78, 86, 93, 94, 98–101, 113, 114, 119, 137–140, 142, 143, 157, 158, 160, 164, 165, 181, 186–188, 197, 201
Castells, Manuel, 110, 116
Categorisation, 16, 113, 151, 152, 154
Civil society, 13, 25, 42, 84, 85, 88, 96, 106, 109, 111, 114, 120, 121, 151, 165, 166, 172

Climate change, 28, 68, 75, 76, 89, 120, 152, 159, 160, 162, 163, 184
Cluster analysis, 29
Coalition, 52, 53, 56, 65, 94, 107–109, 113–120, 143, 153, 159–162, 165, 184, 185
Coding, 6, 58, 74, 76, 77, 98, 136, 167, 197
Cognitive mapping, 73
Collaboration, 75, 77, 83–102, 155, 163, 197
Collective action problem, 42, 43, 45–47, 53
Commodification, 135–137
Community, 1, 2, 5, 6, 11, 23, 25, 33, 34, 42, 44, 46, 47, 57, 63, 65, 67–68, 73–76, 78, 84–86, 90–93, 100, 105–107, 111, 114–123, 131, 133, 135–138, 151, 164–166, 176, 178–182, 185
Community of practice, v, 5, 67–68, 74, 76, 78
Complex systems, 24, 173, 175
Consensus, 13, 33, 44, 53, 71, 73, 77, 87, 89, 99–101, 105, 112, 120
Content analysis, 54, 58, 71, 98
Corporate interest, 109
Corruption, 55
Crisis, 52, 83, 92, 107, 109, 111, 127–145, 158, 200, 201

D

Data, v, 3, 8, 10, 12, 20, 22, 26, 27, 29, 30, 36, 38, 55–58, 69, 70, 72, 76–78, 93, 96–100, 113, 114, 116, 118, 120, 121, 136, 138, 139, 141, 144, 154, 160, 161, 166, 173, 182, 183, 195–197, 201

Decision support system (DSS), 22, 26, 27
Deliberation, 11, 70, 71, 73, 85, 87, 89, 91, 92,
    97–101, 112, 178
Discourse, 14, 58, 61, 64–67, 69, 99, 122,
    149–167, 179–181, 193
Discourse analysis, 8, 71, 152, 160, 162–164,
    166, 167
Discourse coalition, 153, 159–161
Dispossession, 58, 135, 137–140, 180
Document analysis, 35, 52, 77, 95, 100,
    186, 197
Douglas, Mary, 66, 152

E
Eco-city, 29, 30, 186, 187
Economic planning, 93, 96
Energy, 3, 26, 27, 161, 162, 197
Entrepreneurial state, 135, 140–144
Environmental Impact Assessment, 32, 154, 162
Environmental justice, 87, 106, 107, 115,
    117, 118
Ethnography, 66, 99
Evaluation, 13, 25, 26, 28–35, 38, 76, 178
Evidence-based planning, 22–23
Experiment, 28, 57, 59, 143, 144, 186, 187
Expertise, 7, 27, 29, 30, 38, 70, 74, 113, 122,
    152, 161, 162, 164
Externalities, 19, 49, 56, 57, 65

F
Faludi, Andreas, 2
Feedback loop, 37, 174, 185
Fieldwork, 74, 100, 114, 163, 165, 187,
    189, 201
Financialisation, 111, 134, 135, 140–144
First mover problem, 52
Fishing, 22, 117, 118, 182
Forestry, 37, 159, 160
Foucault, Michel, 14, 15, 94, 149–167,
    177, 194
Framing, vi, 4, 9–11, 16, 19–21, 26, 27, 31,
    36, 37, 41–43, 51, 55, 56, 61–65,
    67, 71, 73, 75, 76, 83–85, 93, 96,
    99, 101, 105–107, 118, 127–130,
    136, 139, 142, 149–151, 160, 162,
    164, 171–173, 186, 189,
    193–197, 200

G
Game theory, 43, 51–53
Geddes, Patrick, 1

Gentrification, 100, 106, 111, 117, 134,
    135, 180
GIS (Geographic Information System/
    Science), 24, 36, 38
Governance, 13, 14, 52, 83–102, 105, 107,
    109, 111, 112, 114, 120, 139, 155,
    157, 163, 172, 177, 180–182, 185,
    186, 193, 194, 197, 200
Governmental approach, 7, 14, 15, 21,
    22, 24, 172
Governmentality, 149–167
Governmental technology, 151, 153, 156, 166,
    180, 197
Gramsci, Antonio, 110
Grid-group, 66, 67

H
Habermas, Jürgen, 87
Harvey, David, 131, 132, 138, 140, 142
Healey, Patsy, 87
Historical data, 141
Housing, 19, 27, 29, 32, 47, 49, 54, 57, 65, 83,
    92, 93, 113, 116, 120, 128, 129,
    131, 137, 139–141, 143–145, 157,
    158, 179, 180, 188, 200

I
Ideal speech, 97, 98, 101
Identity, 45, 85, 106, 110–112, 117, 120, 155,
    162, 163, 180
Implementation, 20, 22–26, 29–34, 36–38, 42,
    59, 67, 73, 84, 88, 92, 93, 98, 107,
    108, 144, 164
Indicator, 28–30, 34, 37, 45, 74, 75, 88,
    154, 156
Informality, 135, 175
Infrastructure, 4, 5, 19, 22, 23, 28, 31, 34,
    52, 70–73, 106, 113, 118, 119,
    128, 131, 141, 143, 161,
    186, 187
Institution, vi, 5, 13, 47–51, 58, 61–70, 73, 76,
    77, 79, 85, 86, 111, 118, 134, 139,
    140, 150–152, 157, 166
Institutional capacity, 64, 69, 109
Institutional economics, 42, 48
Interpretive approach, 65
Interview, 6, 8, 28, 33, 35, 36, 52, 58, 59, 69,
    72, 74, 76, 77, 92, 98–100,
    113–116, 118–121, 123, 136–139,
    144, 158, 159, 161, 163, 164, 166,
    179, 181, 182, 184, 186–188, 195,
    197, 201

J

Justice, 7, 75, 87, 105–123, 140, 180

K

Knowledge, 2, 3, 6–12, 20–22, 24, 26, 27, 29, 34, 38, 49, 50, 56, 67, 68, 72–76, 78, 85, 89, 95, 96, 99, 113, 118, 119, 121, 122, 140, 149–167, 178, 188, 200

L

Land ownership, 52, 55, 58, 115, 129, 134
Lichfield, Nathanial, 20, 21, 34
Local economic development, 31, 33, 66, 67, 93–95
Local government, 23, 30, 53, 64, 69, 75, 84, 88, 90, 95, 96, 100, 108, 109, 133, 135, 139–141, 152, 159, 180
Logic of appropriateness, 63, 67, 78

M

Mapping, 8, 26, 27, 30, 38, 57, 62, 69, 70, 73, 150, 152, 157, 161, 179
Market failure, 19, 41, 42, 44, 49
Marx, Karl, 127, 130, 131
Methodology, vi, 2, 3, 8, 16, 28, 30, 33–35, 54, 73, 74, 95, 98, 99, 113, 119, 137, 142, 159, 161, 164, 165, 179, 186, 187, 197, 198, 201
Modelling, 28, 42, 43, 50–53, 55, 59, 73, 177, 178
Monitoring, 20, 30, 36, 37, 57, 65, 76, 88, 93, 120, 121, 154, 182, 183, 187
Mouffe, Chantal, 112
Multi-level governance, 89, 177, 181
Mutuality, 90, 91

N

Narrative, 3, 8, 9, 12, 26, 30, 61, 62, 71, 74, 92, 93, 95, 99, 100, 113, 119, 122, 136, 139, 143, 157, 159, 163, 166, 183, 186
Natural hazard, 73
Neo-liberalism, 134, 136–138, 143, 144, 155, 156, 159, 163, 166
Network, 13, 14, 27, 30, 55, 74–78, 83–102, 111, 113, 131, 166, 172, 173, 176–178, 189, 197

New public management (NPM), 45, 72, 88, 156
NIMBY, 47, 50, 51. 112
Norm, 7, 23, 61, 62, 64, 68, 70, 76, 78, 79. 90, 91, 159
Normative approach, 2

O

Observation, 8, 70–72, 74, 76, 92, 99, 114, 119, 120, 123, 136, 139, 144, 163, 164, 186, 195

P

Participatory observation, 72
Path dependency, 62, 64, 68–71, 79
Performativity, 151
Phronesis, 10, 11
Plan, 1, 4, 5, 22–27, 29–33, 35–38, 44, 46, 47, 51, 55, 63, 70, 73, 78, 83, 95, 99, 100, 105, 116, 117, 120, 121, 141, 142, 152–154, 161–163, 175, 177–179, 184, 187–189
Planning theory, 2, 5, 12–14, 87, 112
Policy formulation, 25–26, 69, 84
Policy integration, 68
Political economy, 2, 14, 15, 58, 108–110, 127–145, 150, 193, 197, 200
Politics, 7, 14, 42, 56, 101, 102, 105–123, 134, 135, 141, 153, 154, 159, 160, 162, 165, 166, 180
Pollution, 19, 32, 49, 66, 83, 152, 154, 174, 178
Power, 7, 11, 14, 15, 19, 25, 38, 48, 52, 53, 63, 69, 70, 74, 88, 92, 93, 98, 99, 101, 102, 105–123, 129, 132, 142, 150, 151, 153–155, 161, 162, 164, 171–190, 193
Practitioner, 2, 6, 7, 13, 34, 62, 64, 67, 68, 100
Pressure group, 106, 110
Principal-agent problem, 42–44
Privatisation, 84, 134
Profession, 4, 6. 7, 79, 158
Property ownership, 55, 58
Property right, 42, 43, 47–50, 56–58, 71, 116, 117, 119, 144
Public administration, 4, 13, 19–38, 42, 49, 59, 62, 70, 74, 173, 174
Public goods, 19, 49, 50
Public interest, 4, 19–21, 23, 34, 41, 44, 59, 66, 79, 127, 136, 145, 151, 188

Q

Qualitative, v, 36, 58, 59, 101, 121, 123,
    136, 197
Quantitative, v, 36, 55, 56, 101, 123, 137, 154,
    195, 197
Questionnaire, 161, 188

R

Racism, 112, 115–118
Rational choice, 13, 14, 41–59, 61, 62, 91, 156
Rational planning, 22, 25, 30, 38, 41
Reciprocity, 90, 91
Reflective practitioner, 67
Regime, 57, 58, 107–109, 112–115, 118
Region, 5, 53, 56, 83, 93, 94, 142, 157, 187
Relational approach, 94, 155, 171–190
Rent-seeking, 42, 47, 50, 53–56
Research design, 3, 194, 196, 197, 200, 201
Research question, 2, 53, 69, 77, 120, 136,
    173, 184, 185, 195–197, 200, 201
Resilience, 73, 173, 175
Resistance, 15, 112, 123, 129, 136, 157, 159,
    164–166, 180, 184
Resource-interdependency, 109
Resource management, 37, 118
Right to the City, 107, 127, 143, 165
Risk, 22, 28, 52, 75, 86, 131, 141, 143,
    160, 161
Routine, 44, 61, 62, 74, 79

S

Scenario, 22, 26, 28, 31, 50, 73, 175
Self-organisation, 172, 175, 179, 185–188
Self-responsibilisation, 155, 156, 164
Social capital, 85, 90–91, 115, 117
Social constructivism, 62
Social learning, 67–68, 73–78
Social Network Analysis (SNA), 55, 56, 91,
    95–97, 101, 172, 176
Spatial planning, 25, 28, 34–37, 48, 49, 65, 94,
    157, 161, 162, 188
Squatting, 136, 137
Stakeholder, 5, 13, 21, 24, 26–29, 33, 34, 38,
    69, 72–78, 83–102, 114, 120, 139,
    179, 200
State, 4, 13, 14, 22, 24, 25, 41, 42, 44, 48, 52,
    56–58, 70, 71, 73, 77, 83–85, 87,
    88, 92–94, 105, 108, 109, 111,
    114–116, 118, 120, 121, 127–132,
    134, 135, 137–145, 151, 155, 157,
    162, 164, 171, 172, 175, 181, 184,
    188, 196, 197, 200

Storyline, 69, 70, 119, 157, 159–161
Strategic Environmental Assessment (SEA),
    24, 34–36, 162
Survey, 1, 6, 8, 28, 35, 77, 78, 98, 116,
    197, 201
Sustainability, 7, 15, 24, 27, 30, 35, 69,
    74, 75, 84, 87, 89, 92, 93,
    152, 154, 161, 162,
    182, 185–187
Sustainability Appraisal (SA), 35, 36
Sustainable development, 5, 35, 65, 75,
    84, 89, 154

T

Tourism, 30–32, 73, 100, 113, 116, 118
Transcript, 6, 71, 76, 159, 181
Transport, 3, 5, 20, 23, 25, 30, 31, 35, 69, 70,
    89, 113, 119, 120, 131,
    150, 185–187
Trust, 51, 52, 76, 78, 90, 91, 115, 143

U

Urban activism, 106
Urban containment, 47
Urban design, 2, 23, 113
Urban gardening, 165, 166
Urban growth, 106, 129
Urban regeneration, 23, 63, 89, 111,
    115, 116, 132, 133, 158,
    173, 180
Urban regime, 87, 88, 107–109, 112–115
Urban social movement (USM), 107,
    109–111, 116, 117

V

Value, 2, 4, 5, 7–11, 14, 16, 25, 27,
    29, 33–36, 38, 42, 46, 48,
    52–56, 59, 61, 62, 76, 78,
    79, 91, 111, 114, 120, 123,
    128–130, 132, 133,
    135–137, 140–143, 155,
    159, 160, 185, 194, 196
Vulnerability, 26, 28, 29

W

Water, 5, 19, 25, 30, 31, 33, 34, 70–73,
    77, 78, 152, 154, 162,
    183, 184
Workshop, 73, 139, 182
Worldview, 5, 61, 64–67, 72